STRATEGY STRIKES BACK

STRATEGY
STRIKES
BACK

How *Star Wars* Explains
Modern Military Conflict

EDITED BY MAX BROOKS, JOHN AMBLE,
ML CAVANAUGH, AND JAYM GATES
FOREWORD BY STANLEY MCCHRYSTAL

POTOMAC BOOKS | *An imprint of the University of Nebraska Press*

All rights reserved. Potomac Books is an imprint
of the University of Nebraska Press.
Manufactured in the United States of America.

Library of Congress Control Number: 2017044550

Set in Arno by Mikala R Kolander.
Designed by N. Putens.

This book is not licensed, authorized, or
endorsed by Lucasfilm Ltd. LLC.

This book is proud to support the Wounded Warrior Project. For more information about the organization, or its mission to honor and empower Wounded Warriors, please visit woundewarriorproject.org.

CONTENTS

FOREWORD

STANLEY MCCHRYSTAL

I remember the attack on the Death Star. Its approach threatened defeat of the Rebel cause, but destroying the ominous warship required a perfectly precise bombing run conducted through a gauntlet of enemy fighters and fire. Pilot and budding Jedi knight Luke Skywalker does it with notable skill and awesome courage. The Death Star explodes across the screen, and the movie concludes with a triumphant ceremony.

The Rebel attack was dramatic and successful but hardly decisive or strategic. The very title of the next film in the series, *The Empire Strikes Back*, signaled that the war was far from over, and we see Luke Skywalker journey to his roots in order to develop the Jedi skills he will need for an extended struggle. Luke's preparation is reminiscent of Mao Tse-tung's doctrine of three phases of a people's war.

The study of strategy is a never-ending labor. In its best practice, we identify the necessary *ways* and *means* to achieve our desired *ends*—or more simply put, we determine an outcome that is realistically achievable and commit ourselves to devoting the resources and taking the actions necessary to gain that outcome. It demands rigorous integrity in predicting the costs we must bear to attain success and a moral pledge to stay the course.

Too often we produce faux strategy by underestimating the difficulties we must overcome, by ignoring the limitations of our force, or by assuming a level of commitment to the cause that proves illusory. Rebellions, whether against the Galactic Empire or another powerful entity, are frequently ignited by firebrand ideologues but, after the romance has faded, are typically the progeny of relentlessly dedicated, harshly realistic operators. Strategies produced at the outset of almost every war give way to less ambitious but more realistic plans when tempered and shaped in reality's forge.

It can feel frivolous to ascribe lessons in strategy to popular movies, much less to science fiction in particular. The characters and events spring from the imaginations and keyboards of clever people, but they aren't real—none of this really happened (yet).

But that's a narrow view, the kind that proclaims art impractical or history irrelevant. In fact, fiction offers an extraordinary opportunity to craft a narrative that highlights both the challenges and criticality of viable strategy while controlling for other considerations. In weighing history, we often argue over the facts or allow aspects of personality to color our view. There are an infinite number of variables to be factored and disputed, which often distracts us from a clear-eyed assessment of strategy.

Of course, with science fiction, we often suspend disbelief to accept the excitement of the story; but as with *Stars Wars*, that's no reason the concepts of strategy shown have to be unbelievable. In fact, throughout the series there are repeated depictions of characters and situations that invite the analysis of serious students of strategy.

Like many things in life, the appropriateness and viability of a strategy is best evaluated in the rearview mirror—but life rarely drives in reverse. Many readers of this book have developed and executed strategies of significant importance and will continue to do so, but no one could ever master the craft beyond the need for continuous study.

Wisdom is where you find it. Don't be afraid to look in unexpected places. This is a great place to start.

PREFACE

ML CAVANAUGH

In teaching strategy at West Point, I learned something important about myself. I've been on both the wrong end of incoming insurgent fire and the receiving end of cadets' blank stares; and if I were forced to decide between the two, I'm not sure I could. Bullets whizzing versus eyes blinking? Deafening shells or awkward silence? A radio malfunction at our unit's most dangerous moment, or a smartphone reach during my lecture's most boring minute? Who could choose? Or the never-sure calculation about whether my soldiers, or students, were laughing at my joke—or at me. But above all else, the classroom left me with the distinct fear that I hadn't adequately prepared my soon-to-be second lieutenants for the battlefields to come. The stakes are higher in military classrooms. War and teaching about war stiffen the spine and sharpen the senses, because in either one, failure carries a steep price.

Author Neil Gaiman once advised college students to "make good art"; but if you're a U.S. Army major assigned to teach the subject I taught, in the place I was, your professional obligation to society is somewhat different— you want your undergraduates to "make good war."[1] This instilled a certain paranoia that propelled me to earn several teaching and strategy awards in 2014 and 2015, which provided a fleeting sense of validation.[2]

But a few shiny trophies didn't prevent reflection on what more I could've done during my time teaching. By the summer of 2015 I moved on from West Point to an assignment in South Korea, where I wrote the war plan for a forward-stationed infantry division roughly a half marathon from the DMZ. Distance didn't relieve me from my chief concern—in my mind the greatest challenge in teaching—which was to find common and interesting terrain to use for the study of strategy.

For two people to talk strategy, both must be familiar with the case in question, whether in business, politics, or war. To discuss even something as studied as American Civil War strategy requires both parties to be deeply knowledgeable about the conflict. This necessary knowledge baseline quickly creates communication problems, particularly across national divides, like with my South Korean army colleagues in the combined command in which I served (the staff included both South Korean and American officers, working together). Our challenge was to find shared frames of reference. A conflict we all knew a lot about.

But this common terrain also had to be fascinating, and inspiration intervened on a dark winter's morning. While running near Camp Red Cloud, north of Seoul, I listened through headphones to cartoonist and teacher Randall Munroe, of XKCD fame, talk about electrifying his physics students by challenging them to solve how much force (lowercase f) Yoda would have required to lift Luke Skywalker's Dagobah-bound fighter off the ground.[3] Munroe described how genuinely excited his kids were to work the problem then and how much more motivated they were to learn physics afterward—all because Star Wars provided common ground they cared about and could actually visualize. Light appeared in the blackness of my predawn run in South Korea when I realized that discussion on strategy similarly demands widespread, relatable scenarios that cross lingual, cultural, and generational divides.

Star Wars is perfect. Blockades. Coups. Armies. Elite forces. Ultimate weapons. Battles. Rebels. An Empire. Star Wars is global culture's most recognized conflict, which makes it the ideal canvas on which to study the art of strategy. It's everywhere, not just in stores and on screens, but also on dog tags and license plates, and it regularly invades the good-night rituals of tiny tots.[4] It has even influenced religion and language.[5]

In a real sense, *Star Wars* is the modern version of Thucydides's *History of the Peloponnesian War*. Both illuminate multiple aspects of epic struggles, and epic they were—while the Greeks fought for twenty-seven years, the Senate and Rebels battled the Empire and First Order for roughly sixty-five.[6] By exploring the lessons of such a widely known long war, strategic educators can avoid lecture and instead lure cadets and citizens alike to greater understanding of strategic competition and societal conflict, which matters because both groups directly contribute to national performance at war.

To test this theory, I shared the idea with my South Korean army colleagues. They all agreed it would be a valuable way to talk about strategy by providing a common tongue. So it seemed the concept would work across nations, military officer to military officer—but would it work beyond? Would it be of value to civilians? How could I know for sure?

As Seoul's spring came, I sent the idea off to two other Modern War Institute (at West Point) fellows, authors Max Brooks and August Cole, as well as to two editors, John Amble and Jaym Gates (since then, August has left the Modern War Institute for other opportunities, and John has come on board). We wrote back and forth and hardened and honed our focus on the films of the *Star Wars* canon, ganging up to write an edited book with diverse, expert contributors that would feature strategic analysis and commentary on *Star Wars*. Deriving support from noted Prussian war theorist and general Carl von Clausewitz, we concluded that each contribution would orient the reader to some topic featured in the films, apply a strategic idea or theory, and then describe how and why that element of the films' story line aids the reader's understanding of current or coming conflict.[7] "Make good art" would help "make good war."

Three unique aspects underpinned what became known as the *Strategy Strikes Back* project. For budding strategic practitioners, this is a way to use familiar terrain to practice strategic analytical skills that will be vital to their success as guardians of their own republic (or home). Second, *Strategy Strikes Back* is a meaningful attempt to grapple with ethical, social, and political issues certain to be central in future conflict, always considering an important question: How might we face this coming, crucial issue? Lastly, the book's premise sets it apart. Writers often use a factual foundation on which to generate fiction; whether springing from history or journalistic accounts, fiction often begins with the real world and imagines adjustments from that base. *Strategy Strikes Back* reverses the process, instead emanating from a work of fiction and then applying real theories, analysis, and concepts to better explain and understand our world. If, as Mark Twain observed, truth can be stranger than fiction, then in this case, perhaps, fiction can be stronger than truth—and help us to more clearly see what may come.[8]

In the summer of 2016 I flew home from my year on the Korean DMZ and drove to my new assignment at U.S. Army Space and Missile Defense Command in Colorado, an organization the movies touched in 1983 when Senator Ted Kennedy coined the immortal "Star Wars" nickname for the Reagan administration's Strategic Defense Initiative.[9] I couldn't help but reflect on just how thin the wall between film fiction and defense reality really is—*Star Wars* is just another bloody galaxy where we can learn how strategy strikes back.

Notes

1. "Neil Gaiman: Keynote Address 2012," University of the Arts, May 17, 2012, http://www.uarts .edu/neil-gaiman-keynote-address-2012.
2. I received the Apgar Award for Excellence in Teaching in 2014, drawn from West Point's six-hundred-plus instructors; was the Defense and Strategic Studies Program Teacher of the Year in 2015; and was, at the time, the youngest recipient of the Order of Saint Gabriel the Archangel in 2015, a professional honor bestowed by the U.S. Military Strategists Association (now known as the Army Strategists Association).
3. See explanation at XKCD, "Yoda: 'How Much Force Power Can Yoda Output?,'" *What If?*, accessed August 9, 2016, https://what-if.xkcd.com/3/. See also Randall Munroe, "How Can Math Help You Imagine the Impossible?," *TED Radio Hour* video, 9:25, March 6, 2015, http:// www.npr.org/2015/03/06/390934908/how-can-math-help-you-imagine-the-impossible.
4. A good friend of mine listed "Jedi" in place of the religion listed on his official military dog tags. Also, I recently followed another driver through the gate at Peterson Air Force Base in

Colorado who had an "xjedi" license plate. And my daughters currently prefer the Little Golden Books edition of *Star Wars* to *Goodnight Moon*.

5. The 2001 United Kingdom census found that nearly four hundred thousand people claimed Jedi as their religion, making it the fourth-largest surveyed. See Charles Q. Choi, "How 'Star Wars' Changed the World," Space.com, August 10, 2010, http://www.space.com/8917-star-wars-changed-world.html.

6. The time period from *Episode I*, when Anakin Skywalker is a young boy, until *Episode VI*, when Luke Skywalker is a fully grown man, is roughly thirty-five years. J. J. Abrams, *Episode VII*'s director, said that approximately thirty years had passed between *Episode VI* and *Episode VII*, making the films' sum total time period sixty-five years. See Bill Whitaker, "The New Force behind Star Wars," interview with J. J. Abrams, *60 Minutes*, December 13, 2015, http://www.cbsnews.com/news/60-minutes-the-new-force-behind-star-wars/.

7. See Carl von Clausewitz, *On War*, ed. and trans. Michael Howard and Peter Paret (Princeton NJ: Princeton University Press, 1976), 156.

8. Mark Twain, *Following the Equator: A Journey around the World* (Hartford CT: American Publishing; New York: Doubleday and McClure, 1897).

9. On March 23, 1983, the *Washington Post* quoted Senator Edward Kennedy, who described the president's Strategic Defense Initiative proposal as "reckless *Star Wars* schemes." Lou Cannon, "President Seeks Futuristic Defense against Missiles," *Washington Post*, March 24, 1983.

INTRODUCTION

MAX BROOKS

How do you teach someone about a niche topic they don't know much about? More importantly, how do you even get them interested? Military strategy is a pretty narrow field of study. Unless you're actually in the military, a history buff, or a dedicated scholar of strategy, chances are you've never given it any serious thought. And why should you?

To be blunt, war affects everyone. Right now, every person on this planet, from a Tibetan village to an American suburb, has had their lives altered by war. It might not be dramatic, and it might not be obvious, but it is real. Our whole way of life, from the language we speak to the land we live in to the god we choose or don't choose to worship, all came down to some military choice that changed the course of history.

That's why it's important for all of us, particularly voters in democratic societies, to understand how and why these choices are made. We elect the people who make those historic choices; and so when they outline their strategies to, say, get involved in the Middle East or to not get involved in Ukraine, we need to know what the hell they're talking about.

As informed citizens, we should all have a basic knowledge of how war affects us. But how in the world do we do that? The problem with classic military texts like Clausewitz and Sun Tzu is that they're total snoozefests. Trust me, if you're not already into this stuff and you have trouble sleeping, just curl up with Alfred Thayer Mahan's *Sea Power and World History*. You'll be out in five minutes.

And the modern stuff isn't any better. The problem with strategists, from either the military or academia, is that they all write for each other. Again, if you're not a lifelong fan, it's like a foreign language, like a medieval Latin bible that only the priest could translate.

We need a new language, with references that we can all understand. That's the idea behind this book, and it came from the brain of Maj. Matt Cavanaugh. Matt's both a serving U.S. Army officer and a total sci-fi nerd. You could say that he's bilingual, which is why he had the idea for this book.

Matt thought the best way to help people understand strategy is through a story we all know and love: *Star Wars*. With the exception of my wife (who still refers to everything sci-fi as "Dungeons and Dragons"), the rest of the human race is pretty well versed on the saga that took place "a long time ago in a galaxy far, far away." The appeal of *Star Wars* is international and multigenerational, and it's got plenty of fans in uniform. Matt tested fiction as a tool in his West Point classroom; after refining it while serving overseas, he decided to take it mainstream with *Star Wars*. He put out a call to those in the military, academia, and fiction (like myself) and asked us if we'd be interested in writing essays about real warfare told through the lens of George Lucas (and now J. J. Abrams).

The result is this book.

Here you will find the real-life applications of the *Star Wars* saga, from the political fallout of targeting civilians to toxic, top-down leadership to the long-term consequences of abandoning postwar allies.

As a reader, you won't need a military background or a PhD in geopolitics. Like me, all you need is a love of *Star Wars* and an interest in the events that shape the world around us.

May strategy—the real Force—be with you.

STRATEGY STRIKES BACK

PART 1

Society and War

Armies alone don't fight wars. Societies do.

The moment individuals began to organize into small bands, larger tribes, and ultimately wide-ranging political societies, these sovereign entities—whether calling themselves an empire or an order, republic, or rebellion—began to exert distinct influence over the use of force. As Charles Tilly said in *The Formation of National States in Western Europe*, "war made the state and the state made war."

How should civilians relate to soldiers and soldiers to civilians? Why should advanced societies send aid to heal war-scarred foreign soil? How have women's wartime roles evolved—and where might they go? What happens when military forces shrink and separate from the society they serve? And how might smarter weapons and superwarriors impact future war?

This set of essays covers the intersection between society and war—how culture and cause, politics and strategy, ethics and beliefs impact the decisions of, and for, war.

1

The Case for Planet Building on Endor

MAX BROOKS

My fellow senators, I write to you on the one-year anniversary of our glorious victory over the Empire, to remind you of those forgotten allies whose courage and sacrifice made that victory possible. Many worlds rose in defiance of Emperor Palpatine's tyranny. Many cultures contributed to his downfall. And yet when the entire rebellion hinged on a final, desperate battle, one race leapt heroically into the fray to strike the critical blow for freedom. Of course it was the Ewoks of whom I speak, those eleventh-hour allies who made the difference between victory and defeat and who need our help as badly as we once needed theirs.

On that momentous day of our liberation, as cheers erupted, from Tatooine to Bespin, I danced among the bonfires of Endor, beneath stars once hidden by the looming shadow of the Death Star. With me danced our small, courageous allies, who drummed on the emptied helmets of stormtroopers as they sang songs of peace and freedom. We laughed and cheered and thanked our new comrades from the bottom of our hearts. And then we left them. No provision was made for postwar nation building. No plans were drawn for restoring their land. In our rush to return to private lives and personal interests, we abandoned a deeply traumatized world.

While the moon of Endor may still look idyllic from above, the tranquil forest canopy cloaks deep and festering scars. The horrific battle, combined with years of brutal Imperial occupation, has devastated the fragile terrestrial ecosystem. Ewoks are a subsistence-based society who now find their gathering flora poisoned and their hunting fauna massacred.

Like their environment, the Ewoks' civilization has proven too fragile for the calamity of combat. They govern by extended family groups, or "tribes," and have no concept of centralized leadership. This is why, in answer to previous queries, they have had difficulty comprehending the notion of a galactic representative to the Senate (to say nothing of electing one). Not only were a substantial number of tribal elders killed in the Battle of Endor (Ewoks always lead from the front), but those who survived the carnage have found their legitimacy threatened by the starvation and depredations that have followed.

As the delicate web of traditional order frays, corruption, intimidation, and fraternal bloodshed are now the law of the land. Younger, more militant warriors are now asserting themselves into the power vacuum. Many are veterans of the battle against the Empire, hardened by loss and tempered by violence. As I write this, my friend and former ally Wicket leads a patchwork Northern Alliance in a civil war against a growing faction of religious fanatics.

These younglings refer to themselves as "students," followers of an ancient belief we used to coerce their people to our cause. Never forget, my fellow senators, that we cynically stoked the fires of their religious faith to turn those flames against our enemy. But how quickly do flames spread out of control? Should the students defeat Wicket's Northern Alliance and seize control of Endor, we may one day find those fanatical flames before us. Control your laughter. I mean this in all sincerity.

I do not suggest the possibility of future Ewok starships emerging from hyperspace to threaten the heart of the Republic. Quite the opposite. They may never come to us, but we may have to return to them. The Republic still faces numerous threats both from rogue worlds and from non–state actors. What if the latter launches a devastating terror attack against densely populated Coruscant? And what if that attack is launched from the militarized sanctuary of Endor? What would happen to the pursuit force that attempted to land?

My fellow senators, do not for a moment underestimate the ingenuity, tenacity, and utter ferocity of the Ewoks in battle. Do not be misled by the "sticks and stones" stories of the Battle of Endor. Those primitive weapons soaked Endor's soil in the blood of the galaxy's most advanced warfighters.

Ewoks are masters of stealth and ambush. I personally witnessed a company-sized unit creep within bowshot range of an Imperial legion to launch a surprise attack. Ewoks are also superb logisticians. Without roads, without wheels, without anything but vines and muscle, they somehow managed to preposition both falling and swinging logs that destroyed two Imperial AT-ST Scout Walkers. While you may laugh at the story of the wood-and-hide glider that fecklessly dropped rocks on another AT-ST, remember that behind this seemingly comical device is a mind capable of comprehending the physics of flight. And it is that mind that saw two Ewoks assist my comrade Chewbacca in not only capturing another AT-ST but learning to operate its controls! And this, my fellow senators, this ability to adapt at near lightspeed, is what makes the Ewoks supremely dangerous, because while we may not have showered our former allies in emergency relief aid, we did leave them with mountains of discarded Imperial weapons.

I can still remember the image of a victorious Ewok, arms raised in triumph, brandishing an Imperial blaster; and my stomach tightens at the thought of that blaster aimed at us. How long before he and those like him decide that they were merely pawns in our grand strategic struggle, and how long before that resentment boils over into rage?

That is why I encourage—I implore—this august body to make Endor's reconstruction a prime objective. It will take time—years, perhaps decades. Remember, we are essentially starting at year 0 and must rebuild from the ground up. The Imperial occupation and subsequent postwar neglect has nurtured an entire generation of Ewoks on chaotic conflict. This must be reversed. We must engage with Endor long enough to train up an entirely new generation whose formative years are anchored in peace and stability. That stability can only be accomplished by an army of aid workers. Every security detachment must be matched by an equal, if not larger, force of doctors, engineers, and ethnoecologists just to name a few. They must be dedicated, highly trained, and deeply, deeply sensitive to the cultural peculiarities of their host planet. Never forget: we are rebuilding Endor, not re-creating Naboo. We must work within their ancient society in order to repair it. We must tread the razor blade's width between the twin dangers of hostility and dependency. Lack of societal awareness, no matter how well intentioned, will place us in the role of foreign occupier. Likewise, bottomless charity further erodes the system we seek to save. We must not help the Ewoks but rather help them to help themselves. In doing so, we must practice the strictest strategic flexibility. We cannot be afraid to replace failed programs and always consider contingency plans. The kind of fluid thinking that Captain Solo took to navigate an asteroid field is exactly what is needed here. That and a great deal of money.

Healing Endor will be expensive. It may require cuts to other programs throughout the Republic. It might even require additional taxes on our citizens. Some of those citizens will grumble. Some will openly resist. They may ask—*demand*—why their hard-earned credits are siphoned off to a faraway land they have never seen to help strange foreign creatures they have never met. We must be brave and honest when dealing with this backlash. We must educate our citizens about the role Endor played in our fight for freedom. We must admit our mistakes at that fight's end. We must explain to them, as I explain to you, the dangers of neglecting a former ally. Of course I understand that many worlds have been devastated by decades of Imperial rule. And as an orphan of a destroyed planet, of course I can sympathize with the plight of those tasked with re-fusing the shards of a shattered Republic. But while we debate on the future of Jedha refugees and Kashyyyk's Truth and Reconciliation Courts, I urge you to consider the crossroads between empathy and security. Make no mistake, my friends, those roads converge on Endor. We must win peace today to avert war tomorrow.

2

The Jedi and the Senate

JIM GOLBY

Jedi guard themselves, they cannot. Try, they may, but fail, they will.

When the Galactic Empire rose from the ashes of the Republic after more than one thousand years of democratic rule, many Rebels focused their blame on Anakin Skywalker and his betrayal of the Jedi. Yet this simplistic story ignores the much deeper structural and institutional flaws that undermined civilian control of the Jedi Order. While there is no doubt that Skywalker is at least partially culpable for the fall of the Republic, it nevertheless remains the case that the system of civilian control—based on the Senate's granting of complete autonomy to the Jedi Council in matters of personnel policies, professional education, and strategy—was ultimately doomed to destroy the very system the Jedi Order was designed to protect.[1]

The Jedi Order, like all large organizations, was only as good as the sentient beings who inhabited its ranks. Unfortunately, elitist Jedi and their sheltered professional military education system were bound to create a warrior caste of arrogant and entitled polymaths who resented the very life forms they were sworn to protect.

The Jedi accession system was largely hereditary, drawing a small pool of recruits exclusively from families predisposed to high midi-chlorian counts. As a result, the inhabitants of many solar systems were drastically under-represented among the Jedi, and some species were completely excluded from the Jedi Order, with no hope of joining the ever-shrinking ranks of this elitist organization. This exclusivity, combined with distinctive Jedi attire and impressive lightsabers, helped set the Jedi apart from other life-forms in the galaxy and created a mystique around the Jedi. It also drove unprecedented levels of confidence in the Jedi Knights, demonstrated con-sistently by the nearly complete deference shown to the Jedi in public, and decreased public scrutiny of the Jedi Council. Many sentient beings simply had little or no direct contact with the Jedi. Since they did not understand the Jedi, many citizens of the Republic no longer felt qualified to criticize even obvious strategic or ethical failures committed by the knights. And since the Jedi were seldom questioned by the public or the Senate, they too began to believe that their actions shouldn't be questioned and grew increasingly irritated and incensed on the rare occasions when they were.

This sense of Jedi entitlement was exacerbated by a sheltered professional education system that separated Jedi candidates from their families at a very young age and indoctrinated them in the ways of the Force. As young padawan learners, aspiring Jedi were sequestered from other life-forms and constantly reminded of how unique they were and how they were among only a small percentage of citizens in the Republic who could even hope to become part of the elite order of Jedi. Although they often traveled on missions to the farthest reaches of the galaxy during their training, they were held at arm's length from the general population. They observed but did not interact with—or learn to appreciate, understand, or respect—the diverse cultures and citizenry of the Republic spread throughout the far corners of the galaxy. And since Jedi themselves came from traditional Jedi families, over time they became more and more detached from the Republic itself.

Jedi attempts to become apolitical and completely unbiased were also ultimately self-defeating. The Jedi were instructed to be selfless, detached, and altruistic. However, their lack of real and enduring relationships with members of other species, combined with the belief that the Jedi Code was not something to which most life-forms in the galaxy could even aspire, caused these humble servants to begin to believe that they were morally and ethically superior to other, more primitive species. Comments like Obi-Wan Kenobi's sarcastic question upon meeting the Gungan Jar Jar Binks, "Why do I sense that we've picked up another pathetic life-form?" sadly had become commonplace among the Jedi. By the time they completed their training, most Jedi had developed the belief that they were better and morally superior to the citizens of the Republic they served. In fact, this sense of arrogance and entitlement was impossible to deny. As even Master Yoda admitted upon hearing Kenobi's complaints about young Anakin Skywalker's lack of humility, "Arrogance is a flaw more and more common among Jedi. Too sure of themselves, they are. Even the older, more experienced ones."

The ethical foundations of the Jedi professional education system also rested primarily on the belief that the Jedi, in fact, could subvert their desires and passions to achieve a state of total emotional detachment. Yet while the attempt to master one's emotions and to subvert one's own desires was a laudable goal, Jedi often believed that self-abnegation was a challenge they had overcome rather than a continual—and perhaps ultimately impossible—process. This failure to recognize the ways their emotions, biases, and parochial interests could cloud their own judgment would have devastating consequences. The belief among a small yet misguided band of heterodox Jedi that the Jedi could never fully escape their own passions led to the establishment of the Order of the Sith and the rise of the dark side of the Force, the greatest threat the Republic would ever see. Although remaining Jedi rightly criticized the lust for power and eternal life sought by these dissident Sith, they also failed to recognize that they had not, in fact, achieved the unbiased state of complete selflessness that they believed they had. The Jedi Knights' failure to subvert their own emotions and desires was evident on many occasions, particularly in Qui-Gon Jinn's emotional deathbed plea, during which he begged his former padawan Obi-Wan Kenobi to promise to train young Anakin Skywalker. Neither Jinn's request nor

Kenobi's loyal pledge to his master was even remotely rational, detached, or bereft of passion and emotion. As a result, Jinn's prideful belief that Anakin would bring balance to the Force began a chain of events that would lead to the emergence of Darth Vader and the death of millions.

Jedi arrogance and entitlement also led to Jedi suspicion of—and disregard for—political leaders themselves. Obi-Wan Kenobi and Qui-Gon Jinn both repeatedly and openly expressed their disdain for politicians and admonished Anakin Skywalker that Padme Amidala and other members of the Senate were "not to be trusted." This lack of trust in political leaders is difficult to understand given the limited interactions between the Jedi Council and the Senate and the immense autonomy granted by the latter to the former in all matters of strategy. Yet Jedi increasingly became more and more willing to pursue their own interests while asserting impartiality and hiding behind their claims of expertise and knowledge of the Force.

It is true that the Jedi developed a knowledge of the Force that allowed them to wield amazing telekinetic powers and unparalleled skill with lightsabers. Yet the Jedi Council failed to recognize the limits of their expertise, ignored the prevalence of uncertainty on galactic battlefields, and underestimated the ability of Sith adversaries to adapt to Jedi tactics and strategies. As a result, the Jedi were completely surprised and unprepared for the rise of the Sith on multiple occasions, most notably at the start of the Clone Wars.

In fact, even in the face of compelling evidence that the Sith had returned—when Qui-Gon Jinn encountered Darth Maul—Mace Windu and Master Yoda were unwilling to recognize that there might be limits to their expertise, with Windu asserting, "The Sith would not have returned without us sensing it." After the creation of the Clone Army finally forced the Jedi Council to recognize their tragic mistake, Master Yoda nevertheless refused Windu's plea to "inform the Senate that our ability to use the Force has diminished." Rather than notifying their elected civilian leaders of the immense vulnerabilities in the Republic's defenses with enough time to develop alternative options to counter the growing threat, the Jedi instead tried to take matters into their own hands and actively avoided political control. Mace Windu led a small group of Jedi in a failed attempt to remove

Chancellor Sheev Palpatine and, when faced with a decision of whether to arrest his adversary or serve as his judge and executioner, chose to ignore the rule of law. It was at this moment when Palpatine manipulated Anakin's passions and Darth Vader was born. Yet it is telling that—when faced with a true crisis—the Jedi trusted only themselves.

While this was clearly the most extreme case, it was not the only time the Jedi revealed that they did not believe in the system they were sworn to defend and instead pursued their own goals in the face of conflicting civilian goals. During the Republic's most trying times, Jedi could often be counted on to pursue their own personal battles or parochial interests rather than answer the call to defend the citizens of the Republic. During the darkest hours of the Republic, both Master Yoda and Obi-Wan Kenobi were derelict in their duty and went into self-imposed exile for decades. Similarly, before the Battle of Endor, Luke Skywalker also offered himself up as a prisoner so he could attend to Jedi business—settling a personal vendetta with his father in a lightsaber fight that was operationally and strategically irrelevant to the ongoing conflict. Yet these Jedi were too easily able to rationalize and reconcile their selfish, personal actions with the ideals of the Jedi Code. Whereas the Sith believed they could master the power of their passions, the Jedi fooled themselves into believing that they had subverted their desires when, in fact, they had not and could not. As a result, Jedi delusions that they were unbiased and apolitical frequently put the strategic and political goals of the Republic, and later the Rebellion, at great risk.

The system of civilian control in the Republic relied entirely on an implicit bargain that as long as the Senate granted the Jedi autonomy, the Jedi would develop expertise that they would use to advance the interests of the Republic. However, this system relied entirely on the ability of the Jedi to police themselves and to willingly use their expertise and abilities only to advance the interests of the Republic. Yet as we have seen, Jedi arrogance and self-righteousness often caused the Jedi to conflate their legitimate expertise with their own interests or political preferences. Growing Jedi pride and entitlement, combined with a lack of scrutiny by the public, would have been an extremely difficult challenge to overcome even in the best system.

Yet the Galactic Republic had no discernable structures or institutions with which to direct, monitor, or discipline Jedi attempts to pursue their own preferences when they came into conflict with those of the Senate or the Republic itself. And in cases where Republican and Jedi preferences diverged, the Senate simply had no tools with which to control the Jedi.

For a while, the Jedi Code had provided a way for the Jedi to discipline themselves; but as each generation of Jedi became more detached from the galaxy than the last, the code began to falter in practice. Jedi lies, such as "there is nothing to see here" or "these are not the droids you are looking for," became increasingly prevalent. The Jedi Knights also began to use their infamous mind tricks to violate individual sovereignty and force other life-forms to act against their will. Additionally, they frequently began to claim "Jedi business" backed by the threat of a lightsaber, to take whatever they wanted, or to escape responsibility for the destruction they left in their wake. With no one willing or able to question them but themselves, Jedi discipline began to wane. Since Jedi operated in small, independent teams spread throughout the galaxy, it became increasingly difficult for Jedi to call their brothers or sisters to account, especially when they were exposed to risks that other citizens of the Republic simply did not and could not understand.

In the face of slipping Jedi discipline, the Senate also lacked any real ways to shape Jedi behavior or punish Jedi disobedience or noncompliance with Senate directives. Political leaders had granted total control over Jedi recruiting, education, and personnel policies to the Jedi Council. They had also relinquished any control over the appointment of Jedi knights or membership on the Jedi Council itself. In the face of Jedi complaints about senatorial meddling in Jedi business, the Senate eventually backed off its responsibility to dictate legal standards of service, instead allowing the Jedi Council full authority to set and enforce its own rules. And since the Jedi formally shunned material belongings, despite living in ostentatious quarters and acquiring anything they needed or desired through the use of Jedi mind tricks or appeal to necessity and their lofty reputation, the Senate lacked any means to incentivize Jedi compliance with civilian directives.

As a result, over time, Jedi personal and parochial interests inevitably began to overtake the interests of other life-forms in the galaxy. Jedi arrogance, entitlement, and overconfidence often meant that Jedi did not realize that their expert judgments were clouded by their own personal and parochial interests. Moreover, the lack of structural and institutional checks at the Senate's disposal left its members with little influence over the Jedi. The best they could hope for was that the Jedi understood the Republic and respected all its life-forms so much that they would subordinate their own desires and interests for the greater good.

Yet therein lies the lesson of the Jedi and the state. At moments of great crisis, the galactic system could only rely on the benevolence of individuals with immense power. Although the Jedi may have been the best and the brightest the Republic had to offer, there were no institutions or structures in place that would allow the Senate to check or control the Jedi. And there were no mechanisms to ensure that Jedi preferences and expertise remained subordinate to and integrated with the policies and political realities of the Senate. As exemplified by the passions and selfishness of Kenobi and both Skywalkers, even the best men and women cannot be counted on to pursue the greater good when faced with a choice between their own interests and the interests of many. And even if they can do so in some exceptional cases, such a system can only be tested for so long before human frailty will again place it at risk. Anakin Skywalker may have been the proximate cause of the fall of the Republic, but it was only a matter of time before another Jedi would have failed a similar test. Jedi autonomy and expertise came with significant risk, and there were simply no institutions or structures that political leaders in the Senate could use to guard the galaxy from the Jedi themselves.

Although the Jedi lived long ago in a galaxy far, far away, the failure of civil-military relations in the *Star Wars* universe remains relevant today. Political leaders in the United States undoubtedly have stronger institutions and mechanisms by which they can exercise control over military leaders, and the system of civilian control enshrined in the U.S. Constitution that has been refined through statute and tradition remains truly exceptional.[2] This system has weathered many crises and survived despite some challenging military and civilian personalities.

Yet even the most exceptional systems cannot maintain themselves, and there are some causes for concern in U.S. civil-military relations that the lessons of *Star Wars* might help illuminate. Similar to the Jedi, the United States' all-volunteer force is becoming smaller, more insular, and increasingly detached from American society.[3] In a large and diverse republic, these trends are understandable, and perhaps even inevitable, especially during an extended period without a major-power war or mass mobilization.[4] Throughout U.S. history, however, civil-military relations have been marked by a deep civilian skepticism of military leaders and institutions, allowing the public and its political representatives to exercise effective—though sometimes uncomfortable—civilian control over the military's personnel policies, professional education system, and role in the advisory process. Yet this skepticism has begun to break down in recent years. As it did with the Jedi, increasing public confidence in the armed forces and a lack of familiarity with the military over time could erode public willingness—and consequently decrease the incentives for political leaders—to question military leaders and force them to adhere to civilian policy guidance.[5] When we place Jedi knights or modern U.S. generals and admirals on a pedestal on which they cannot be questioned, it becomes extremely difficult to maintain the political primacy and civil-military integration necessary to make successful strategy.[6]

At the same time, if a creeping sense of arrogance or entitlement takes hold among military leaders or in the ranks of the armed forces following fifteen years of war, it could lead to a military similar to that of the Jedi—one that doesn't recognize the limits of its own expertise and begins to put its own parochial interests ahead of the society it serves, perhaps without even recognizing that it is doing so. U.S. military leaders today must also avoid the temptation to reinforce the impression that they are at the center of the galaxy or that those in the military are the only Americans who serve or sacrifice.[7] While we should not expect today's military leaders to be able to achieve the unbiased emotional detachment that even the Jedi could not, they can do more to recognize their own biases, be transparent in dealing with political leaders, and subordinate themselves to civilian control.

The American Republic has a set of institutions that are far more suited to maintaining civilian control over the military than the Galactic Republic ever had to control the Jedi. In fact, Senate influence over senior Jedi appointments—combined with statutory authorities, the power of the purse, and clearer lines of command responsibility along with the constitutional power of civilian oversight—might have even been enough to keep the Jedi Council firmly under the Senate's control. Nevertheless, absent a willingness among political leaders and the American public to question the military and a commitment by military leaders to integrate military expertise with political guidance, all the institutions in the galaxy will not prevent the United States from meeting the fate of the Jedi and the Galactic Senate. Exceptional generals—Marshalls or Eisenhowers, Powells or Schwarzkopfs, McMasters or Mattises—may be able to show restraint or demonstrate remarkable leadership during a rare crisis. But without strong institutions to implement civilian control and a commitment by civilian policy makers to question the military and its leaders, eventually our own Vader will come along and our republic would be lost.

Notes

1. In his classic work *The Solider and the State*, Samuel Huntington describes this form of civilian control as "objective civilian control." Under Huntington's theory of objective control, civilian leaders assert control over the military by professionalizing it and granting military leaders total autonomy within the military sphere. This theory contrasts with subjective civilian control, which involves placing legal and institutional restrictions on military autonomy to maximize control. See Samuel P. Huntington, *The Soldier and the State: The Theory and Politics of Civil-Military Relations* (Cambridge MA: Belknap Press, 1957).

2. In his book *Armed Servants*, Peter Feaver describes legal and political tools that civilian leaders in the United States use to control the military. See Peter Feaver, *Armed Servants: Agency, Oversight, and Civil-Military Relations* (Boston: Harvard University Press, 2003).

3. For a more detailed analysis of trends in the United States, see Hugh Liebert and James Golby, "Midlife Crisis? The All-Volunteer Force at 40," *Armed Forces and Society* 43, no. 1 (2016): 115–38.

4. For a more in-depth discussion of how fifteen years of war have affected civilian and military attitudes in the United States, see James Golby, Peter Feaver, and Lindsay Cohn, "Thank You

for Your Service," in *Warriors and Citizens: American Views of Our Military*, ed. Kori Schake and Jim Mattis (Stanford CA: Hoover Institution Press, 2015).

5. For additional evidence that senior military leaders already have significant influence over public opinion, see James Golby, Peter Feaver, and Kyle Dropp, "Elite Military Cues and Public Opinion about the Use of Military Force," *Armed Forces and Society*, February 6, 2017, doi:10.1177/0095327X16687067.

6. For a framework outlining how best to integrate military advice into national-security decision making, see James Golby, "Beyond the Resignation Debate: A New Framework for Civil-Military Dialogue," *Strategic Studies Quarterly* 9, no. 3 (2015): 18–46.

7. Martin Dempsey, "The Military Needs to Reach out to Civilians," *Washington Post*, July 3, 2013; ML Cavanaugh, "No, Soldiers Aren't the Only Ones Who Serve," *Baltimore Sun*, June 13, 2017.

3

Distant Warriors

Are Clones and Troops Too Separate from the Societies They Serve?

CRISPIN J. BURKE

On thousands of far-flung worlds throughout a galaxy far, far away, clone troopers are the face of the Republic. Much closer to home, the 2.4 million men and women of the U.S. armed forces serve in nearly 150 countries across the globe.[1] As the Clone Wars raged on screens both large and small, hundreds of thousands of U.S. service members fought in Iraq and Afghanistan—together, the longest period of sustained war in U.S. history.

Of course, U.S. service members aren't clones. Those fictitious soldiers were bred in a laboratory and trained specifically and solely for combat from birth; the United States' armed forces are made up of millions of volunteer troops. But despite this fundamental difference, there's much that the clones and the modern U.S. military have in common, including one particularly noteworthy feature: they represent just a small portion of the population and are charged with waging remote wars on behalf of a society that often seems to barely know they exist. With war largely outsourced to a separate warrior class, what does this say for civil-military relations in both galaxies, and how can the lessons of the Clone Wars inform efforts to reduce a real and growing civil-military divide in the United States?

Clones can think creatively; you will find them immensely superior to droids.

Taun We, *Attack of the Clones*

Clad in identical body armor, helmets, and dark eyeglasses, U.S. troops might *look* like clones at first glance. But looks are deceiving. The U.S. military is a diverse group of men and women from across the country, performing thousands of jobs across the five distinct services. But despite the homogeneity suggested by their name, even the clones couldn't resist the need to specialize, with dozens of clone trooper variants trained for every imaginable climate and special mission. And like their U.S. military counterparts, each clone trooper is more than just a serial number—they sport unique tattoos and hairstyles and even adopt their own monikers. Most importantly, they have their own individual quirks and talents—a fact that gives them considerable advantages on the battlefield over their droid adversaries.

But clones' diversity does have its limits; all of them, for example, share the same genetic material. By contrast, U.S. service members come from every conceivable social and economic background. The racial makeup of today's military generally replicates that of the U.S. population.[2] And contrary to popular stereotypes, U.S. troops come from predominantly middle-class neighborhoods—poorer Americans are underrepresented, largely because the military generally precludes recruiting those with criminal backgrounds, high school dropouts, and the medically unfit.[3] Although those standards might not sound like they match a genetically modified supersoldier like Jango Fett, they're high enough that less than a quarter of Americans between the ages of seventeen and twenty-four meet them.[4]

Clones may grow on Kamino, but U.S. troops don't. It takes battalions of recruiters to bring in nearly two hundred thousand qualified service members every year and meet the needs of the five branches of the armed forces, active duty and reserves.[5] And maintaining the all-volunteer force requires more than just recruiting the right people; it also means keeping them in uniform for years, even decades. In many ways, this retention is even more important than initial recruitment. After all, only maintaining a certain number of career soldiers can ensure mastery of the U.S. military's arsenal of high-tech equipment.

Shortly after abolishing the draft in 1973, the Defense Department realized it needed to offer better pay and benefits if it wanted to attract and keep the best and the brightest troops. In the early 1980s, Congress boosted military pay and offered generous educational benefits, including the Montgomery GI Bill. As a result, the number of troops who volunteered to serve a full twenty-year career increased nearly sixfold between the draftee era and that of the all-volunteer force. More importantly, the services quickly began to attract recruits who were better educated, more disciplined, and less likely to desert.[6]

But preserving the all-volunteer force became exceedingly difficult during the wars in Iraq and Afghanistan. Whereas the Republic could simply snap its fingers and grow a new battalion of clones, the U.S. Army was nearly stretched to the limit by the requirement to field an additional twenty-five thousand soldiers to support the 2007 Iraq troop surge.

Ultimately, the U.S. Army could only keep up with the relentless pace of the war by adding nearly eighty thousand soldiers to its ranks in the course of just a few years.[7] Doing so, however, inevitably forced the U.S. Army to lower recruiting standards; prevent leaders from booting out poorly performing soldiers; and most controversially, institute a backdoor draft through a policy called "stop-loss." By 2010 the signs of stress on the force were apparent, with the military reeling from spikes in high-risk behavior—including drug and alcohol abuse—divorce, and suicide rates.[8]

The Clone Wars last for about three years in the *Star Wars* universe, with many clones serving in constant combat. But as viewers, we see little of how years of war wear on the clones individually or the consequent stress on the Clone Army as a whole. Would the clones turn to alcohol abuse, drug use, and suicide? Would the Republic, in a rush to press more clones into service quickly, cut corners and grow less capable clones? Where do badly wounded clone troopers go for long-term medical care, and how do civilian political authorities manage the need to plan for and provide such care?

[The success of the all-volunteer force] has come at significant cost. Above all, the human cost, for the troops and their families. But also cultural, social, and financial costs in terms of the relationship between those in uniform and the wider society they have sworn to protect.

Secretary of Defense Robert Gates, September 29, 2010

In both the *Star Wars* galaxy and modern America, the public outsources the dirty business of warfighting to a separate warrior class. In *Star Wars* it's the clones; born, bred, and educated on a planet not even in the Jedi Archives, the clones fight a war that's largely out of sight and out of mind for the average Republic citizen. Closer to home, the all-volunteer force of the U.S. military serves in every corner of the globe, working on behalf of a public to which its connection seems worryingly tenuous.

Nearly half of all troops are stationed in just a handful of states, with most based in sparsely populated areas where troops have room to drive tanks, fly fighter jets, and fire heavy artillery without waking the neighbors.[9] Not to mention, over two hundred thousand service members currently serve outside the United States, with over fifty thousand more in Alaska and Hawaii.[10] Add in the long hours, frequent field exercises, and back-to-back deployments, and you quickly see a military *physically* separated from the U.S. public.

But this separation is not a one-way dynamic. The American public, likewise, is just as detached from the military. The war in Afghanistan is the longest in American history, but it's largely neglected by Americans. Over five hundred American troops died in Afghanistan during 2010, the highest annual total of the war.[11] Yet just one in six Americans reported following the war closely that year.[12]

The war in Afghanistan is even less popular than the war in Vietnam—typically considered the touchstone of societal disapproval—with just 17 percent of Americans approving.[13] Yet there has been no widespread, demonstrative opposition to the war in Afghanistan on the scale seen during the Vietnam War, or even Afghanistan's contemporary conflict in Iraq. Early opposition to both post-9/11 wars reached a crescendo in 2007 before subsiding almost completely by the end of 2008, suggesting they might have been little more than a wedge issue for partisan politics. Most Americans have chosen to completely tune out military affairs.

On one hand, it's a credit to the military that civilians don't think about it often. After all, some days, the government seems to barely function, but the U.S. military just *works*. Civilian control of the military, however, relies on an informed public voting for informed leaders—and surveys suggest the public is growing more disinterested and misinformed regarding the military.

Americans offer their opinions on nearly every political issue; but when it comes to military matters, they're unusually silent. When asked about issues ranging from women in combat to military pay, a surprising number of Americans respond that they don't know enough to offer an opinion—even as the military becomes the go-to solution for everything from Ebola to ISIS.[14]

The overwhelming majority of both service members *and* civilians believe the public does not understand the problems faced by U.S. men and women in uniform. But while fewer Americans serve in the military than ever before, the American public fails to see the burden borne by the United States' troops as unfair; an overwhelming majority of Americans view this as just "part of being in the military."[15]

The clones have it worse. The Republic has not just figuratively but literally outsourced the entire Clone Wars to them. In the *Star Wars* universe, we rarely even see clones mingling with Republic citizens. Those rare few who wind up stationed on Coruscant, the galaxy's capital planet, congregate among one another at bars almost exclusively tailored for clones. Born and bred a world apart, the clones just don't understand nonclones, and it seems that feeling is mutual.

> CLONE TROOPER FIVES: I do know that some day this war is going to end.
> CLONE CAPTAIN REX: Then what? We're soldiers, what happens to us then?
>
> "Carnage of Krell," *Clone Wars*

We don't see much from the clones after the Clone Wars, so we don't know how, or even if, the clones return to reintegrate with society. We can assume that a handful live to survive the wars, but what then? Growth acceleration means that the clones won't survive long after retirement, even if they lived that long. Not to mention, the average clone trooper, raised for nothing but combat since birth, doesn't have many employment opportunities. It's safe to say that following the war, the Galactic Empire is more focused on building space-based superlasers than benefits programs for clone veterans.

While U.S. service members don't have it as bad as the clones, many feel out of place after leaving the military. Nearly half of post-9/11 veterans report difficulty reintegrating into civilian life, double the rate of troops in the Vietnam era.[16] Soldiers feel an obligation to look out for one another, but veterans lose that support system when they leave the service, leaving many to experience feelings of helplessness and a lack of purpose.

Veterans face real struggles upon leaving the military, but the greatest obstacles are negative stereotypes of them. Civilians believe that veterans are more likely than the average American to have mental health issues (including post-traumatic stress), die by suicide, and be homeless—all of which are false. Yet the popular stereotype of the veteran made crazy by war persists, deterring would-be employers from hiring vets.

Fortunately, U.S. veterans, by and large, have overcome the stereotypes. By nearly every conceivable metric, veterans lead happier and more fulfilling lives than most Americans—and certainly much better than those of the clones.[17]

The clones aren't the only soldiers to do thankless work in oft-forgotten regions. Neither are today's troops. Underappreciated volunteers throughout history have long borne the burden of their government with too little thanks from the people they served. Rudyard Kipling's 1890 poem "Tommy" gives voice to this seemingly timeless experience:

> You talk o' better food for us, an' schools, an' fires, an' all:
> We'll wait for extry rations if you treat us rational. . . .
> For it's Tommy this, an' Tommy that, an' "Chuck him out, the brute!"
> But it's "Saviour of 'is country" when the guns begin to shoot;

Indeed, soldiers from Rome to Rodia know all too well the thankless work done on behalf of a disinterested republic. Fortunately, while clone troops might have helped usher in a military dictatorship, the U.S. military has never been put in such a position—perhaps a testament to its strong tradition of political neutrality. That, indeed, may be the most important difference between the civil-military split in our galaxy and in one far, far away.

Notes

1. Defense Manpower Data Center report from September 2016. Reports are posted at the DMDC website and updated monthly, https://www.dmdc.osd.mil/appj/dwp/dwp_reports.jsp, accessed January 7, 2017.

2. Department of Defense, *2014 Demographics: Profile of the Military Community* (Arlington VA: Office of the Deputy Assistant Secretary of Defense, 2014), http://download.militaryonesource .mil/12038/MOS/Reports/2014-Demographics-Report.pdf.

3. Thomas E. Ricks, "Population Representation in the Military Services: Endless Fun for Tom Once More," *Foreign Policy*, February 9, 2015, http://foreignpolicy.com/2015/02/09 /population-representation-in-the-military-services-endless-fun-for-tom-once-more/.

4. U.S. Army Recruiting Command, USAREC *2013 Talking Points*, May 6, 2013, http://www.usarec .army.mil/hq/apa/download/May2013talking-points.pdf.

5. Harvey M. Sapolsky, "What Americans Don't Understand about Their Own Military," *Defense One*, May 6, 2015, http://www.defenseone.com/ideas/2015/05/what-americans -dont-understand-about-their-own-military/112042/.

6. Bernard Rostker, *I Want YOU! The Evolution of the All-Volunteer Force* (Santa Monica CA: RAND, 2006), 508.

7. Defense Data Manning Center figures reflect manning levels between September 2001 and September 2010.

8. General Peter Chiarelli, then the vice chief of staff of the U.S. Army, wrote about stress factors at great length in a 2010 study commissioned by the U.S. Army titled ARMY: *Health Promotion, Risk Reduction, Suicide Prevention*, http://www.armyg1.army.mil/hr/suicide/docs /Commanders%20Tool%20Kit/HPRRSP_Report_2010_v00.pdf.

9. Rosa Brooks, "Civil-Military Paradoxes," in *Warriors and Citizens: American Views of Our Military*, ed. Kori N. Schake and James Mattis (Stanford CA: Hoover Institution Press, 2016), 34.

10. Data accumulated from the Defense Manning Data Center.

11. Data collected from iCasualties, http://icasualties.org/oef/, accessed January 7, 2017.

12. Pew Research Center, "Top Stories of 2010: Haiti Earthquake, Gulf Oil Spill," December 21, 2010, http://www.people-press.org/2010/12/21/top-stories-of-2010-haiti-earthquake -gulf-oil-spill/.

13. CNN Political Unit, "CNN Poll: War in Afghanistan Arguably Most Unpopular in U.S. History," *Political Ticker*, December 30, 2013, http://politicalticker.blogs.cnn.com/2013/12/30/cnn -poll-afghanistan-war-most-unpopular-in-u-s-history/.

14. Jim Golby, Lindsay P. Cohn, Peter D. Feaver, "Thanks for Your Service: Civilian and Veteran Attitudes after Fifteen Years of War," in *Warriors and Citizens: American Views of Our Military*, ed. Kori N. Schake and James Mattis (Stanford CA: Hoover Institution Press, 2016), 127.

15. Benjamin Wittes and Cody Poplin, "Public Opinion, Military Justice, and the Fight against Terrorism Overseas," in *Warriors and Citizens: American Views of Our Military*, ed. Kori N. Schake and James Mattis (Stanford CA: Hoover Institution Press, 2016), 147.

16. Jason Ukman, "The American Military and Civilians, Worlds Apart," *Washington Post*, October 5, 2011, https://www.washingtonpost.com/blogs/checkpoint-washington/post/the-american -military-and-civilians-worlds-apart/2011/10/04/gIQAhIDgLL_blog.html?utm_term =.973ecf864af9.

17. Brooks, "Civil-Military Paradoxes," 29.

On Destroying Alderaan

MICK COOK

"No star system will dare oppose the Emperor now . . . not after we demonstrate the power of this station."

With these words, Grand Moff Tarkin explained to Princess Leia the strategic logic of his decision to destroy the planet of Alderaan with the newly unveiled Death Star. It was a move intended to send a message to the Rebellion: capitulate or face certain and total annihilation. Tarkin's decision was proven unwise, both militarily and personally—it ultimately contributed to the Death Star's destruction itself, an event in which he would die. But it also offers an illuminating incident through which to examine two aspects of strategic decision making: the moral component of war—in particular the tenets of just war theory—and the criticality of considering long-term ramifications of using new and destructive weapons.

It might credibly be argued that Tarkin's destruction of Alderaan was as much an act of vengeful malice as it was a means of establishing a strategy of deterrence across the galaxy, as he claimed. There was limited military benefit to be achieved from the destruction of a planet that he recognized was not used as a base by the Rebel Alliance.

What Tarkin evidently failed to understand was that Alderaan's destruction would strengthen the very Rebel force he was seeking to destroy, both politically and morally. Tarkin's failure to fully consider the implications of his decision echoes the difficulty that real-world political and military leaders face in properly taking into consideration an array of complex factors when weighing whether and how to use newly introduced technologies, often of significantly increased lethality. This has been true throughout the history of modern warfare—from the dawn of the nuclear age through to the cyber era.

Before returning to an assessment of the practical, military logic of the strike against Alderaan, considering the decision alongside that of targeting Hiroshima and Nagasaki with nuclear weapons offers a useful means of conceptualizing just war theory. These comparative cases—one from a galaxy far, far away and the other from here on Earth—also illustrate how the application of a new weapon without full consideration of its practical employment can not only backfire politically but also cede the moral high ground to an opponent.

There is no doubt that Alderaan was not a legitimate military target when measured against the criteria of just war theory. It is possible that Princess Leia's claim that the Rebel base was elsewhere could, of course, have been a deliberate deception; however, Tarkin gave no indication that he believed this to be the case. This implicit acknowledgement left Alderaan devoid of any military value. Still, could the strike be deemed an appropriate military action? Three basic tenets of just war theory should be considered to answer this question: distinction, proportionality, and necessity.

The tenet of distinction requires the target to be identified as an enemy combatant—a mechanism aimed solely at reducing the likelihood of noncombatant casualties. The tenet of proportionality requires the military response to be proportionate to the threat. In essence, this means that a nuclear weapon should not be used to engage a squad of infantry in an ambush position in the jungle. The nuclear weapon would no doubt remove the threat of ambush, but the response is far greater than that required to achieve this effect and far more severe than any damage that the ambush itself could cause. The final tenet, necessity, requires the act to be necessary to the achievement of the military objective. This prevents the undue loss of life from the engagement of enemy forces that cease to be a threat to the mission.

The strike clearly did not meet the distinction standard. This is made clear after Tarkin informs Leia that Alderaan will be destroyed because she has refused to divulge the star system where the Rebel base is located. "You would prefer another target, a military target? Then name the system!" Tarkin's failure to comply with this tenet is obvious. But what of the other two?

Tarkin, as a regional governor, sought to deter other systems and planets from supporting the Rebels. Even after learning that the Rebel base was on Dantooine, Tarkin sticks to his decision to strike Alderaan because of its proximity to other planetary systems. "Dantooine is too remote," he says, "to make an effective demonstration." It is clear, then, that the target value of Alderaan was as an example. Tarkin, presumably, can only link a single individual from Alderaan to the Rebellion—Leia. Yet he chooses to destroy millions of innocent lives as well as the planet they inhabit to punish that single individual. Proportionate? Hardly.

Finally, there is the question of necessity. Tarkin's threat to destroy Alderaan had worked to persuade Leia to provide the information he required. Again, there is the real likelihood that Leia might be lying in an effort to safeguard both the Rebellion and her home planet. But Tarkin's response to the newly divulged information ("Don't worry," he tells Leia, "we will deal with your Rebel friends soon enough") suggests that he does in fact believe that Alderaan is not home to the Rebel base. As such, beyond demonstrating the ruthlessness with which the new weapon of mass destruction was to be employed, he also acknowledges that the strike is of no military necessity.

So how does the destruction of Hiroshima and Nagasaki compare? President Harry Truman's decision to drop the atomic bombs was taken to shorten a war that had already cost millions of lives and was predicted to continue for several months or even years.[1] From an Allied perspective, the decision to use weapons of mass destruction would cause deaths heretofore unseen as a result of a single weapon but would reduce the overall cost of the war in terms of human suffering.[2] The two cities were chosen to reduce the total number of casualties, yet both also put pressure on *and* preserved the national leadership of Japan, thus enabling capitulation. Still, it is difficult to clearly conclude that the targeting of Hiroshima and Nagasaki satisfied the distinction tenet of the just war theory. The cities' population may have been supportive of the war and involved in the industries that directly supported the war effort, but they remained noncombatants.

To assess the proportionality of the strike on Hiroshima and Nagasaki, the bombs' destruction needs to be measured against the assessment of expected future war casualties made by the Truman administration. In the decision makers' minds, they were preventing the war from continuing to rage across Asia and the greater Pacific region, although the latter was almost completely liberated from Japanese control by this stage. If the war continued in the way it was being fought, Truman's team estimated that millions more would suffer or die. By choosing the perceived lesser of the two evils—destroying two cities, with an estimate that 80,000 to 150,000 Japanese citizens would be killed—these future deaths would be prevented.[3] Immensely destructive, yes, but also arguably proportionate.

The final tenet of necessity is measured based on the bombing's success in achieving the military and political objective of Truman's strategy. Truman's overarching objective was to end the war with Japan as quickly as possible with as few casualties as possible. The use of this immensely destructive weapon was assessed as the method most likely to achieve this objective in the most efficient manner (i.e., with the fewest casualties). More specifically, Truman sought to highlight to Japan that if it continued to fight a total war, it would place its survival as a state in jeopardy. In this sense, the strikes on Hiroshima and Nagasaki could broadly be deemed as meeting that criteria. Although the possibly unforeseen consequences of the radioactive fallout from the explosions highlight that technological advances in war are often employed well before the full repercussions of such a decision are understood, the bombing ultimately conforms to the necessity tenet.

The destruction of Hiroshima and Nagasaki, then, generally did not meet the distinction tenet and generally (although not without ambiguity) did meet the proportionality and necessity tenets—overall, it might be concluded that, all things considered, the decision was ultimately in accordance with just war theory, but just barely. The destruction of Alderaan by a weapon of mass destruction belonging to the Empire, of which the planet was a part, on the other hand, doesn't meet any of the criteria. However, despite this difference in terms of justice, both the strike against Alderaan and those against Hiroshima and Nagasaki highlight a trend evident throughout human history: that great powers will take risks, particularly with great leaps in military technology, to meet their objectives. This utilitarian mindset— the ends justify the means—can blind those wielding power from seeing the likely consequences of their actions, intended or not. With that fact in mind, it's equally important to consider the practical, strategic logic of the strike against Alderaan—separate from moral or ethical considerations.

Not long after the destruction of Alderaan, we witness the ultimate fate of the Death Star; Tarkin and his lackeys die in a fireball after the Rebel forces launch a concerted attack aimed at a specific weakness in the weapon. In two ways, Tarkin's decision to target Alderaan can be shown to have led directly to the new weapon's destruction. First, Tarkin sought to demonstrate the Death Star's destructive capability to encourage submission; instead, this made it a target for the Rebellion's leaders, who knew the Rebels could not withstand its power once it was turned directly against them. Second, the Rebels were able to destroy the Death Star because the station's weaknesses were not fully understood by those wielding its power before putting it to use.

These facts lead to rigorous questioning of Tarkin's strategic decision making. Essentially, by choosing to destroy Alderaan with a new weapon whose destructive power was previously unknown to his opponents, Tarkin effectively created a new vulnerability—that the Death Star would become the target of attack itself. This too has echoes in the real world, this time in the cyber domain.

Operation Olympic Games is the name widely used by the media to refer to the operation that launched the first serious state-versus-state offensive cyberattack.[4] It was the advent of a new way of warfare. The operation's goal was to set back the Iranian nuclear-enrichment program. The weapon, the Stuxnet computer virus, was designed not only to damage the centrifuges Iran used in its enrichment efforts but also to hide from the centrifuge operators that there was anything amiss.[5] The worm virus was introduced into the closed networks through the laptops and personal electronic devices of civilian scientists working on the program. Once it was embedded in the supervisory-control and data-acquisition programs, it began to do its damage, while reporting to the system administrators that the system was performing without any issues. The employment of this new weapon was, based on the assessed aim, successful; however, the unintended consequence was that this new weapon was now also in an adversary's hands (and due to a bug in the virus's code that let it spread beyond the enrichment facility, in the hands of the wider public as well). In short, the target of the operation, or another potential adversary, could reverse engineer the weapon, strengthen their defenses, or even use it for their own ends.

The parallel between the Death Star and the Stuxnet virus is not technological; rather, it is in the failure to identify the consequences of using the weapon in the first place. The destruction of the Death Star after its use against Alderaan was not simply a matter of the Rebels destroying a key weapon system. It was an example of Rebels removing the means with which the Empire intended to implement its new strategy of deterrence. The Rebel forces could, essentially, respond in kind to the destruction of Alderaan and score both a moral victory by avenging innocent lives lost and a political one by undermining the Empire's new strategy. The employment of Stuxnet opened a discussion of the moral ambiguity of cyberweapons and endowed the target with the potential ability to re-create its capabilities, a possibility somewhat akin to how the Rebel destruction of the Death Star mirrored the destruction of Alderaan, on a smaller scale.[6] In each case, a new weapon's user had achieved tactical and operational goals, but with a strategy that did not account for second- and third-order effects.

So in addition to being inconsistent with the tenets of just war theory, Grand Moff Tarkin's decision to destroy Alderaan also had devastating practical implications. Contemporary strategists rightfully give deep consideration to the ethical implications of various courses of action under consideration. But what Tarkin's actions—and the decisions to drop atomic bombs on Japanese cities and to employ a cyberweapon against the Iranian nuclear program—make clear is that considering only the direct effects and the morality of a decision to employ a new and powerful capability are not enough. Employing a weapon that is not fully understood is bound to have deep and significant consequences. Only by pairing an accurate assessment of the justness of an action with a detailed understanding of all potential military and political consequences can effective strategy be found. This is the lesson of Alderaan.

Notes

1. Bruno Coppieters and Nick Fotion, *Moral Constraints on War: Principles and Cases*, 2nd ed. (Lanham MD: Lexington Books, 2008), 164.
2. Michael Walzer, *Just and Unjust Wars: A Moral Argument with Historical Illustrations*, 4th ed. (New York: Basic Books, 1991), 264.
3. Coppieters and Fotion, *Moral Constraints on War*, 164.
4. Allan Friedman and P. W. Singer, *Cybersecurity and Cyberwar: What Everyone Needs to Know* (Oxford: Oxford University Press, 2014), 117.
5. Friedman and Singer, *Cybersecurity and Cyberwar*, 98.
6. James P. Farwell and Rafal Rohozinski, "Stuxnet and the Future of Cyber War," *Survival* 53, no. 1 (2011): 28.

5

Civil-Military Relationships in *Star Wars*

DANIEL D. MAURER

Science fiction sets out not so much to explore the possibilities of the future as to comment on the crises that it sees imminent in contemporary life.

Christopher Coker, *Can War Be Eliminated?*

With each *Star Wars* episode's famous opening line—"A long time ago in a galaxy far, far away . . ."—viewers are invited to witness a drama whose iconic characters display the same fundamental menu of fears, ambitions, motives, and loyalties shared by actors throughout the great conflicts of history, both recent and ancient.[1] The themes of *Star Wars*—ego, power, sin, corruption, loyalty, choosing sides, rebelling against tyrannical authority, love for one's brothers-in-arms, accountability for crimes, faith in a power greater than one's natural abilities and intellect can imagine, and hope that the light will overcome the dark in the end—are universal and timeless, as applicable to us as they are to Wookiees and Ewoks, or Hamlet and Henry V.

These themes make compelling story lines that are, at once, fantastic and stingingly accurate. *Star Wars*, then, has a similar value to the contemporary reading of Thucydides and Shakespeare. War, as philosopher Christopher Coker puts it, is part of our cultural and biological heritage; regardless of the character of the conflict, war itself is "resilient."[2] As a *necessary* corollary to this presumption, the often-ugly and often-misunderstood relationship between the political leadership that governs, attempting to determine the shape and results of these affairs, and the military arm that employs the use of force to meet those strategic ends will always be one factor (among many) that defines outcomes. This is what we mean by "strategic civil-military relationships." Samuel Huntington, Peter Feaver, and other scholars in history and political science have much—but not all there is—to say about this subject. *Star Wars*, if we watch closely enough, can introduce us to this subject as well as any historical vignette.

SITH'ING THE EVIDENCE

The original trilogy contains several passages rich in their illustration of enduring civil-military relationship themes. The iconic scene at the end of *Episode V—The Empire Strikes Back* is one of them. When Darth Vader duels Luke Skywalker inside the bowels of the Cloud City, cuts off his hand, and tells Luke that he is his father, Vader then offers him salvation. "Luke, you do not yet realize your importance," Vader tells him. "You've only begun to discover your power. . . . Join me, and together, we can rule the galaxy as father and son!"

Vader, it seems, was dissatisfied with his own mere apprenticeship to the Emperor. He desired ultimate sovereign power for himself and suggested a deal with a leader of the Rebel Alliance to switch sides and participate in a coup d'etat that would stamp out the war, not incite more of it.[3] Later, in *Episode VI—Return of the Jedi*, Luke (having by then accepted the truth of his birth) allows himself to be captured on the forest moon of Endor, knowing he will be turned over to Darth Vader. Shackled and unarmed, Luke attempts a reverse coup—to persuade his father that there is still good in him and to turn away from the dark side. Vader, perhaps beginning to doubt his obligations and beginning to feel swayed by his positive emotions toward his son, rejects this entreaty but appears to do so reluctantly, as if he has no choice. "You don't know the *power* of the dark side," he tells Luke. "I *must* obey my master. . . . [It is] too late for me, Son."

Here, Peter Feaver might apply agency theory. Using microeconomic concepts and a good deal of math, Feaver would suggest that this scene encapsulates essential features of the strategic military agent (Vader) struggling to abide by (but eventually acquiescing to) the dictates of his civilian principal (his "master") that he knows to govern his more limited scope of authority.[4] Here, Vader has no independent discretion on the matter of turning Luke to the dark side and over to the Emperor ("What is thy bidding, my master?" he often asks).[5] Yet it would seem contrary to his conflicted conscience. It raises the specter of the so-called agency problem, where the agent—whose legitimate range of actions should be cast only for the benefit of his principal's interests and within limits imposed by that principal—starts to *freelance* based on internalized moral considerations.[6]

James Burk, approving of this spike of conscience, this heart-over-head decision making, would offer that there *is* such a thing as "responsible disobedience" or a "protected space" where senior military officers may not only disagree but *disobey* their civilian political master when acting for the benefit of the larger national security interest. That may be true, but very often the "good" of that national security interest may not be visible until much, much later, vindicating the hero's disloyalty perhaps decades after his or her retirement or death. How is the civilian leader—or military antagonist—to know, in the moment, when that disobedience is responsible? Indeed, the Emperor had already permitted the Rebels to land on Endor and access the shield generator that defended the new Death Star. He had also pre-positioned his massive fleet to attack the Rebels' ships when they later arrived. Capturing Luke, given the larger climactic battle on the horizon, seemed like a politically motivated waste of a precious resource (a Sith lord surely is in short supply) that did not satisfy any obvious strategic military objective. At best, it was the Emperor's attempt to keep his enemies closer than his friends and to share some of his political power rather than risk being overthrown completely. Moreover, Vader seemed helpless to act contrarily. The Emperor, no doubt relying on his prescience, was able to "monitor" (to use Feaver's term) his agent extensively to deter or react to perceived "shirking" that could lead to ineffective military decision making or tactical loss or, in the extreme, a coup against that principal.[7]

Fortunately, the history of American strategic civil-military relations suggests that fear of a future military-led coup d'etat is probably unrealistic.[8] Therefore, these iconic scenes of duty and obedience variously illustrate the furthest, darkest, and scariest consequence of the pathological civil-military relationship. Much more common throughout history and the foreseeable future are the subtler symptoms of fracturing or unhealthy relationships at that strategic level. The effective translation of policy (driven by politics) to military activity is one such recurring source of civil-military crisis and anxiety. It, too, is well portrayed in *Star Wars*.

WHO WIELDS THE LIGHTSABER?

During *Episode IV—A New Hope*, before Luke, Leia, Chewie, and Han find themselves battling stormtroopers in the detention block and escaping the squeeze of the trash compacter, the audience becomes privy to a gathering of senior Imperial officers inside a large, sterile conference room aboard the soon-to-be-completed Death Star.[9] General Tagge, we can immediately discern, is fraught with anxiety. With the station not yet fully operational, he warns that they are still vulnerable to an attack by the well-equipped Rebel Alliance. (On the Union side, General George McClellan, sitting inside Washington during the first year of the American Civil War and terrified of the large Confederate forces assembling across the Potomac River, would have understood this concern well.)[10] Moreover, Tagge fears that the Death Star's *use* might mean the Rebel Alliance will "continue to gain support in the Imperial Senate"—at which point he is abruptly cut off by the entrance into the war room by Grand Moff Tarkin and Darth Vader. The grand moff, a position of great influence that seemingly serves as the most senior uniformed officer, is in charge of the Empire's most important weapon and is a regional governor-general—beholden only to the head of state, the Emperor.[11] Interrupting Tagge's fretful whining, Tarkin seeks to alleviate the general's concern over the interference of the political branch that had previously offered some check on the Emperor's sovereign war-making discretion.

"The Imperial Senate," Tarkin confidently relates, "will no longer be of any concern to us. I have just received word that the Emperor has dissolved the council *permanently*. The last remnants of the Old Republic have been swept away."

"That's impossible!" Tagge replies. "How will the Emperor maintain control without the bureaucracy?"

"The regional governors now have *direct* control over their territories. *Fear* will keep the local systems in line. Fear of this battle station."

After a petty but nearly murderous squabble between Vader and Motti, Tarkin once again establishes control over his meeting. "This bickering is pointless," he declares. "Now, Lord Vader will provide us with the location of the Rebel fortress by the time this station is operational. We will then *crush* the Rebellion *with one swift stroke*." The Death Star, it becomes clear, will be used to both deter and punish, intended to firmly collapse organized resistance to the Emperor's unilateral mastery over the galaxy.

This scene, though probably more violent (and shorter) than most meetings of the Joint Chiefs of Staff inside the Pentagon's Tank, offers us a point of departure for thinking about perhaps the most consequential of all challenges that strategic civil and military leaders suffer. Translating policy into military action, in a way that is politically useful, to achieve the ends of that policy is what ultimately animated Carl von Clausewitz's thinking and description of war in general.[12] This, in Colin Gray's terms, is the "strategy bridge" between ends and means.[13] It is such a challenge because—at least in a modern democracy—the strategic military leaders are sometimes excluded from the civil political process. Even when they are allowed inside the tent, so to speak, they may misunderstand the overarching policy and therefore misuse the military instrument in its defense.[14]

Such bureaucratic disorder is often compounded. Strategic civilian leaders often lack any empirical or experiential knowledge of how and why the military works at the strategic level. They risk under- or overutilization of those deadly means.[15] The military leadership fears recklessness or fecklessness; the civilians, ultimately, worry about results of their decisions—their freedom of maneuver in the political space. These parties speak different dialects of the same language and therefore often miss the intimate connection between policy and military force (whether threatened or used). As Clausewitz wrote, "No major proposal for war can be worked out in ignorance of political factors; and when people talk, as they often do, about harmful political influence in the management of war, they are not really saying what they mean. Their quarrel is with the policy itself, not with its influence. If the policy is right—that is, successful—every intentional effect it has on the conduct of war can only be to the good."[16]

The use of the Death Star to bully star systems into compliance is clearly not for the good, and yet this scene hints at the greater issue. On one level, it illustrates that politics acts as a restraint on the unfettered ability of the sovereign to use military force to effectuate policy.[17] By dissolving the Galactic Senate by fiat, the Emperor removed a source of democratic debate, counsel, and formal opposition to his grand designs for the Empire. The only checks on his authority, then, became the uncertainty of military victory over his armed enemies—an uncertainty that his Death Star was built to overcome.

The ease with which Tarkin executed an entire planet—and *his* choice of which planet—also suggests either the tacit or explicit delegation of authority from the supreme political sovereign (the Emperor) to his expert military agents. This is yet another aspect of strategic civil-military relationships that worries pundits and politicians. Though certainly taking a form that would be tantamount to President Dwight Eisenhower allowing General Douglas MacArthur to use tactical nuclear weapons in Korea or China at his sole discretion, such a trusting relationship is not limited to science fiction or alternative history. Consider General Maxwell Taylor's relationship with President John F. Kennedy during his one-of-a-kind stint as military representative to the president (placing himself between the Joint Chiefs of Staff and the president and distinct from the national security advisor). He notes the "importance of an intimate, easy relationship, born of friendship and mutual regard, between the president and the Chiefs [and which] is particularly important in the case of the Chairman [of the Joint

Chiefs of Staff].... The Chairman should be a true believer in the foreign policy and military strategy of the administration which he serves."[18]

Tarkin, if nothing else, was such a "true believer" in the Emperor's strategy. This, of course, begs the question, Are such relationships—blurring the distinction between spheres of political responsibility and military expertise and action—healthy or desirable for the functioning of the strategic use of military might? As is often the case in these scenarios, context and personalities matter. Point of view (and often political party affiliation) ultimately shapes opinions of how degraded these relationships are or whether they simply reflect pragmatism under the circumstances—essentially, if it helps win the war, let it be.[19] Morris Janowitz, in the 1960s, argued that such clear-cut distinctions or spheres exclusively held by one or the other was unrealistic—that, in fact, a blurring may be routinely necessary for some senior military officers tasked with direct planning and negotiation with civilian leaders.[20]

On the other hand, Samuel Huntington—the father of civil-military relations theory—would have argued that Tarkin and company seemed to discredit all social and political disputes as mere military problems to be attacked. So did the political leader and head of state, the Emperor. When such modes of thinking through problems align perfectly between these two parties, the polity risks a failure in what Huntington termed "objective control" over the military.[21] Without objective control, the military becomes the government and the government becomes the military, a wholly risky state of affairs. It would suggest an opportunity for the military to pose a political threat to the existing leadership (surely something an emperor would need the Force to foresee and avoid), and it meant a Napoleon- or Alexander-type command—the sovereign himself on horseback leading the charge and taking the field of battle. This leaves the military fighting not just the enemy but also fighting for a sense of professional autonomy and to secure its distinct, internally cohesive sense of corporateness. Huntington's ideal military was, on the contrary, completely apolitical.[22] The role of the military officer, by which he meant strategic military leader, was, under his view, threefold but severely limited: first, to *represent* the military's expert views to the political and civil leadership; second, to *advise* those leaders by presenting various military courses of action that could be feasible under the circumstances; and third, to *execute* those decisions of the political leadership, even if those decisions deviate from the military's preferences.[23] Plato and Aristotle would have agreed with this stay-in-your-lane approach.[24] Under no circumstances would the state's and military's cultures or strategic leadership philosophies blend as they so clearly do in that cold and sterile Death Star conference room.

Tarkin, Vader, and the others in the room were not under the objective control of a legitimate civil authority, because *their* scope of authority was nearly boundless, only constrained by the will and discretion of one person sitting on the throne (remember, Tarkin was regional governor *and* military leader, responsible for law enforcement, security, civil governance, and military operations). As such, their actions were *aprofessional*, not *apolitical*. Under a traditional view of strategic civil-military relations, first articulated by Huntington, the translation of policy goals into military action would have been, and should be, a far messier process engaging in what Eliot Cohen has termed the "unequal dialogue."[25] It would have been akin to a lawyer carefully recommending a plea strategy to a distressed client accused of a serious crime or a doctor advising a patient facing a long illness and uncertain recovery. The agent has the expert knowledge and is the source for recommendations, but the client/patient has the authority to adopt them, ignore them, or modify them.

Rather than a bright-line rule keeping the military firmly entrenched on one side and devoid of political influence, each individual circumstance would be resolved differently—the balance between those two unequal voices—because of the different personalities, particularized problem sets, preferences, priorities, and prejudices. For Cohen, it ought to be a "question of prudence, not principle" that shapes how intrusive or hands-off that civilian leader is with respect to military affairs.[26] In other words, the unequal nature of the dialogue between Lincoln and McClellan was in no way binding on how it would play out later between Lincoln and Grant.[27] What worked for Kennedy and Taylor did not work for Kennedy and his earlier Joint Chiefs.[28] Secretary of Defense Donald Rumsfeld's dialogue with General Tommy Franks between 2001 and 2003, to take a more recent example, was unequal in a different way (some would suggest a more negative way) than later dialogue between Secretary Robert Gates and General Stanley McChrystal, fighting in Afghanistan. Under this view, there is no fixed formula that calculates the respective duties of the civil-military leaders and no line painted dividing their lanes.

The *Star Wars* universe demonstrated the absence of such strategic dialogue. No questions about the Emperor's quest for power arose, and none seemed to have been burning the consciences of those in the room. No thought was given to whether this tool, with all its menacing brutality, was the *right* tool within the arsenal to achieve the purposes of order and stability the Emperor envisioned. While never imposing an obligation on the master (the principal or client *always* maintains absolute sovereignty and direction over the representation), their military expertise and experience would have been useful to the civil authority, at least as a way to work through potential political objections or plan ahead for potential military setbacks. In a pure dictatorship, such as the Galactic Empire under Palpatine illustrates, those fruitful (even if time-consuming and inefficient) councils are less likely to occur. In a more democratically based system of war powers, such as the U.S. Constitution establishes, the civilian principal retains ultimate discretion and command authority.[29] But this does not mean the voice of reason or alternatives is never heard. Quite the opposite, American political tradition tends to still follow Huntington's model for objective control and suggests that nagging voice of subject-matter expertise is mandatory, especially at that critical juncture when policy becomes expressed by military means.[30] As General Martin Dempsey, a recent chairman of the Joint Chiefs of Staff, wrote, "Military professionals hold unique expertise and their input is vital to formulating and executing effective policy. This requires that the military's unique perspective and advice be heard in the formulation of laws and policies that create, support, and employ our armed forces, or its effectiveness can be reduced to the detriment of the Republic."[31]

President Kennedy expressed this same sentiment in the gloomy days following the failed Bay of Pigs invasion of Cuba in 1961. Disappointed in the strategic advice he was given, Kennedy wrote a memo to his Joint Chiefs, reminding them of what his expectations were for their counsel: "I expect the Joint Chiefs of Staff to present the military viewpoint in governmental councils in such a way as to assure that the military factors are clearly understood before decisions are reached. . . . While I look to the Chiefs to represent the military factor without reserve or hesitation, I regard them to be more than military men and expect their help in fitting military requirements into the over-all context of any situation, recognizing that the most difficult problem in Government is to combine all assets in a unified, effective pattern."[32]

Unquestionably, at some point, strategy-making practice necessarily involves both civilian and military elites. Both must understand the "basic and prevailing conception of what any war existing or impending is really about and what it is attempting to accomplish."[33] As the complexities of organizing and building the material, training the manpower, and employing the weapons of modern war seem to ever increase, war generates the need for an ever-expanding technocratic professional staff expertise to wisely manage the processes that aid civilian leaders in translating policy into strategy and strategy into military operations with tactical objectives.

WHAT LESSONS FROM A GALAXY FAR, FAR AWAY?

We look to the future for a reason: to redirect our attention to the present.

Christopher Coker, *Can War Be Eliminated?*

Whether it is the Emperor's unilateral control over all aspects of military strategy (U. S. Grant once had some disparaging comments on President Jefferson Davis's own inclination to do the same) or co-opting Tarkin's military expertise and blurring the line between civil and military decision making, the story lines of *Star Wars* offer clear-cut examples of universal and timeless themes that animate all discussions of strategic civil-military relationships.[34] Duties of obedience and scope of authority under principles of agency, the sovereign's source of political legitimacy, a military command-er's discretion, and loyalty pop up within these hallowed scenes. They can be instructive starting points for thinking through present difficulties and future civil-military crises. If we are careful, we can target them as easily as Luke did with womp rats in his T-16 back home.

Notes

1. Thomas Hobbes, *Leviathan* (1651), quoted in Steven Pinker, *The Better Angels of Our Nature: Why Violence Has Declined* (London: Penguin Books, 2012), 33. Hobbes was a scholar and translator of the first historian of war (or true historian, period), Thucydides; see Thucydides's epic *The History of the Peloponnesian War*, trans. Rex Warner, bk. 1.76 (New York: Penguin Classics, 1954), 80, describing Athens's fear, honor, and self-interest as rationally determining its relations with the other Greek city-states, including Sparta. See also Donald Kagan, *On the Origins of War and the Preservation of Peace* (New York: Doubleday, 1995), 8, quoting Thucydides; Colin S. Gray, *The Strategy Bridge: Theory for Practice* (Oxford: Oxford University Press, 2016), 101–2, 111, referring to Thucydides's "timeless triptych" as a "powerful universal formula" explaining—in general terms—why people go to war. See also John Rawls, *The Law of Peoples* (Cambridge MA: Harvard University Press, 2001), 28–29, recasting but adhering to Thucydides, using the terms *power, prestige,* and *wealth.*
2. Christopher Coker argues that "war remains ubiquitous because we are still in thrall to our inherited biology"; Christopher Coker, *Can War Be Eliminated?* (Cambridge: Polity, 2014), 6–17.
3. Here, I simplify. The offer to Luke implies what would amount to a coup, and there are many types of coup that need not be distinguished here. For a description of the various types, see Rebecca L. Schiff, *The Military and Domestic Politics: A Concordance Theory of Civil-Military Relations* (New York: Routledge Press, 2009), 21.
4. Peter D. Feaver, *Armed Servants: Agency, Oversight, and Civil-Military Relations* (Cambridge MA: Harvard University Press, 2005), 54.
5. In fact, in *Episode V*, it is Vader who first suggests to the Emperor that "if [Skywalker] could be turned, he would be a powerful ally."
6. Kathleen M. Eisenhardt, "Agency Theory: An Assessment and Review," *Academy of Management Review* 14 (1989): 57, 58; see also James Burk, "Responsible Obedience by Military Professionals: The Discretion to Do What Is Wrong," in *American Civil-Military Relations: The Soldier and the State in a New Era*, ed. Suzanne C. Nielson and Don M. Snider (Baltimore MA: Johns Hopkins University Press, 2009), 149, 151–54.
7. Feaver, *Armed Servants*, 58–68.
8. But for a creative and interesting counterargument, see Charles J. Dunlap Jr., "The Origins of the American Military Coup of 2012," *Parameters*, Winter 2011–12 (reprint from Winter 1992–93), 107.
9. "Holding a sword" is often used as a metaphor for the divided control over the use of military force. See, for example, Mackubin Thomas Owens, "What Military Officers Need to Know about Civil-Military Relations," *Naval War College Review* 65, no. 2 (Spring 2002): 67, which

states, "At the institutional level, there are 'two hands on the sword.' The civil hand determines when to draw it from the scabbard and thence guides it in its use. This is the dominant hand of policy, the purpose for which the sword exists in the first place. The military's hand sharpens the sword for use and wields it in combat"; see also Vincent Brooks, Thomas C. Greenwood, Robert C. Parker, and Keith L. Wray, *Two Hands on the Sword: A Study of Political-Military Relations in National Security Policy* (Carlisle PA: U.S. Army War College, 1999).

10. James M. McPherson, *Tried by War: Abraham Lincoln as Commander in Chief* (New York: Penguin Press, 2008), 52–53.

11. He is the only one in the room apparently capable of restraining Darth Vader's use of the Force to strangle Motti when he notes that Vader's "sad devotion to that ancient religion" has been so far useless in preventing the Empire from defeating the Rebels.

12. In *On War*, Clausewitz argues that "war is a pulsation of violence . . . [but] subject to the action of a superior intelligence . . . war is not merely an act of policy but a true political instrument, a continuation of political intercourse, carried on by other means" and that "war is only a branch of political activity . . . in no sense autonomous." Carl von Clausewitz, *On War*, indexed edition, ed. and trans. Michael Howard and Peter Paret, with Bernard Brodie (Princeton NJ: Princeton University Press, 1984), 87, 605.

13. Gray, *Strategy Bridge*, 7, 15.

14. Gray, *Strategy Bridge*, 204.

15. Eliot A. Cohen, *Supreme Command: Soldiers, Statesmen, and Leadership in Wartime* (New York: Anchor Books, 2002), 2–3. Some exceptions, tending to prove the rule, include Ulysses S. Grant after the American Civil War, Dwight Eisenhower after the Second World War, and Winston Churchill as prime minister during that war.

16. Clausewitz, *On War*, 608.

17. See, for example, U.S. Department of the Navy, *Warfighting*, Marine Corps Doctrine Publication (MCDP) 1 (Washington DC: Department of Defense, 1997), 23–25, http://www.marines.mil /Portals/59/Publications/MCDP%201%20Warfighting.pdf. See also Gideon Rose, *How Wars End: Why We Always Fight the Last Battle* (New York: Simon and Schuster, 2010), 3; Colin S. Gray, *Modern Strategy* (Oxford: Oxford University Press, 1999), 30, 5; Lawrence Freedman, *Strategy: A History* (Oxford: Oxford University Press, 2013), 86–87.

18. Maxwell D. Taylor, *Swords and Plowshares* (New York: W. W. Norton, 1972), 252.

19. Linda Robinson et al., *Improving Strategic Competence: Lessons from 13 Years of War* (Santa Monica CA: RAND, 2014), http://www.rand.org/pubs/research_reports/RR816.html.

20. Morris Janowitz, *The Professional Soldier* (New York: Free Press, 1971), 20.

21. Samuel P. Huntington, *The Soldier and the State: The Theory and Politics of Civil-Military Relations* (Cambridge MA: Belknap Press, 1957), 83–85.

22. Huntington, *Soldier and the State*, 71.

23. Huntington, *Soldier and the State*, 72.

24. Plato, *The Republic*, bk. 4; Aristotle, *Nicomachean Ethics*, bk. 1; see also Russell, *History of Western Philosophy*, 113, 183.

25. Cohen, *Supreme Command*, 12.

26. Cohen, *Supreme Command*, 12.

27. T. Harry Williams, *Lincoln and His Generals* (New York: Knopf, 1952), 6–11.

28. "After the Bay of Pigs, Kennedy had little regard for the JCS and their recommendations." Arthur M. Schlesinger Jr., *A Thousand Days: John F. Kennedy in the White House* (Boston: Mariner Books, 2002), xvi, 295.

29. U.S. Const. art II, § 2, cl. 1; but see David Luban, "On the Commander in Chief Power," *South Carolina Law Review* 81 (2008): 477, 483, which argues, "The Commander in Chief Clause is a sphinx, and specifying its powers and the theory generating them is its riddle."

30. Cohen, *Supreme Command*, 229. Eisenhower also argued that "there must be a clear and unchallenged civilian responsibility in the Defense establishment . . . [which] is essential not only to maintain democratic institutions, but also to protect the integrity of the military profession." Dwight D. Eisenhower, "Special Message to the Congress Transmitting Reorganization Plan 6 of 1953 Concerning the Department of Defense," *The American Presidency Project*, April 30, 1953, http://www.presidency.ucsb.edu/ws/?pid=9831.

31. Martin Dempsey, *The Profession of Arms: An Army White Paper* (Washington DC: U.S. Army Training and Doctrine Command, 2010), 26, http://cape.army.mil/repository/white-papers /profession-of-arms-white-paper.pdf.

32. President John F. Kennedy to the Chairman, Joint Chiefs of Staff, "Relations of the Joint Chiefs of Staff to the President in Cold War Operations," National Security Action Memorandum 55, June 28, 1961, https://www.jfklibrary.org/Asset-Viewer/sjtthyMxu06GMct7OymAvw .aspx. General Maxwell Taylor was, according to Matthew Moten, the primary author of this memorandum, as a recommendation to President Kennedy followed Taylor's personal investigation of the Bay of Pigs operation. Matthew Moten, *Presidents and Their Generals: An American History of Command in War* (Cambridge MA: Belknap Press, 2014), 279–80.

33. Bernard Brodie, *War and Politics* (New York: Macmillan, 1973), 439.

34. Grant sarcastically reflected that Jefferson Davis held an "exalted opinion of his own military genius." U. S. Grant, *Personal Memoirs of U. S. Grant* (Cambridge MA: De Capo Press, 2001), 344.

6

How General Grievous and Vulture Droids Foreshadow Conflict's Fast Future

RAQ WINCHESTER AND FRAN WILDE

No battle plan ever survives first contact with the enemy.

Helmuth von Moltke

According to leadership guru Simon Sinek, great leaders start with *why*. Why is action important? The leader needs to know this, and a great leader will tell her followers the reasons. As Yoda might say, "Start with *why*, great leaders do."

Sinek and Yoda mean leaders of people, but what happens when the troops aren't people? Where does the leader start then? Very soon, our military leaders will command autonomous mechanicals—drones and robots with limited onboard artificial intelligence, or AI. As a result, the United States' military must expand and clarify Sinek's maxim, integrating it with the "OODA loop" (Observe, Orient, Decide, and Act) for the future of warfare. If correctly implemented, this will allow military AIs to assess what they observe against the why of the strategic goals and to orient correctly, making the right decisions and taking effective action.

Let's think about this from the perspective of a drone swarm defending some airspace. If one drone falls out of the swarm, the others immediately *observe*, "Drone X was killed," and *orient*, "We have a hole in our formation." Because they know why they are there, they *decide*, "We must fill that vulnerability," and *act* with all drones in the swarm adjusting spacing until there is no gap.

This capability won't be found only in tactical swarms; leadership itself will operate from intimately composite constructs, because the leaders of this military must start from a multifaceted why. The commanding officer must communicate *why* the action is necessary to the individual mechanical or organic as well as to the swarm. Near-future warfighting is going to involve a lot of swarms.

This means commanding officers must communicate at computer speed, considering and addressing all the possibilities the drone swarm or robot will consider. To address this need, military command will be human officers advised by artificial intelligences, giving orders framed as *why*s to autonomous swarms, which then determine the best way to achieve the goal.

Think General Grievous and his vulture droids, rather than individually piloted UAVs (unmanned aerial vehicles).

Grievous's contribution to the combat capability of the Separatist Alliance is the vulture droid, officially known as the Variable Geometry Self-Propelled Battle Droid, Mark I, or more commonly, the Vulture-class starfighter. The vulture droid was initially a remote-controlled, small, space-based weapon; but during the Clone Wars, Grievous upgraded them with limited AI, making them increasingly autonomous. The vulture droids are fast, cheap, and spatially controlled kinetic force (lowercased *f*) projections.

These autonomous mechanicals can dominate the future's three-dimensional battlespace; they can deploy in water, in atmosphere, or in orbit. In 2016 the United States began to lose the air dominance it had enjoyed since the end of World War II, as scrappy adversaries like ISIS weaponized hobby drones and took asymmetric warfare to the skies. In response, the Department of Defense's Strategic Capabilities Office developed swarm intelligence for flying drones, allowing each machine to communicate with others in the swarm at speed. The swarm intelligence worked like a flock of birds or school of fish, reconfiguring the swarm as units were lost or directives altered, because it understood the why and used the OODA loop to come up with the how on its own as illustrated in our example.

These drone swarms, like vulture droids, answer the three big drawbacks to human warfighters: while humans process faster than current supercomputers, they can't process all possible data types, and they tend to select biased data sets; they can be hurt, confused, or killed; and because the military seeks to avoid or limit casualties, a great many high-risk/high-reward operations don't happen. Droid swarms will allow the military to attempt those. Oh, and humans don't work well in space.

Grievous's vulture droids show us how future generals will command swarms, starting from why. Grievous gets an objective ("Kill Anakin Skywalker"), develops a strategy ("Because Anakin is human and can't survive space, getting to him with mechanical minions when he's limited in melee combat has the best chance of success"), and decides on an operation ("Intercept Anakin in his Jedi starfighter when he comes out of lightspeed alone in this zone"). Grievous deploys his vulture droids with the mission parameters in their programming and leaves the tactical decisions to their limited swarm AI. While each vulture droid individually attempts to do the most damage where it contacts the Jedi starfighter, Anakin and his astromech droid fight back as the swarm reconfigures to attack key targets like the life support, astromech, and cockpit, applying the OODA loop against the why of "We're here to kill Skywalker."

Grievous also demonstrates the power of a combined human(oid) and AI officer, which we will need to command mixed troops. General Grievous started life as a red-skinned reptilian humanoid from Kaleesh, but he expanded his fighting ability with mechanical body alterations. While his brain remains organic, he relies on information and advice from astromech droids and battle droids. This makes him a *centaur*—a composite person-AI who makes decisions by synthesizing human and machine intelligence.

This usage of "centaur" comes from chess, where it refers to a human and a computer playing as a team to take advantage of their complementary strengths. For the past two decades, the combination of human and computer has created the strongest chess players, far surpassing top human players and beating even the best chess computers. The centaur model is being adopted by the Department of Defense to create the best possible military strategists and analysts, combining the speed and depth of artificial intelligence with the creativity and strategic vision of a human expert.

This is the U.S. military's Third Offset Strategy, the newest how addressing the why of countering adversaries such as the Russian or Chinese militaries. Centaurs give human commanders breadth of awareness, knowledge, and speed to keep up with droid troops; but the decision to engage is human. The Jedi would want it that way.

With the drone swarms, our brilliant strategic centaurs will have warfighter resources that are expendable, have more and different senses, and be able to OODA at near-human speeds. It's a seemingly winning combination, but Grievous and the vulture droids did not win. What might go wrong?

The current U.S. military hierarchy isn't big on sharing the why or on pushing decisions down to the lowest possible level at which they can be made. Historically, the military has been a "Just do what I told you" culture. Some of the military will need to stay that way, but the warfighters must follow the example set in Iraq by General Stanley McChrystal's Joint Special Operations Task Force. However, despite the success of the task force, military culture and conventional wisdom have not yet embraced this new paradigm. It will be very difficult to implement the Third Offset Strategy in the U.S. military culture, and it will need to be implemented differently for autonomous mechanicals than for human soldiers. While meat and metal squads should be flexible and effective in support of each other, the ability to communicate the why and the ability to process multiple hows will require a lot of specialized training and practice in the officer corps, and the military is likely to segregate mechanicals from organics for decades.

Even if implemented well and properly, this approach isn't without risks. The biggest risk to removing humans from harm's way? It will be an easier decision to engage in conflict. The cost-benefit analysis of "Should we fight?" will skew toward "yes."

More wars more frequently will stress our computing power and other resources. And of course, limited AI and swarm intelligence will—as all technology does—proliferate and escalate. While the U.S. offset strategies are designed to offset some Russian and Chinese relative advantages, the United States can expect to see rapid advances in autonomous minions from Russia and in AI from China. Both adversaries pose significant cyberwar threats as well, which will doubtless be deployed against military AIs. We already see decentralized networks organized around a central why, in the Taliban, Al-Qaeda, and ISIS.

Another downside is that algorithms are philosophies, not proofs—and in a swarm the algorithms that drive drone decision making must be tested and retested against the geo-socio-political landscape in order to avoid becoming outdated or worse. While a human-AI centaur at the core of a General Grievous or the Third Offset Strategy could balance out these risks, overreliance on algorithms and outdated technology patches is something we already suffer. A strategy for swarm maintenance would be well advised, as would plenty of war games and battle labs to check the assumptions inherent in the algorithms.

This future is coming. Military drone swarms will initially be defensive, but air- and sea-based small UAVs will enact strategies like this within the next five to ten years, damaging or destroying planes, helicopters, cars, and boats. The centaur with full AI will come online a little later; and because this isn't a scripted show where Grievous must lose, we can expect the military centaurs and swarms to see much more combat success with many fewer human casualties.

As Obi-Wan says, "Only a Sith lord deals in absolutes." Centaurs and drone swarms will likely give us safer, quicker war, but may come with the loss of the very human *why*.

7

From Princess to General

The On- and Offscreen Rise of the Woman Warrior

ERICA IVERSON

Leia wigs. Action figures. Halloween costumes. Christmas ornaments. Forty years after the release of *Star Wars: Episode IV—A New Hope* in 1977, the far-reaching influence of the *Star Wars* franchise is deeply rooted in global pop culture. Beyond marketing, one discernible impact of *Star Wars* is the advancement of female characters throughout the movie series. Leia Organa's character progression from princess to general throughout the series of films showcases the evolution of her character depth over time. Leia's trajectory has featured several roles of tactical and strategic importance: diplomat in the Imperial Senate, leader in the Rebel Alliance, Hutt killer, and commanding general in the Resistance. As a catalyst for change in Hollywood, Leia helped set the stage for women serving in nontraditional gender roles both in film and the real world. Posters of Leia as Rosie the Riveter and of Leia posing with her blaster have inspired millions. With exposure to Princess Leia as an action figure in the late twentieth century, fighting alongside and even saving male counterparts in battle, American strategic culture began a transformation. Women characters in the *Star Wars* saga are inspiring generations. Young girls are now opting to dress up as superheroes instead of princesses, trading scepters for lightsabers.[1] Over the last four decades, *Star Wars'* portrayal of women in myriad roles has facilitated an important cultural shift on the role of women serving in strategic leadership positions.

Through the 1970s and 1980s, archetypal female roles in Hollywood were often hypersexualized, glorifying physicality over capability, like the infamous Bond girls. With the release of the first *Star Wars* movie in 1977, audiences were exposed to the duality of a female character who fights, shoots, kills, and looks good doing it. Fans responded. Princess Leia as the heroine became an icon. Her character memorabilia are showcased in conventions, video games, apps, toys, costumes, blogs, and books. The public demand for women in nontraditional roles launched a paradigm shift of traditional gender stereotypes within the sixteen-year gap between *Episode VI—Return of the Jedi* (1983) and *Episode I—The Phantom Menace* (1999). Americans started opening historically male-held senior management roles and accepted more leadership positions for women. In the 1990s, for the first time, women in the United States became U.S. surgeon general (1990), an African American senator (1992), an African American astronaut (1992), a military service secretary (in the U.S. Air Force, 1993), attorney general (1993), and secretary of state (1997). Many supported these firsts in government, but it took a little more Leia, Queen Amidala, and Mon Motha to help garner mainstream acceptance of women in key leadership roles.

The Clone Wars animated series was a game changer for *Star Wars* fans. Airing six seasons (2008–13) between the release of *Episode III—Revenge of the Sith* and *Episode VII—The Force Awakens,* the series introduced female characters in myriad roles not conventionally seen in other Hollywood genres. These characters appealed to younger audiences, who could identify with the challenges they faced. Young girls could dream beyond being a princess and envision themselves as a Jedi master, fighter pilot, Rebel soldier, or ship captain. *The Clone Wars* was a nexus of change, shifting the gender paradigm on what female characters were capable of doing and achieving. Fans embraced Ciena Ree (captain of a Star Destroyer), Hera Syndulla (captain of the *Ghost* freighter), Shaak Ti (Jedi general on the Jedi

Council), and Aayla Secura (Jedi knight and general who led the 327th Star Corps of clone troopers). Through *The Clone Wars*, younger audiences saw empowered women characters give orders, make critical decisions, balance personal issues, and fight for what they believed in—and those audiences were thereby empowered themselves. Strong female leaders were now operating at all levels of conflict on both sides of the good-evil continuum. The wider success of the animated series set the pace for a promising Hollywood trend, giving voice to an expanded demographic fan base who challenged producers to cast more-relatable characters.[2] When Kathleen Kennedy, one of Hollywood's most powerful women, took over from George Lucas as president of Lucasfilm in 2012, a new era of *Star Wars* began.[3] Her influence as movie producer, beginning with the 2015 release of *The Force Awakens*, has had a colossal impact, bringing in more women roles in the films.

In the first six movies, there are only a few speaking roles for women besides Leia; conversely, newer releases *Episode VII—The Force Awakens* and *Rogue One* feature not only female leads but women in more varied and disparate roles as well. *Star Wars* set the trend by promoting influential role models whom both men and women could identify with and aspire to be and who challenged traditional norms. More important for a younger-generation audience is to see real-life women redefining gender roles, both on- and offscreen. Taking protagonists Rey and Jyn Erso, for example, and comparing them to corporeal women with similar, proven capabilities helps legitimize these characters. Rey is a female Luke Skywalker. Her resourcefulness, intuition, quick wit, and scavenger skills ensure her survival. Her mastery—as a pilot, a captive, a fighter with any weapon—is instinctive. Rey is a departure from the helpless damsel, demonstrated so clearly—and in the moment's brevity, powerfully—when she tells Finn, "I know how to run without you holding my hand."

A small number of U.S. Army officers who also don't need any handholding set a historical precedent by graduating from the U.S. Army's arduous Ranger School since it opened to women in 2015. Physical and mental grit, tactical proficiency, weapons expertise, industriousness, and self-survival are just a few of the traits needed to survive the rigorous sixty-one-day course. These women defied the odds and, after earning the coveted Ranger Tab, became overnight legends—with real-world echoes of Jyn Erso, who led her all-male team of Rebels in a self-sacrificial mission to get the Death Star plans to Rebel leadership. Defiant and determined, Jyn Erso's character also reflects the traits of Jennifer Matthews, a Central Intelligence Agency analyst whose experience and knowledge in targeting and hunting al-Qaeda operatives was unmatched.[4] Tragically, Matthews was killed in a targeted attack; however, she was one part of the Band of Sisters, who collectively, using their experience, leadership, and strategic vision, were able to hunt down Osama bin Laden.[5] These Army Rangers and Band of Sisters illustrate how over forty years our cultural perceptions have changed and our strategic culture has revolutionized social acceptance of women as strategic leaders. Look no further than the full gender integration of women into all combat roles in the United States' armed services, which began in April 2016.

Retired Major General Robert Scales used the term "Strategic Jedi" to describe those individuals who possess qualities that align with Carl von Clausewitz's definition of strategic genius.[6] The U.S. government has been expanding its force of strategic Jedi. It is now commonplace to see women serving as strategic advisors, directors, commanders, administrators, and executives in national and international leadership roles. The Obama administration brought on a record nine women to cabinet-level positions. Three female judges sit on the United States' highest court. Positions historically held by men have opened to women, to include the directors of the U.S. Secret Service and the CIA's National Clandestine Service; the White House national security advisor; the head of the National Geospatial Intelligence Agency; the ranking member of the House of Representatives Appropriations Committee; and a four-star combatant commander. Three branches of the U.S. armed services have had a woman reach the rank of four-star general. The same trend can be seen in corporate America. Yahoo CEO Marissa Mayer was a major influence in Google's success, starting as their first female engineer and rising through the ranks to be a top executive before taking the helm at Yahoo. Mayer famously claimed that she "refused to be stereotyped," much like Leia, Rey, and Jyn, while further promoting the idea that "passion is a gender-neutralizing force.[7] Indeed.

Allowing for the most-qualified individuals to fill leadership positions brings in fresh perspectives as well as a credible and varied range of expertise and talent.[8] To accommodate the growing trend of women holding key leadership roles around the globe, the United Nations Security Council unanimously adopted UN Security Council Resolution 1325 (UNSCR 1325) as an international framework to address the pivotal role women should and do play in conflict management, conflict resolution, and sustainable peace.[9] Dr. Theo-Ben Gurirab, president of the Security Council when UNSCR 1325 passed in October 2000, remarked that "women are half of every community. . . . Are they, therefore, not also half of every solution?"[10] Decidedly so. UNSCR 1325 recognizes—then and, more importantly, today—the pivotal role women play in the prevention and resolution of conflict. Women in our world are now recognized as active agents of change, at the forefront of national security, politics, defense, peace building, and peace keeping.

The *Star Wars* franchise shows no sign of waning interest. Over forty years ago, only five of the original ninety-three action figures available represented a woman; and of those five, all were Princess Leia. Today, fans have abundant options of male and female action figures, in many different roles. *The Force Awakens* features women as medics, X-wing fighter pilots, computer technicians, weapons analysts, mechanics, intelligence officers, Senate leaders, and even a stormtrooper captain. *Star Wars* continues to change perceptions and surpass expectations of the capabilities its characters perform.

The cultural transformation over the past four decades is so clearly illustrated by comparing *A New Hope* to the newest films: Princess Leia became General Leia, while Yoda and Jedi Luke gave way to Maz and Jedi Rey. In the true test of battle, victory requires an unequal sum of stamina, courage, strength, will, intelligence, and honor, an alchemy that may be different for all yet is fundamentally gender indifferent. In 2017's *Wonder Woman*, fans cheered in theaters across the country as Diana Prince commanded her ragtag team of men amid battle: "Stay here. I'll go ahead." Strategic Jedi come in many shapes and forms, using the tools they are given. More integral, pivotal, and diverse characters in *Star Wars* has expanded the series' fan base well beyond the success of the early films. In the closing scene of *Rogue One*, we get a glimpse of Princess Leia looking at the stolen plans of the Death Star, saying one word: "Hope." We are forging toward the next frontier of leadership with women taking their rightful place at the helm. Soon we will not need to rely so heavily on fictional characters for inspiration, as we increasingly have enough real-life women Jedi to choose from. They are our new hope.

Notes

1. Hailey Middlebrook, "Halloween Costume Showdown: Superheroes Beat Princesses This Year," CNN, October 19, 2016, http://www.cnn.com/2016/10/19/health/halloween-costumes-superhero-princess/.

2. Social media sites like *FANGirl Blog*, Tumblr's *Women of Star Wars*, and podcast *Fangirls Going Rogue* continue to recruit and unite a global audience, generating interest to demand more roles for women on-screen.

3. Michal Lev-Ram, "How the Star Wars Producer Went from Secretary to Studio Boss," *Fortune*, September 10, 2015, http://fortune.com/2015/09/10/kathleen-kennedy-lucasfilm-star-wars/.

4. Robert Windrem, "Hunting Osama bin Laden Was Women's Work," NBC News, November 14, 2013, http://www.nbcnews.com/news/other/hunting-osama-bin-laden-was-womens-work-f2D11594091.

5. Windrem, "Hunting Osama bin Laden Was Women's Work."

6. Robert H. Scales, "Are You a Strategic Genius? Not Likely, Given Army's System for Selecting, Education Leaders," Association of the United States Army, October 13, 2016, https://www.ausa.org/articles/are-you-strategic-genius-not-likely-given-army%E2%80%99s-system-selecting-educating-leaders. "Every special calling in life, if it is to be followed with success, requires peculiar qualifications of understanding and soul. When these are of a high order, and manifest themselves by extraordinary achievements, the mind to which they belong is termed genius." Carl von Clausewitz, *On War*, ed. and trans. James John Graham (London: N. Trübner, 1873), 23.

7. Breeanna Hare, "How Marissa Mayer Writes Her Own Rules," CNN, March 13, 2013, http://www.cnn.com/2013/03/12/tech/web/marissa-mayer-yahoo-profile/.

8. Adding a gender perspective into leadership and the decision-making process has far-reaching impacts in the fields of foreign policy, defense, and international peace and security. In national defense, inclusion of women into nontraditional roles like female engagement teams (FETs), tiger teams, and gender field advisors has transformed the gender paradigm with regards to women in combat, in which all combat roles are now open to qualified individuals, gender notwithstanding. Female soldiers and marines on assigned teams help inform and shape

operational and tactical missions through their interactions with local women. Women serving on FETs have influenced local populations by improving situational awareness and collecting intelligence from local women. Diverse perspectives, albeit gender, cultural, religious, or other, can derive unique viewpoints, innovative approaches, and alternative solutions.

9. Office of the Special Adviser on Gender Issues and Advancement of Women, "Landmark Resolution on Women, Peace and Society," United Nations, accessed August 25, 2017, http://www.un.org/womenwatch/osagi/wps/.

10. Brenda Oppermann, "Hawks, Doves and Canaries: Women and Conflict," *Small Wars Journal*, August 13, 2014, http://smallwarsjournal.com/jrnl/art/hawks-doves-and-canaries-women-and-conflict.

PART 2

Preparation for War

Wars require weapons; weapons require arsenals; arsenals require planning.

Every society needing protection must make provisions that include all kinds of high and low tech: swords and shields, fighters and blasters, destroyers and droids. The ancient adage applies, even in space: *Si vis pacem, para bellum* (If you want peace, prepare for war).

How should we construct our future fighting tools? Not just technically, but mentally? How should we connect ideas about weapons for war to a theory of victory? And how can we spot early flaws that might lead to failure downstream?

These essays describe prewar preparedness across several dimensions and in two broad categories: physical (logistics, economics, organization, and technology) and intellectual (intelligence structure, doctrine development, and strategic theory). Whether forming the iron fist or thinking through how to use it, these efforts are an attempt to create some order before the chaos.

Tarkin Doctrine

The Empire's Theory of Victory

KELSEY D. ATHERTON

The regional governors now have direct control over their territories. Fear will keep the local systems in line. Fear of this battle station.

Grand Moff Tarkin

Wilhuff Tarkin has only twenty-three lines in *A New Hope*. Thirty-nine years later, he gains three more in *Rogue One*. It is from such a thin canon that we get Grand Moff Tarkin, the ill-fated architect of Imperial strategy whose mind gave form to an audacious strategic theory. Outside of the films, Tarkin enjoyed a strong showing in both *The Clone Wars* and *Rebels*, which fill in the great gaps between the collapse of the Old Republic and the emergence of the Galactic Empire. While Palpatine orchestrated his ascent to power, while Anakin Skywalker claimed tactical success after tactical success, Tarkin theorized a path for the Empire to hold power, forever.

The Old Republic died from a thousand cuts, and none were clearer than the lack of a flexible military response to growing unrest. With Tarkin's proposed oversectors, a single high-ranking military commander would have extra resources on hand and the authority to quell rebellions. We can see in this a response to the chaos of the Clone Wars, where the Republic found itself in a civil war and without an army. Tarkin's entire career was a response to the failures of the Jedi Order, whose diplomat-knights had failed to prevent the war or, on their own, win it.

The Tarkin Doctrine was a theory for Imperial supremacy over the entire galaxy, motivated by fear and held in check by a stunning, staggering technological development: the Death Star. We first see the Tarkin Doctrine spelled out as a memorandum to Emperor Palpatine, in the *Death Star Technical Companion*, a supplement to the *Star Wars* Roleplaying Game. Like all grand statements of strategy, it describes a specific threat and several overarching tools for controlling that threat.

First is the threat: the persistent problem of rebellions—except for those, Palpatine's Empire was poised to control the galaxy for a long time, after decades of civil war. Tarkin acknowledged that peace might eventually be achieved through permanent occupation by force of the entire galaxy, but having the military on hand to do that was a distant proposition. To meet the immediate and future needs of the Empire, Tarkin had three major proposals: rapidly form new military districts, rule through fear, and create a superweapon that would inspire terror in anyone who ever even thought about tolerating a rebellion on their planet.

Military governors, with sweeping authority over their sectors, were one part of Tarkin's solution. The Empire, as we see it in *Rogue One* and *A New Hope*, was powerful but not all powerful. There were hard limits based on the number of Star Destroyers, TIE fighters, and stormtroopers. Darth Vader was the penultimate tool in this arsenal; an ace pilot and deadly weapon unto himself, he cowed all around him into obedient surrender or death. But Vader was one man, the last of a religious faith, and it's clear that Tarkin had contempt for all Jedi.

"The Jedi are extinct; their fire has gone out of the universe," Tarkin told Vader, in response to Vader sensing the presence of Obi-Wan Kenobi. "You, my friend, are all that's left of their religion."

Tarkin was hardly the first commander, tasked with ending an insurgency, to find that the religious Rebels he had been sent to quash still persisted.

But Tarkin wasn't thinking of the Galactic Civil War in terms of religious conflict. He was focused on stopping all possible rebellions, and for that he needed fear. To Tarkin's eye, a galaxy where everyone is in mortal fear of the consequences of rebelling is a galaxy that can be garrisoned at a fraction of the cost of one where punishment is lenient. The second component of the Tarkin Doctrine is rule through fear, and that fear came from a weapon never before seen in the history of the galaxy: the Death Star.

By the time of *Rogue One*, the Empire had no external threats. There were rebellions, but the Clone Wars were over, the separatists were defeated, and the whole military apparatus was devoted to killing stragglers and cementing Palpatine's rule. It was at this same time that the Empire began to develop the Death Star, a weapon conceptualized in the Old Republic but not yet fielded in the universe. The Death Star was a tool of fear, not just for Rebels, but for anyone who harbored Rebels. The ability to destroy a planet was, potentially, galaxy changing. Insurgencies thrived by finding places they could hide before striking out again. With the Death Star, Tarkin had a weapon that could destroy an entire planet simply for the crime of harboring Rebels.

The Death Star was an offset strategy, turning the Empire's monopoly on power and deep pockets into a tool that could force any planet to choose between surrender or nonexistence. The first planet destroyed was Alderaan, formally peaceful but with Rebel sympathies. To the extent that news traveled in the galaxy, the sudden destruction of a planet from a brand-new superweapon must have been all anyone talked about. And it was power concentrated nominally under the Emperor's control; but in effect, the power to end worlds was Tarkin's alone.

With Alderaan destroyed, Grand Moff Tarkin had every reason to believe that the Rebellion would soon suffer a similar fate. Tracking an escaped prisoner back to her Rebel base put a bullseye on the greatest foe to stable Imperial rule, and Tarkin almost got away with it.

We know how this ended; a flaw, designed into the Death Star, became the target of choice for several Rebellion fighter squadrons. Darth Vader, together with TIE fighter escorts, attempted to stop the fighters on their drive to the thermal exhaust port. A force-sensitive ace pilot fired the salvo that destroyed the Death Star, and Tarkin perished in the ensuing fireball.

Was the Tarkin Doctrine worth it? It certainly seemed so to the Emperor, who oversaw construction of a second Death Star. Destroying Alderaan, intended to convince the public that harboring Rebels was a fatal mistake, instead galvanized existing Rebels against the Empire. What was supposed to be rule through fear floundered at the first sign of Imperial fallibility.

Still, no one else in the entire *Star Wars* universe offered as clear a path to peace through superior firepower. Tarkin's vision, forged in civil war and counterinsurgency, was a military technology so powerful that it changed the politics of the galaxy, so threatening that it made insurgency a death sentence not just for the would-be insurgents but for anyone even distantly related to a possible insurgent. Palpatine supported the tool and likely the tactic, and the First Order, a bloodthirsty Imperial successor sect, imitated the destructive power in their own Starkiller weapon.

How to create peace after decades of insurgency is a maddening question. Tarkin's answer was elaborate, brutal, and focused on human cowardice. In a galaxy defined by war, Wilhuff Tarkin was one of the few even attempting to answer the right question.

How Not to Build an Army

The Empire's Flawed Military Force

MICK RYAN

Publisher's note: This editorial is from the esteemed historian of the Galactic Civil War Mora Akbar. Born on Mon Cala, Mora Akbar studied history at the Mon Cala City Academy and at the Coruscant Academy. He has served as official historian for the Galactic Alliance Defense Force and is currently the historian in residence with the Galactic Alliance Senate. As we recognize the centenary of the Palpatine Dialog, Mora Akbar's article examines how the Grand Army of the Republic and its successor, the Imperial Military, underpinned the rise and fall of the Galactic Empire between 19 BBY and 4 ABY.

> It is with great reluctance that I have agreed to this calling. I love democracy. I love the Republic. The powers you give me I will lay down when this crisis has abated. And as my first act with this new authority, I will create a Grand Army of the Republic to counter the increasing threats of the separatists.

Senator Sheev Palpatine, Palpatine Dialog, 16 BBY

This week marks the one hundredth anniversary of what we now know as the Palpatine Dialog. This was a moment in galactic history that, perhaps more than any other, marked the descent of the old democratic polity into several decades of authoritarian rule, suppression, and destruction of democratic systems. It was underpinned by the rise of a powerful technomilitary elite that facilitated the emergence of the centralized, political-religious dictatorship of Emperor Palpatine.

Like many despots throughout history, Palpatine justified authoritarian rule through allegations of Senate corruption disempowering democratic rule. He pressured the Senate (supported by devious yet brilliantly opportunist political backroom deals) to grant him extraordinary powers to deal with a separatist crisis. An example of his double-dealing at the time was his promise—while secretly fermenting the downfall of the Senate—to Queen Amidala: "I promise, Your Majesty, if I am elected [chancellor of the Republic], I will restore democracy to the Republic."[1]

But Palpatine's political deviousness and tyrannical approach to power was also founded on one other element: the reliance on a powerful and brutal military to generate fear in the people and systems of the galaxy. While his exploitation of the dark side of the Force—and his manipulation of Anakin Skywalker—are well known and studied, the powerful and long-reaching Imperial Military forces played a key role in the rise and eventual fall of Palpatine's Galactic Empire.

The Clone Army—unbeknownst to the Jedi and other members of the Senate—had been secretly commissioned by Jedi Master Sifo-Dyas sometime around 32 BBY.[2] This was done allegedly to assist the small band of around ten thousand Jedi in the increasingly difficult task of keeping the peace throughout the galaxy. With the election of Palpatine as grand chancellor, this new army was officially sanctioned. Tasked to respond to the separatist threat to the Republic and charged with the destruction of separatist droid armies, this force was known originally as the Grand Army of the Republic.

Fighting for three years under the leadership of the Jedi, the Kamino-trained clones were a very disciplined and effective military force. However, the successes of the Grand Army of the Republic underpinned the political maneuvers of Palpatine and ensured his consolidation of power. By 19 BBY the Grand Army of the Republic was on the verge of victory over the separatists. It was this point at which Palpatine's grand design was revealed.

During the final battles of the Clone Wars, Chancellor Palpatine issued the now infamous Order 66. Portraying the Jedi as traitors to the Republic and designed to destroy their power throughout the galaxy, Order 66 resulted in the near extermination of the ancient Jedi Order. With the clones conditioned for absolute loyalty, clone troopers of the many legions and sector armies exterminated their Jedi officers, leaving fewer than a handful remaining. It also left the reins of the Grand Army of the Republic—previously commanded by the Jedi—in the hands of Palpatine. As he proclaimed at the time, in his declaration of a New Order, "And the Jedi rebellion has been foiled. The remaining Jedi will be hunted down and defeated. In order to ensure our security and continuing stability, the Republic will be reorganized into the first Galactic Empire for a safe and secure society."

Following the Declaration of the New Order in 19 BBY, Palpatine focused on the elimination of all other competing forms of influence. This was characterized by the elimination of Galactic Republic organizations, with the institutions of the Old Republic being dismantled or appropriated for use by the new Galactic Empire. One institution appropriated by the new Emperor was the Grand Army of the Republic.

Palpatine transformed the Grand Army of the Republic into a new Imperial Military. Continuing the massive military buildup that had commenced during the preceding Clone Wars, the new Imperial Military became a key instrument of the Emperor's strategy to control the galaxy. In a speech shortly after the Declaration of the New Order, Palpatine stated that "the Jedi Order is a lesson to us that we cannot permit any agency to become powerful enough to pose a threat to our designs, or the freedoms we enjoy. That is why it is essential we increase and centralize our military, both to preserve the peace and to protect the Empire against inevitable attempts at insurrection."[3]

This new military organization was transformed in appearance and function from its predecessor. Functionally, the Imperial Military shifted from fighting conventional ground and space conflicts against highly capable droid armies, to one that was focused on suppression of uprisings and insurgencies throughout the galaxy. Composed of naval, army, and storm-trooper commands, the Imperial Military possessed a mass, training, and rapid galactic deployability that was foundational to the Emperor's political power in the First Galactic Empire.

The appearance of the new Imperial Military also changed from its pre-decessor. Many classes of new starships were commissioned. New uniforms and equipment were brought into service, and the personnel composition changed. Primarily raised as a clone force under the Old Republic, the new Imperial Army inducted millions of male humans after the Clone Wars. With the vast resources poured into this military expansion, the enormous fleet of starships and legions of ground forces could be applied to the Imperial-ization of the galaxy under the leadership of Palpatine.

Where the Empire required resources from a particular planet, it would be seized by the Imperial Military. Planets that possessed nonhuman gov-ernors had their leaders replaced with human Imperial governors. This bias toward humans by Palpatine and his Imperial Military was particularly odious. Despite the many other sentient species throughout the galaxy—comprising trillions of individuals—only humans were considered worthy to hold most of the command positions in the Imperial Military (the author, a native Mon Calamari, would certainly have not made the cut at the various Imperial military academies).

As the Empire expanded toward the galaxy's periphery, many worlds were ecologically devastated. Local populations saw their children drafted into Imperial service, while corrupt regional governors with Imperial Mil-itary support exploited local people. Compulsory attendance at military parades and the construction of stormtrooper barracks and garrisons on various worlds across the galaxy became the norm.

Palpatine was implementing his plan of ruling the entire galaxy while unlocking the secrets of the Sith masters. But the pervasive Imperial influence, merciless brutality, and massive cost of maintaining numerous stormtrooper legions and fleets of starships, only emboldened a growing Rebellion across the galaxy. The Declaration of Rebellion in 2BBY marked a turning point in the power of the Empire. The declaration noted, "We, the Rebel Alliance, do therefore in the name—and by the authority—of the free beings of the Galaxy, solemnly publish and declare our intentions: To fight and oppose you and your forces, by any and all means at our disposal; To refuse any Imperial law contrary to the rights of free beings; To bring about your destruction and the destruction of the Galactic Empire; To make forever free all beings in the galaxy. To these ends, we pledge our property, our honor, and our lives."[4]

This represented the first large-scale, organized military resistance against the Imperial Military. Some two years after this declaration, the rebellion achieved its first major victory over the Imperial Military with the destruction of the first Death Star during the Battle of Yavin. This provided the Rebel Alliance with a level of credibility that it had not previously been able to achieve.

Contrary to the intentions of Grand Moff Tarkin, the destruction of Alderaan in the lead-up to the Battle of Yavin only provided more evidence of the brutality and tactics of fear employed by the Imperial Military. It served as a rallying call for the resistance against the Empire and its Imperial Military forces. Acts of terror by the Imperial Military, such as the infamous release of the Candorian plague at Dentaal and the subjugation of the Tion Cluster, only served to further delegitimize the Imperial Military forces and to pry more worlds from the grasp of Palpatine and his dark, corrosive Empire.

But it was the Battle of Endor that demonstrated the ultimate weakness of the Imperial Military forces. Its command structure was highly centralized, emphasizing loyalty to the Empire and to the supreme commander, who reported directly to the Emperor. The ethnocentric bias toward humans in the Imperial Military denied them the intellectual variety that may have allowed them to anticipate the plans and intentions of nonhuman sentient races within the Rebellion.

The Empire had relied on the employment of Imperial forces from distant planets to keep the peace throughout the galaxy, eschewing the more effective use of local forces possessing greater cultural awareness. Having concentrated its most talented and experienced forces for the destruction of the Rebellion at Endor, most were killed either on the second Death Star or Darth Vader's command ship *Executor*.

The destruction of the Imperial Military's most talented leaders and troops in this battle soon resulted in a paucity of talent throughout the galaxy. It began suffering larger-than-normal losses of warships and troops, which resulted in an Imperial Military death spiral as it was forced to employ poorly performing personnel drawn from the numerous Imperial academies across the Empire, who continued to perform poorly and suffered ever-increasing loses—in personnel and legitimacy. The Rebellion—through an increasing number of victories over Imperial forces—greatly enhanced its credibility, and many planets seceded to join the New Republic.

With the remove of one hundred years, it is perhaps easier for contemporary historians to review this dark time in our collective history. The pervasive cruelty, brutality by Imperial legions on thousands of worlds, and the economic demands of sustaining the hundreds of millions of members of the Imperial Military provided fuel for the growing Rebellion across the galaxy. This military-heavy approach to security and stability (incorporating a combination of combat and policing duties) ultimately failed in a galaxy composed of many different sentient races. We must continue to study this approach for the lessons it can provide to future galactic leaders, policy makers, and senior leaders of the Galactic Alliance Defense Force. There are several key lessons that stand out in particular.

First, choosing appropriate grand strategic objectives should be an obvious lesson for contemporary political and military leaders, regardless of their system of origin. Not only should these be ethical (i.e., not pursuing complete domination), but the means by which these objectives might be achieved should not require massive use of force, fear, and brutality—or the consumption of enormous amounts of public funding. The Empire possessed a singular declared objective of sustaining a Galactic Empire as a means to a "safe and secure society." It relied exclusively on military solutions and was unsustainable over time.

Second, legitimacy in governance is critical. While many systems will have local cultural variations, leaders should be selected in a method that is considered just and fair by a majority of local people. This legitimate government should be able to provide security, encourage popular participation in government, understand the local cultural norms, and minimize corruption. The Empire's preference for human governors across the galaxy and for senior leadership in the military compromised their legitimacy.

Third, the military instruments available to our contemporary leadership must only be used for the achievement of legal political ends. Palpatine's rule, while ultimately political in nature, was personality based, lacked legitimacy, and was reliant on brute force from a gargantuan military instrument. The military forces that are employed by contemporary political leaders must be schooled in civil primacy, the appropriate use of force, and the delegation of authority and must—at all costs—nurture a learning culture.

Finally, the ethical basis of military forces is brought into stark relief by the events of the Clone Wars and the Galactic Civil War. Despite the murky genesis of the Clone Army, the Grand Army of the Republic possessed a clear political mandate for its existence and operations. It was led by well-trained, ethical Jedi leaders and possessed a legitimacy that was generally highly regarded throughout the galaxy. In contrast, the successor Imperial Military lacked legitimacy due to its unethical conduct against multiple star systems, its press ganging of recruits into Imperial service, its ethnocentric approach to recruiting mainly from a single race, and its absolute loyalty to the tyrannical Emperor. This should provide a worthy case study for all cadets at military academies throughout the galaxy.

It has now been several decades since the scourge of Snoke and the eradication of the New Order. It has been even longer still since the death of Emperor Palpatine during the Battle of Endor. Palpatine was a cunning politician, a tyrannical and ruthless emperor, and a Sith lord who mastered the dark side of the Force. As we commemorate the centenary of the Palpatine Dialog this week, we must recommit ourselves to ensuring that this dark period of our history is understood by this and future generations. We must not repeat the mistakes of our ancestors, who, through all their best intentions, gave power through the Imperial Senate to a maniacal character and his vicious Imperial Military machine.

Notes

The epigraph was spoken by Senator Palpatine in *Attack of the Clones*. BBY and ABY indicate before the Battle of Yavin and after the Battle of Yavin, respectively. In 25 ABY the New Republic commissioned the New Republic Historical Council to restandardize the Galactic Calendar. The council chose the Battle of Yavin, instead of the Battle of Endor, calling the former the more significant galactic event. From that point on, the year in which the Battle of Yavin occurred was the epoch used for the dating system.

1. Terry Brooks, *Star Wars Episode I: The Phantom Menace* (New York: Del Rey, 1999), 238–39.
2. Sifo-Dyas was a Jedi master who served during the last decades of the Galactic Republic. When the Sith were revealed to have returned during the Invasion of Naboo in 32 BBY, he secretly commissioned the creation of the Clone Army, before he was murdered by Count Dooku.
3. James Luceno, *Dark Lord: The Rise of Darth Vader* (New York: Del Rey, 2005), quoted at "Imperialization," *Wookieepedia*, accessed August 8, 2017, http://starwars.wikia.com/wiki/Imperialization.
4. Paul Murphy, *The Rebel Alliance Sourcebook* (Honesdale PA: West End Games, 1990), quoted at "Declaration of Rebellion," *Wookieepedia*, accessed August 8, 2017, http://starwars.wikia.com/wiki/Declaration_of_Rebellion/Legends.

10

The Jedi and the Profession of Arms

STEVE LEONARD

> For over a thousand generations, the Jedi Knights were the guardians
> of peace and justice in the Old Republic . . . before the dark times . . .
> before the Empire.
>
> Obi-Wan Kenobi, *Star Wars: Episode IV—A New Hope*

At the height of its power and influence, the Jedi Order was already a
profession in crisis. What began as a slow decay had advanced into a
precipitous decline, one from which recovery would prove inexorably
unlikely. Before Anakin Skywalker was seduced by the dark side of the
Force, before Supreme Chancellor Sheev Palpatine issued Order 66, the
Jedi were already at a tipping point, desperately clinging to a storied past
while confronting an uncertain—and increasingly bleak—future. It was
a decline that could not be avoided, could not be stopped. It was as inevitable as the Force itself.

With Order 66, Darth Sidious launched the Great Jedi Purge, and the
fall of the Jedi was all but complete.

The Holy Order of the Jedi Knights—the Old Jedi Order—evolved over the millennia into "the guardians of peace and justice" in the galaxy. Ancient and monastic, the Jedi Order emerged from the ashes of the Force Wars on Tython, united by its belief and observance of the light side of the Force, which reflected the values of the order itself: honesty, compassion, selflessness, and humility.[1] Despite their victory, the Jedi would commit much of the ensuing twenty-five thousand years locked in mortal combat with the devotees of the dark side—the Sith—who embraced a corrupt and wanton disregard for the natural order of the universe and an equally disturbing willingness to draw power from the evil that lurked in the dark side of the Force.

Over the subsequent millennia, the Jedi faced countless challenges from the Sith, including their near extinction at the end of the Jedi Civil War.[2] The battle between light and dark waged for thousands of years, the balance between them always in flux. But adhering to their core values and beliefs, the Jedi Order persevered as a *profession*, weathering each successive storm. Despite the mysticism surrounding their order, the Jedi were in fact, by their very nature, a profession sworn to protect and preserve balance in the Force, "the guardians of peace and justice" in the Old Republic.

Historically, professions are sources of uniquely expert work. Medicine, jurisprudence, and the military are all examples of established professions. Members of these professions commit years of study and practice to their chosen "orders" before they are capable of producing expert work. Professions earn the trust of society through their ethic—the core values, principles and virtues that frame the culture of the profession—and are granted significant autonomy to develop and safeguard expertise in the best interests of society.[3] Finally, professions are motivated by servant ideals and the lifelong pursuit of expert knowledge, and membership bears the status of "an ancient, honorable, and revered occupation."[4]

Nowhere is this more important than in the profession of arms, which is entrusted to provide security for a society unable to do so for itself and without which the society cannot survive. The lethality inherent in the profession of arms bears with it a deep moral obligation not just to the profession but to society itself. This makes the ethic—and the responsibility to police those who abandon its values, principles, and virtues—all the more essential to the profession.

By any definition, the Jedi Order was a profession—a trusted, disciplined, and often revered vocation. At the very core of the order was the Jedi Code, the fundamental values and beliefs that framed their profession:

> There is no emotion, there is peace.
> There is no ignorance, there is knowledge.
> There is no passion, there is serenity.
> There is no chaos, there is harmony.
> There is no death, there is the Force.[5]

The Jedi bore all the hallmarks of a professional order. Within the Jedi Order, there were seven degrees (or tiers) of seniority based on mastery of the Force. A Jedi initiate, or youngling, was a Force-sensitive child undergoing the early stages of training at the Jedi academy. Upon completing the initiate trials and being chosen to continue training with a Jedi knight or master, the initiate would advance to become a padawan, or Jedi apprentice. An apprentice who completed the Jedi trials was then bestowed with the title of Jedi knight. The path to Jedi master typically involved the successful mentoring and development of a number of padawans to Jedi knights, while a Jedi weapon master was the title given to those masters who pursued years of study of physical combat with the Force.[6] Jedi councilors were those few selected to serve on one of the four Jedi councils; the master of the order presided over the Jedi High Council.[7]

The Jedi served a unique and vital role in society, one that allowed the Old Republic to survive and flourish over a thousand generations. In this role, the Jedi continuously developed expertise within their profession and leveraged that expertise to the greater good of the society they served. In particular, they provided for the citizens of the Old Republic what they could not provide for themselves—peace and security.

The Jedi were able to serve successfully in this capacity because they possessed expert knowledge of the Force, drawing on its power to safeguard the peace and justice essential to the survival of the Old Republic.

This expert knowledge was the lifeblood of the Jedi Order, created and maintained through a steadfast commitment to maintaining balance in the Force. Mastery of the Force, earned through years of study and practice, was the hallmark of a Jedi.

From the systems on the outer rim to the planets at the deep core of the galaxy, the Jedi were trusted to promote peace, resolve conflict, and maintain order. The Jedi Code established the values, principles, and virtues that guided their efforts and defined their service on behalf of society. The Jedi weren't just respected members of society, they were revered within the Old Republic. They earned that trust, that reverence, though the proper practice and policing of their profession, through years of training, discipline, and professional acculturation bound by a core ethic—the Jedi Code. Galactic society granted them the necessary autonomy to develop expertise and— guided by their professional ethic—to self-police the order in honorable service to the Old Republic.

Within the Jedi Order, the practice of their chosen vocation motivated and inspired others, fostering a commitment to the profession itself—the lifelong pursuit of mastery of the Force, earning a position of respect within ranks of the order, and the validation that came with selfless service in the name of the Jedi Code. For the Jedi, their chosen profession was much more than a "sad devotion to that ancient religion," as General Motti described it to Darth Vader before the Battle of Yavin. It was a calling. It was a way of life.

Finally, the Jedi established and upheld the discipline and standards of their profession through the Jedi councils, including responsibility for the training and development of initiates into the order. From its founding, the Jedi Order—the Jedi profession—had been governed by a council of masters. The Jedi High Council was the first and, ultimately, primary administrative governing body of the order, comprised of twelve Jedi masters, including five permanent members who accepted a lifetime appointment to the council. Led by the master of the order, the High Council also served as the principal advisors to the supreme chancellor.

In time, other councils were convened to coordinate and oversee other professional elements of the Jedi Order. The Council of First Knowledge, led by the caretaker of first knowledge, oversaw the training, education, and professional development of the order. Comprised of five Jedi masters, the Council of First Knowledge was responsible for the Jedi academy and its curriculum and guarded and maintained the Temple Archives. They oversaw the collection and proliferation of Jedi knowledge and accepted responsibility for eradicating Sith teachings and artifacts from the archives.

Similarly, the five master consulars chosen to lead the Council of Reconciliation worked closely with the Galactic Senate and the Republic Diplomatic Corps to prevent and resolve political impasse among the different governments and peoples of the Old Republic. The Reconciliation Council drew on a corps of Jedi trained as diplomats and ambassadors, as well as Jedi seers, specialized knights who assisted the master consulars and could sense the will of the Force. In most diplomatic scenarios, the Council of Reconciliation was the face of the Old Republic.

The Council of Reassignment managed the Jedi Service Corps, an alternative to service for those initiates who failed to pass their trials or were not selected as padawans by a master but still desired to serve the order. These former initiates could thus continue service in one of four branches: the agricultural, medical, educational, or exploration corps. Members of each corps operated under the oversight of a satellite council and served the order—and galactic society—just as a knight would but through and with the mastery of a different set of skills.[8]

By all measures, the Jedi Order was a noble calling—a strong profession with a legacy of service and commitment and a powerful ethic. Here, the words of Obi-Wan Kenobi were prescient: "For over a thousand generations the Jedi Knights were the guardians of peace and justice in the Old Republic." The Jedi Order was born out of the ancient conflict to restore balance to the Force; and over the course of more than twenty-five thousand years, that conflict had remained central to their existence.

But in the years leading up to the Clone Wars, the Sith had been seemingly reduced to a mere shadow of the threat they once presented. The threats the Jedi did face—many of them not threats at all but the challenges confronted in holding together a vast Galactic Republic—failed to yield the type of cataclysmic conflict posed by the Sith. The Jedi had become complacent. An order organized, trained, and equipped to engage in major conflicts with a peer opponent was left to negotiate trade agreements, combat terrorism, and maintain peace and stability across the galaxy.

The citizens of the Old Republic, too, had become complacent. The Jedi Order bore responsibility for security, stability, and justice across the entire galaxy. The people themselves had not had to fight for their own rights for over a thousand generations. That burden was shouldered by the Jedi, who—by their very way of life—were increasingly separated from the people they served. Nearly four thousand years before the Great Jedi Purge, the Sith lord Darth Traya predicted what would one day come to pass: "If you seek to aid everyone that suffers in the galaxy, you will only weaken yourself . . . and weaken them. It is the internal struggles, when fought and won on their own, that yield the strongest rewards. . . . If you care for others, then dispense with pity and sacrifice and recognize the value in letting them fight their own battles."[9]

The divide between the Jedi and the people of the Old Republic had grown into a yawning chasm. The Jedi Order, a profession once recognized as a paragon of courage and honor, was now as distant and foreign as any world on the outer rim. The Jedi were insular, sequestered, and utterly unknown to the very people they were sworn to protect. For a profession that owed its existence to society, the connection to the people was sacrosanct.

Ultimately, the profession itself was in decay. Despite the presence of the Jedi councils to ensure the operational efficacy of the practitioners, no single entity bore responsibility for safeguarding the Jedi Code—the very ethic of the profession. Initially, the rot might have been difficult to recognize, but it would slowly begin to spread across the profession, leaving the order weakened and exposed. And as the ethic faltered, so then did the profession.

Even as the shadow of the Sith loomed dark over the Old Republic, the Jedi High Council remained largely unaware. They were easily manipulated into deploying a Jedi force under Master Dooku into a misguided and disastrous fight with the True Mandalorians during the Battle of Galidraan.[10] As a result, Dooku, disillusioned with the High Council, began his own journey to the dark side of the Force. At the same time, the High Council was oblivious to the manipulations of Darth Plagueis, who was already orchestrating the rise of his apprentice, Palpatine, through the political ranks of the Galactic Senate.[11]

The council's decision to employ clone troopers as proxies in the conflict with Count Dooku's Confederacy of Independent Systems signaled yet another schism in the Jedi Order.[12] Addressing the High Council, Jedi Knight Bardan Jusik underscored the threat the decision posed to the core values of the Jedi: "So how do we justify what we are doing now? Breeding men without choice, and without freedom, to fight and die for us? When do the means cease to justify the end? Where is our society heading? Where are our ideals, and what are we without them? If we give in to expedience in this way, where do we draw the line between ourselves and those we find unacceptably evil? I have no answer, Masters. Do you?"[13]

In turning away from the tenets of the Jedi Code in the name of expedience, the High Council found the tipping point that pushed the fate of the Jedi Order—the Jedi profession—to the precipice. The elevation of Anakin Skywalker to a seat on the council—the first and last Jedi to be appointed by the supreme chancellor—set in motion the sequence of events that would end with Operation Knightfall and launch the Great Jedi Purge.[14]

When Palpatine—secretly Darth Sidious—issued the command "Execute Order 66," he triggered an order programmed into the clone troopers through a biochip implanted during their creation on Kamino. The chip, which controlled the behavior and ensured the absolute obedience of the clones, caused troopers across the galaxy to turn on the Jedi and kill them. The same clone troopers that Bardan Jusik cautioned the High Council against using became the instrument of their own destruction.

The Old Jedi Order had fallen. The profession was dead.

Not the last of the old Jedi, Luke. The first of the new.[15]

Obi-Wan Kenobi

The Great Jedi Purge marks a catastrophic moment for the order as a profession and serves as a convenient backdrop for a contemporary discussion of the decline of the profession of arms and its ultimate impact on future conflict. The same symptoms of professional decay that plagued the Jedi—a gradual disassociation with the society and people it served and a slow erosion of its ethic—can be seen today in our own military forces.

In a 2001 article in *Time*, author Mark Thompson discusses the drift between the U.S. military and civilian society: "Neither the U.S. military nor civilian society is to blame for the drift. In fact, fundamental changes in each have made it inevitable. Only 1.5 million of the 240 million Americans over 18—about half of 1 percent—are in uniform today. Without a draft or a good civilian economy, they tend to stay in uniform longer, further isolating them from the American mainstream."[16]

The profession of arms, to a large degree, owes its existence to the trust bestowed on it by the society it protects and defends. But as the relationship that underpins that trust erodes—when society demands more sacrifice of the profession than the society demands of itself—the fabric that ties the two together inevitably frays. And as that fabric becomes increasingly threadbare, so does the moral obligation the profession extends to the people it defends.

The other significant source of decay—the erosion of the values, principles, and virtues of the professional ethic—symptomatic of the fall of the Jedi is as prevalent today as it was at the outset of the Clone Wars. As we struggle to self-police our own with any vestige of consistency, we are as culpable for the decline of the profession of arms as was the Jedi High Council when they failed to contain the rise of Darth Sidious. And the increasing politicization of current and former members of the senior ranks of the military threatens to tear asunder an already threadbare ethic.

Historian Richard Kohn, writing in *World Affairs Journal*, noted these trends with some sense of foreboding: "Professions that cannot change themselves from within, cannot respond to the needs of their clients, and cannot enforce standards of behavior so as to maintain the confidence of their constituencies while also inspiring the admiration and loyalty of their own members are in trouble."[17]

In assessing the failure of an incredibly well-funded, well-equipped, and well-organized military force to defeat two insurgencies and a nascent civil war, Kohn placed the blame firmly at the feet of a profession of arms in decline—a profession, much like the Jedi Order, already in chaos, already balancing on a precipice.

Notes

1. Daniel Wallace and Jason Fry, *Star Wars: The Essential Atlas* (New York: Del Rey, 2009); Jan Duursema and John Ostrander, *Star Wars: Dawn of the Jedi—The Prisoner of Bogan* (New York: Marvel, 2015). The values reflected in members of the Jedi Order and commonly associated with Force sensitives aligned with the light side of the Force are referred to throughout the *Star Wars* films as well as the broader literary canon. In general, these are captured as positive emotions, where adherents to the dark side embrace the opposite.

2. The Jedi Civil War, also known as the Second Sith War or the Old Republic Insurrection, occurred approximately four thousand years before the Battle of Yavin (which led to the destruction of the first Death Star) and is addressed widely in the broader literary canon. During the war, Darth Revan, a Jedi who had turned to the dark side, reduced the Jedi to fewer than one hundred, either killing them outright or seducing them to the dark side.

3. T. O. Jacobs and Michael G. Sanders, "Principles for Building the Profession: The SOF Experience," in *The Future of the Army Profession*, ed. Don M. Snider and Lloyd Matthews, 2nd ed. (New York: McGraw-Hill, 2005), 441–62.

4. David Segal and Karen DeAngelis, "Changing Conceptions of the Military Professions," in *American Civil-Military Relations: The Soldier and the State in a New Era*, ed. Suzanne C. Nielsen and Don M. Snider (Baltimore MD: Johns Hopkins University Press, 2009), 194–212.

5. Christie Golden, *Dark Disciple* (New York: Del Rey, 2015). Greg Weisman, *Kanan: The Last Padawan* (New York: Marvel, 2015).

6. Daniel Wallace, *The Jedi Path: A Manual for Students of the Force* (San Francisco CA: Chronicle Books, 2010); Drew Karpyshyn, *Darth Bane: Rule of Two* (New York: Del Rey, 2007).

7. Karpyshyn, *Darth Bane*; Wallace, *Jedi Path*.

8. Karpyshyn, *Darth Bane*; Wallace, *Jedi Path*.

9. Obsidian Entertainment, *Star Wars: Knights of the Old Republic II—The Sith Lords* (San Francisco CA: LucasArts, 2004).

10. Daniel Wallace, Ryder Windham, and Jason Fry, *The Bounty Hunter Code: From the Files of Boba Fett* (New York: Chronicle Books, 2014).

11. James Luceno, *Darth Plagueis* (New York: Del Rey, 2012).

12. Luceno, *Darth Plagueis*.

13. Karen Traviss, *Republic Commando: Hard Contact* (New York: Del Rey, 2004), 221.

14. Traviss, *Republic Commando*.

15. Timothy Zahn, *Heir to the Empire* (New York: Bantam Spectra, 1991), 14.

16. Mark Thompson, "An Army Apart: The Widening Military-Civilian Gap," *Time*, November 10, 2011, http://nation.time.com/2011/11/10/an-army-apart-the-widening-military-civilian-gap/.

17. Richard H. Kohn, "Tarnished Brass: Is the US Military in Professional Decline?," *World Affairs Journal*, Spring 2009, 7.

The Right Fleet

Starships for Strategic Purpose

BJ ARMSTRONG

In the climactic moments of the Battle of Hoth, the vast majority of the Rebel Alliance's forces slipped between the fingers of the Imperial strike force deployed into the outer-rim system. In the Battle of Yavin, small fighters overcame the defenses of the Death Star in order to strike the design weakness that made it vulnerable. Repeatedly a small freighter named the *Millennium Falcon,* and its crew and passengers of vital Rebel leadership, escaped what appeared to be overwhelming Imperial odds. These developments in the galactic struggle between the Empire and the Rebel Alliance have been ascribed to luck by some and to the influence of ancient religion by others. However, such events do not require supernatural explanation. Instead, in military and naval terms, they are the result of strategic choices and decisions regarding the architecture of the Imperial fleet. These events were the natural outcome of the Imperial leadership's nearly exclusive and myopic focus on large space battles and the platforms necessary for those battles, while ignoring the strategic role of fleets in constabulary duties and space security operations in peacetime.

From a long time ago to the present day, naval and space forces have struggled to understand their role in the larger galaxy. The officers commanding space forces and developing fleet policy have had a tendency to focus nearly all their attention on the most physically dangerous and violent aspect of their profession: ship and squadron combat in space. The result of this focus is that policy work on fleet design and force architecture attempts to address a single question: what type of force is needed to seize the initiative and dominate the enemy in space battle? This question is certainly an important one, but it should not be the only issue considered when developing the acquisition plans and operational concepts of any fleet. This was particularly true for the Imperial fleet, which served to enforce the will of the Emperor and the dictates of the regional governors, regardless of whether the Empire was in open warfare with another force.

Discussion of fleet design benefits from examination of the history of planetary naval strategy and operations as a guide. Naval forces long played a central role in the power of polities both in peacetime as well as during war. The necessity for fleets during the conflicts between nations, or political groups, that spanned maritime environments seems obvious. The ability to establish command of the sea would be leveraged into the opportunity to cross those nautical divides and project force onto the enemy. Over the course of history, it was determined that the best way to achieve this dominance was to prepare for fleet battles that would sweep the enemy's resistance from the sea. One of the struggles that strategists encountered with this ideal, however, was that once the maritime environment was claimed as the domain of a single competitor, resistance from the shore rarely ended, and a different set of forces and operational concepts were needed to project the power necessary for victory.

The operational history of the Battle of Hoth illustrated this problem for the Imperial fleet in a space-operations context. There was no enemy fleet to engage and no question of who dominated the space environment within the system. Yet the strike force assembled was made up exclusively of large forty-thousand-man Star Destroyers designed to engage other combat vessels in battle. The result of this force architecture was that the Rebel Alliance easily spotted the Imperial arrival, based on the proximity that the strike force came out of hyperspace and because the size and shape of the force of massive battleships made it easy to identify. Once combat was engaged with the Rebels, the Star Destroyers attempted to establish a blockade of the system. But the small numbers of large ships, susceptible to antiaccess weapons like the ion cannon employed by the Rebels, were unable to effectively maneuver to capture fleeing small craft. The base on Hoth was destroyed, resulting in an Imperial tactical success, yet nearly the entire Rebel force was able to escape, giving the Rebels the strategic victory because of their continued survival. With fighter craft focused on defense of the Imperial assault and without small fleet combatants to enforce the blockade and run intercept operations on the escaping transports, fighters, and small craft, the blockade was a dismal failure. Success by squadrons of stunt fighters against the Death Star at the earlier Battle of Yavin also raises similar questions about the balance of the Imperial fleet in operations outside of system- or galaxy-wide wars.

SLIPPING THROUGH IMPERIAL FINGERS

In some ways, misconceptions over the fleet architecture necessary for success in establishing command of space, versus the architecture needed to effectively exercise the control that it provides, are to be expected. Placing first priorities on the initial element of space strategy seems natural. If you cannot win the battle, it will be hard to go on to effectively fight the rest of the conflict. However, moving beyond combat and the responsibilities of ships and squadrons in battle, the Imperial fleet's force design almost completely ignored a second and equally important set of missions: operations and fleet responsibilities in peace.

Particularly within the authoritarian political construct of the Imperial government, the ability of a fleet to transition to constabulary duties during periods without a direct conventional opponent was vital. Yet a force made up almost exclusively of ships the size of Star Destroyers and Super Star

Destroyers—carriers augmented with only stunt ship–sized strikers and fighters—produced a fleet that struggled to effectively pursue these missions. Much as the Imperial strike force at Hoth demonstrated that small numbers of large ships are ineffective at close blockade operations, large numbers of smaller ships are also more effective at the patrol missions and constabulary operations necessary to establish security in the large expanse of Imperial-controlled space.

With few ships optimized for patrol capabilities or operations outside of squadron engagements and with size being the dominant factor in warship design, it becomes nearly impossible for the fleet to provide effective units for space security operations. When Imperial edicts that attempted to control trade, or restrict space commerce, were matched with a lack of capability for patrol and enforcement, the natural result was smuggling and the rise of non–state actors that took advantage of the situation. When local planetary governments were stripped of their authority, after the dissolution of the Imperial Senate and vesting of power in regional governors, responsibility for space security also devolved to the governors. However, the Imperial fleet—designed almost exclusively for squadron- and fleet-level combat and given authority over huge sectors of space—had no chance of keeping up with the space insecurity that developed. The result was that large sections of space, including almost all the outer-rim systems, devolved into safe havens for pirates, smugglers, and illicit droid merchants.

As these non–state groups formed loose organizational structures and safe basing arrangements, the networks between them grew, and contraband activity became ever easier. The Imperial fleet rarely arrived to demonstrate presence or conduct constabulary responsibilities. Smugglers were rarely boarded. When they were threatened with inspection, the volume of traffic on the intragalactic ratlines meant they could dump their cargos without significant effect to the networks themselves (though admittedly sometimes with personal ramifications when kingpins demanded remuneration). This environment of space insecurity, with enormous sectors lacking Imperial patrols or the arrival of only large battleships, created the perfect conditions for the Rebel Alliance to grow. Uncharted settlements of smugglers and illicit merchants became common, but to Imperial probes they were indistinguishable from Rebel activity. The clandestine movement of Rebel personnel and equipment could use the same ratlines that smugglers and other non–state actors had developed. With a fleet design that limited ability to conduct constabulary operations, there was little the Empire could do about it.

Despite the common perception that fleets are only needed for war, governments introduce risk to the peace when they focus their fleet policies on that single element of space power. The insecurity that spread through the galaxy following the Emperor's seizure of power was as much a result of a fleet that could not conduct constabulary duties as it was a sign of political resistance. The leaders of the Imperial fleet desperately sought the glory of squadron battles, which their predecessors had known in the Clone Wars and other conflicts, but they were blind to the challenge they faced and the security requirements of the fleet they led.

EFFECTS ON IMPERIAL COMBAT READINESS

Beyond the strategic impact of poor fleet design on the Imperial fleet's ability to maintain security and reduce the capabilities of the Rebel Alliance, there were also practical and internal implications. The focus on large, gold-plated ships with massive defensive systems and training in the doctrine of squadron battle had a vital effect on the officer corps in the Imperial fleet and on leadership across the force. It created an environment of risk aversion, and it limited decision making and authority to a debilitating degree. This not only affected the performance of fleet units in peacetime but also would have implications during wartime operations as well.

Because of the Imperial fleet's focus on large ships, officers rarely learned how to handle the responsibilities of command early in their careers. It was not just junior officers who struggled. The movement to a Star Destroyer fleet also eliminated the ships and units that midcareer officers would have commanded. The earliest an officer could assume the mantle of command was as a captain, nearing the end of a career. By extension, the size of a Star Destroyer, with a crew of forty thousand and a massive price tag for the equipment involved, meant that when an officer did finally rise to a command position, it was a responsibility of a massive magnitude and one for which the officer had had little practice.

The doctrine of fleet battle in the Imperial fleet focused on procedural compliance and adherence to written orders. There was little room for individual analysis or mission thinking. When an Imperial officer was trained and promoted in this environment, it was smarter to develop rote knowledge of the applicable directives and exact compliance, rather than working to understanding the operational or strategic reasoning behind them. Because there were no small ships to command, officers were never pulled out of this mindset of risk aversion and rote memorization. Suddenly, in the closing years of their career, they were placed in command of a massive warship and told that now everything was up to them and that they had to not only know the directives but understand the reasoning behind them and make their own decisions. The result was a culture that saw regular relief for cause, and occasional executions, of officers who might have followed doctrine exactly but failed in their final objectives.

An Imperial fleet architecture that included smaller ships, with smaller crews and less overall responsibility involved, would have given junior and midcareer officers the opportunity to develop their command abilities over the course of a career. It would have encouraged more-dynamic leadership and would have necessitated that officers learn not only to follow perfect procedure but also to understand the reasoning behind those procedures and exercise their own tactical and operational reasoning. This would have strengthened decision making and would have resulted in better strategic understanding later in a career, just in time to assume command of a capital ship in the Star Destroyer squadrons.

BALANCE AND THE FLEET FORCE

During multiple engagements in space battles, from the Clone Wars to the Battle of the Endor system, the Imperial fleet demonstrated skill and capability in large fleet engagements and in the development of deep-space, squadron-level operations. However, once the Empire attained control of the galaxy, the fleet design constructed around large starships and battlefleet operations became a hindrance to the galactic responsibilities of the fleet. Senior leadership in the Imperial forces continued to emphasize building larger and larger starships and focused training on squadron-level engagements and above. Meanwhile space degenerated into not only a lawless area that offered advantages to pirates, smugglers, and illicit droid merchants but also an environment in which the Rebel Alliance could establish itself. The failure of the Imperial fleet to understand the constabulary duties that are a central part of a fleet's responsibility in the star-studded commons created an improper architecture and resulted in vital gaps in capability. These gaps smoothed the way for the rise of the Rebel Alliance and offered the Rebels tactical and operational opportunities that led to their eventual victory. The Empire's failure to bring balance to the fleet force and to provide capabilities across the range of fleet operational requirements, in both peace and war, is a lesson for fleets across time.

12

Why We Need Space Marines

B. A. FRIEDMAN

They have no idea we're coming. They have no reason to expect us. If we can make it to the ground, we'll take the next chance. And the next. On and on until we win or the chances are spent.

Jyn Erso, *Rogue One*

In a memo labeled #MH2215: "Short Notes on the History of the Rebel Alliance Navy," Mon Mothma laid out why the Rebel Alliance was built around a fleet of starships instead of land forces, especially infantry.[1] These notes reveal the thinking of the Rebellion leadership early in its existence, especially in regard to fleet design. The victory of the Alliance and the establishment of the New Republic are testimony to Mothma's vision and strategic reasoning. A Rebel Alliance built around planetary infantry forces would have been easily isolated and destroyed by the Galactic Empire. Be that as it may, the historical record of the Galactic Civil War is one of strategic constraint and tactical desperation. Battles were won and lost on the flimsiest of margins. It is easy to marvel at the feats of arms performed by legendary Rebels during the war. It is easier still to forget that audacious plans, like the small-unit infiltrations of the Battles of Scarif and Endor, could have just as easily turned into massive victories for the Empire. In the case of Scarif, the Rebel Alliance only gained victory at the cost of massive casualties and the destruction of precious spacecraft.

Given the frequency of orbit-to-planet force projection—operations that involved the rapid deployment of forces onto a planet's surface and coordination between elements both in orbit and on the ground—in the Galactic Civil War, the Rebel Alliance would have been better served had it developed a professional, expeditionary corps. Such a force—akin to forces like the contemporary U.S. Marines—nested within the Rebel Alliance Navy and trained to execute orbit-to-planet operations in support of the fleet could also have achieved victory at a substantially lower cost.[2] A look at key battles and other inflection points during the Rebel Alliance's wars—as well as earlier conflicts that should have informed the Alliance's strategy—offers a number of demonstrative examples.

THE CLONE WARS

The Clone Wars saw a great deal of orbit-to-planet maneuver and, as a result, the Jedi Council's Clone Army found itself on both sides of the orbit-to-planet equation—leading the assault and defending against it in turn. Although the subsequent Galactic Civil War is replete with examples of how an expeditionary marine force would have lent great advantage to the Rebels, many of the trends that underpinned this advantage were already obvious during this previous conflict.

The Battle of Geonosis (22 BBY)

The Battle of Geonosis in 22 BBY (before the Battle of Yavin), the first major conflict of the Clone Wars and the baptism by fire of the Jedi Council's Clone Army, was a demonstration of professional orbit-to-planet maneuver. Although an untested force, the Clone Army—by now dubbed the Grand Army of the Republic—quickly planned and executed a movement from its home port of Kamino. The battle was one of the most complex of the war, featuring a search-and-rescue operation and an assault on droid production facilities, all following a fast and undetected orbit-to-planet phase. Thanks to the ability of the Grand Army of the Republic to quickly and stealthily transition from orbit to the surface of Geonosis, the search and rescue was successful, and so was the assault on the droid factories. The droid military defenders were caught unawares, and the native forces of Geonosis could organize little resistance. The battle led to the loss of the first capital of the Confederacy of Independent Systems as well as the destruction of a major portion of its battle droid production capacity.

Many of the types of operations successfully undertaken during the battle—most notably, rapid deployment from one domain to another—offered a clear sign of the value of marine forces, trained, organized, and equipped for just such a mission. And yet two decades later, as the Rebel Alliance found itself waging war against the Empire, the lesson would be ignored.

The Battle of Kashyyyk (19 BBY)

Turnabout is fair play, and three years after the Battle of Geonosis it was the Clone Army's turn to defend a planet against assault by the Confederacy of Independent Systems. The fight over Kashyyyk occurred during a period of conflict all over the galaxy, as both sides waged concurrent offensive operations. On Kashyyyk, General Grievous, commander of the Confederacy of Independent Systems forces, planned a simple and classic orbit-to-surface attack. His forces used C-9979 landing craft to transport droid troops to orbit over Kashyyyk. The assault itself was spearheaded both by armored assault tanks like the IG-227 Hailfire-class droid tanks and by armored personnel carriers. The defenders employed a standard Clone Army combined-arms task force augmented both by local Wookiee allies and, of note, by a contingent of Clone Marines.[3] Clone Marines were typically tasked with the defense of Republic ships from boarding parties, as well as assaulting and boarding enemy ships. Their use to augment the defense of a planet indicates the importance of controlling territory during the Clone Wars. That the Clone Marines' value was evidently not recognized and a professional marine force was not incorporated into the subsequent Rebel Alliance's formations represented a substantial misappraisal by the Alliance's leadership.

The Kashyyyk Task Force of the Grand Army of the Republic planned and executed a stalwart defense of the planet; however, events beyond Kashyyyk ended the war virtually as the battle was waged. When Sheev Palpatine issued Order 66 and the clone troopers turned on their Jedi officers, Kashyyyk was one of the battles ended by the decapitating effect. Its impacts would reverberate into the Galactic Civil War, although lessons from the Clone Wars about the value of a professional marine force were unheeded, a mistake for which the Rebel Alliance would pay a heavy price in blood.

THE GALACTIC CIVIL WAR

Whereas the control of territory was paramount to both sides during the Clone Wars, the nature of the Galactic Civil War meant that the physical control of planets themselves was much less important. Indeed, the Rebel Alliance simply never had the resources to take and hold territory against the Empire. Mon Mothma understood this fact far better than did Imperial leaders such as Grand Moff Tarkin. Tarkin was completely focused on developing a superweapon—the Death Star—that could annihilate Alliance-held territory, a focus that Emperor Palpatine certainly shared. Mothma's accurate assessment of the kind of war on which the Alliance was embarking—and the Empire's inaccurate assessment of the same—was a key component in the Alliance's success despite the great disparity in resources and capacity.

The Alliance's lack of capability, however, was not without consequence. Although Mothma was correct to focus less on building a Rebel army that could hold planetary territory, the Alliance could certainly have developed a professional corps of troops dedicated to orbit-to-planet assaults, raids, and other expeditionary operations. Lacking such a capability, it was forced to rely on hastily organized groups or small special operations teams without the ability or training for large-scale battles.

The Battle of Scarif (0 BBY)

The Battle of Scarif in 0 BBY, despite its strategic success, was a bloody tactical debacle even before Grand Moff Tarkin's destruction of the Imperial installation on the planet. The proposed mission to retrieve the Death

Star's plans was vetoed by the Rebel council, assessed as too risky. While Jyn Erso forced the issue by undertaking an unsanctioned infiltration with a small, ad hoc team that included a small complement of Rebel Marines, a manning strategy that included a robust, professional corps of marines—ideal for such an operation—might well have persuaded the Rebel council to authorize an orbit-to-surface mission. Such an operation by a force tailored for it would have had greater chance of success and almost certainly would have avoided the heavy death toll inflicted on the hastily planned and improvised assault force and other Rebel Alliance formations forced to support it via an orbital-fleet attack.

Scarif, in particular, demonstrates the paucity of tactical and operational options available to the Alliance combat forces. If a larger complement of marine units were available, these could have been used to effect the capture of the Imperial archives and the Death Star plans. If a portion of the Rebel fleet had been outfitted and trained for the support of orbit-to-planet operations, that detachment could have concentrated on supporting the surface forces while the bulk of the Alliance Navy confronted the Imperial fleet that arrived during the battle. Given Mothma's policy of only developing a deep-space force, the Alliance Navy had to simultaneously support the improvised surface team—a task for which neither fleet nor team was trained—and confront Imperial ships both stationed at Scarif and those that arrived later. Given the complexity of the Scarif mission, it would have been a tricky operation even for a fully professional fleet with a dedicated corps of marines. Since the fledgling Alliance Navy had to handle so many unfamiliar missions at once and with no planning or rehearsal, it was completely overwhelmed. That the Death Star plans were captured—barely—should not hide the fact that the operation was a tactical gamble, and the heavy odds against its success could have been shifted in the Rebel Alliance's favor by the presence of marine units tailored for just such a mission.

The Battle of Hoth (3 ABY)

Although arguably not a victory for the Rebel Alliance, the Battle of Hoth is a clear demonstration of the utility of quick-response orbit-to-planet forces. While the Rebel Alliance was alerted to an impending Imperial attack thanks to the detection of an Imperial probe droid on the surface of Hoth, they were still unable to leave before the arrival of the Imperial forces under Darth Vader.

Vader's task force had its famed 501st Legion, "Vader's Fist." The history of the 501st stretches back to the Battle of Geonosis, and the institutional knowledge of an orbit-to-planet maneuver surely contributed to the Imperial success. Again, because of Mon Mothma's focus on deep-space-faring forces, Rebel Alliance options were constrained, and Echo Base depended more on remaining hidden—and a single shield generator—for defense. What ground troops were available did prepare a fortified defense once the base was discovered, but it stood little chance against the armored task force of AT-AT walkers. The Imperial armored force did suffer casualties, thanks to the creative use of snowspeeder close air support on the part of the Rebels. But in the end, their mission was accomplished: they knocked out the shield generator protecting the base. Once the shield generator was destroyed, the main effort shifted to the 501st Legion, personally led by Darth Vader, which successfully assaulted and captured Echo Base.

Ultimately, the Rebel forces stationed at Hoth were saved by the calm and collected planet-to-orbit withdrawal conceived and executed by the station commander, Leia Organa of Alderaan. Absent her inspired leadership, the Rebel Alliance could very well have lost far more than just Echo Base.

The Battle of Endor (4 ABY)

Occurring four years after the Battle of Scarif, the Battle of Endor again demonstrated the inability of the Rebel Alliance to effectively fight on both the surface and in the orbit of a planet in a coordinated way. After receiving intelligence regarding the construction of a second Death Star and an Imperial shield defense system on the forest moon of Endor, the Rebel Alliance was again forced to turn to a small team that lacked the training and skills necessary to effect an orbit-to-surface landing.

Although the team, led by General Han Solo, managed to evade Imperial naval assets guarding the site, the surface component of the battle nearly met with disaster. During the infiltration and assault phases of the surface battle, Solo's team found itself unable to successfully reach their objective, the shield generator, without being detected by Imperial patrols. The team managed to evade the patrol, only to be captured by local indigenous fighters—Ewoks—that Alliance intelligence had apparently failed to identify during the planning process. After the Alliance team eventually secured their release from captivity and reached their objective, they found themselves completely outnumbered and outgunned by the Imperial garrison and its AT-ST vehicles.

During the entire surface battle, the Alliance troops on the surface and the Alliance naval forces in orbit were completely unable to communicate with each other. Coordination between the two is a basic principle of orbit-to-planet operations that trained and experienced personnel would have immediately identified as an integral planning effort. This left the surface forces unable to transmit vital intelligence regarding the planetary shield to the Alliance Navy or call for fire support.

Just as at the Battle of Hoth, it was the calm and collected leadership of Leia Organa, this time employing her skills as a diplomat even amid battle, that made up for the Alliance's lack of capability for this type of operation. Organa not only effected the release of the surface force from captivity but further convinced the local indigenous troops to join the assault on the shield generator. It was this unplanned—and fortuitous—addition of combat power that allowed the surface force to successfully capture and destroy the shield generator. Fortune favored the Rebel Alliance on Endor, but a dedicated force capable of effective orbit-to-surface operations could have relied on proper organization, training, and equipping for such a mission, rather than on fortune alone.

THE RESISTANCE

Conflicts in the outer rim that arose in the wake of the Galactic Civil War between the Resistance and the First Order then began taking shape. Early evidence suggests that the First Order had a better orbit-to-planet capability than the Resistance. Although a veteran of Scarif, Hoth, and Endor,

General Leia Organa repeated the mistake of the Rebel Alliance and paid little attention to the signs encouraging the development of a corps of orbit-to-surface troops for her Resistance organization. The First Order demonstrated an ability to execute effective and deliberate orbit-to-planet operations, placing trained and organized troops on the surface of both Jakku and Takodana in pursuit of high-value targets. Although the latter landing was disrupted by the arrival of Resistance starfighters acting in a surface-attack role for which they were not designed, the objective of the First Order attack was nonetheless achieved. Based on early reports, the successful Resistance assault on Starkiller Base again relied on a small, improvised team to execute a surface-to-orbit infiltration.

AN ALTERNATE GALACTIC HISTORY

These battles, for all their unique features, show a clear trend: a professional corps of troops trained and organized for orbit-to-planet operations is a key component of galactic warfare. Mon Mothma's decision to build a navy and not an army was understandable. The Alliance faced serious resource constraints and thus could not do both, and a fleet of ships was imperative. Building that fleet was the right choice. However, given the frequency of planet hopping during the Clone Wars, that navy should have included a capability for planetary force projection—an expeditionary marine force nested within and augmenting the Alliance Navy. While victory was achieved in the end, lives could have been saved and opportunities exploited by the adoption of such a force. And the history of a galaxy far, far away might have looked very different.

Notes

1. Alexander Freed, *Rogue One: A Star Wars Story* (Tampa FL: Del Rey, 2016), Kindle edition, 240–42.
2. All dates per "Timeline of Galactic History," *Wookieepedia*, accessed August 31, 2017, http://starwars.wikia.com/wiki/Timeline_of_galactic_history.
3. "Battle of Kashyyyk," *Wookieepedia*, accessed January 11, 2017, http://starwars.wikia.com/wiki/Battle_of_Kashyyyk/Legends.

13

Jedi Mind Tricks

From the Reel to the Real

JEAN MARIE WARD

Stormtroopers at Mos Eisley spaceport detain a speeder carrying a pair of fugitive droids. The speeder's shabbily dressed human passenger, the Jedi master Obi-Wan Kenobi, informs them, "These aren't the droids you're looking for. . . . They can go on their way." The stormtroopers parrot his words and wave the speeder away.

An Imperial officer on the Death Star mocks the futility of Darth Vader's "sorcerer's ways." Vader, standing some two yards away, makes a small hand gesture. The officer starts choking as if being strangled by invisible hands.

In the swamps of Dagobah, aspiring Jedi Luke Skywalker practices psychokinesis by lifting large rocks with his mind. His abilities seem remarkable until his teacher, the small, green-skinned Jedi master Yoda, challenges him to raise his crashed X-wing fighter from the swamp. Luke fails. Yoda closes his eyes. The ship rises, along with a sizeable chunk of water-logged real estate.

The mental powers of the Jedi may be the single most fantastic element in the whole *Star Wars* universe. Sure, faster-than-light travel, cities in the clouds, and planet-killing Death Stars are impossible based on today's science, but their technological trappings let them appear plausible, as long as no one looks too closely. Jedi mind tricks, as well as the training and mental discipline that make them possible, read too much like magic. Everyone knows magic is not real. The laws of physics do not bend to the power of the mind.

The historical record is unanimous on this point. Greek philosophers, Daoist alchemists, Elizabethan secret agents, dedicated materialists, and countless others have spent millennia seeking the real-world equivalent of Jedi mental abilities. Yet none of them have successfully replicated Anakin Skywalker's party trick of floating fruit over a banquet table. But people— and nations—keep trying.

From the 1920s through the 1970s, Soviet scientists spent millions exploring the military applications of telepathy, telekinesis, and other para-psychological phenomena in countless experiments at roughly twenty centers throughout the Soviet Union.[1] Finally, in the late 1960s researchers thought they had found a person capable of moving objects using only the power of her mind. A Leningrad psychic named Nina Kulagina allegedly separated the yolk from the white of a raw egg at a distance of six feet, as well as moving objects such as a crystal bowl, clock pendulums, and bread across the surface of a table via psychokinesis. However, shifting objects on tables without appearing to touch them is standard sleight of hand, the stock-in-trade of fraudulent mediums everywhere. Although no one openly accused Ms. Kulagina of being a fraud, later events suggest her mental powers were far less than advertised. In 1971 she and the scientist in charge of her experiments abruptly disappeared.[2]

Determined not to be outmatched in a psychic arms race, the United States spent another twenty years and around $20 million researching remote viewing, automatic writing, and other forms of paranormal activity.[3] The results were at best inconclusive. What was worse (much worse in the eyes of the Department of Defense, which funded most of the research), they were laughable. After all, *The Men Who Stare at Goats*, the Jon Ronson book that inspired the George Clooney movie, was a *nonfiction* account of the U.S. Army's adventures into parapsychology.

Nevertheless, it would be foolish to dismiss the notion of Jedi mind tricks and the mental discipline that makes them possible out of hand. Some of those so-called tricks are things people do every day. Take Obi-Wan's encounter with the stormtroopers, for example. Strip away the mysticism of the Force, and all he did was lie convincingly to two people conditioned to obedience. Deception is a critical skill in many military operations. For military personnel operating behind enemy lines, the quality of their lies could mean the difference between life and death. As a result, modern special operations forces undergo rigorous training in stealth and deception.

In addition, the prompt acquiescence of those Mos Eisley stormtroopers highlights the flip side of Jedi mind tricks. Military personnel throughout history have been subject to intensive mental conditioning as part of the job. The goal of this mental discipline, however, is the opposite of the stormtroopers' lemming-like obedience. Its purpose is to hone the warrior's mind in the same way physical conditioning hones the body. The mind guides the fist. It is truly the body's primary weapon system.

There is a mental component to every conflict. As conflict escalates to combat, that mental component grows in importance. Therefore, training a fighter's body is not enough. You must also train the mind. The form this mental training and conditioning takes is determined by the nature of the military organization and its values and objectives.

For example, the legendary warriors of Sparta were an aristocratic elite determined to remain at the top of their social heap. They began preparing their children for military life as soon as they were old enough to toddle out of the house. Any Spartan citizen (essentially any Spartan male who successfully completed military training and had been inducted into one of the dining messes that functioned as de facto military units) could discipline anyone's child as if it were his own. This accustomed the children to taking orders at an early age.[4]

At seven the boys were separated from their families and sent to a combination grammar–military prep school, where they wore the same garment in winter and summer. They were never fed enough and encouraged to steal—but they were beaten if caught. This taught them stealth and prepared them for operations behind enemy lines.[5] The education process turned the entire state into an armed camp in an all-out, society-wide effort to forge an undefeatable warrior caste entirely dedicated to the political goals of the Spartan city-state.[6] It also created a dangerous feedback loop of Spartan exceptionalism and siege mentality, which led to the city-state's collapse when it faced a coalition of the other Greek city-states and the threat of internal revolt by unfranchised Spartans.

In contrast, the small city-state of ancient Rome successfully expanded its dominion to encompass large portions of three continents, hundreds of different population groups, and a bewildering array of religions. The Roman Republic and, later, the Roman Empire needed their military to do more than win wars. They needed it to win peace, to create a sense of pan-Roman unity and mutual interest among former enemies. To achieve these goals, the Roman legions developed into a professional force that was largely composed of volunteers drawn from every class of citizen throughout the Roman world.

For recruits, they preferred young men in their late teens but would accept a good candidate as old as thirty-five.[7] The army issued travel bonuses to new recruits, because their units were usually located a great distance from their recruitment site. Once they arrived at their base, they would be issued standardized gear and begin a standardized course of physical training.[8] The drills would continue for the duration of their enlistment, as would the harsh discipline.[9]

Every element of the process reinforced the core values of egalitarianism and respect for the rule of law crucial to upholding Roman authority across Europe and the Mediterranean basin. Assigning individuals from different regions to the same unit and immersing them in the shared experience of barracks life underscored the essential equality of all Roman citizen soldiers—and by extension all Roman citizens—regardless of their origins. The enforcement of standardized military regulations provided an ongoing education in the power of law, the universality of its application, and its benefits to society as a whole. More importantly, the impact of this conditioning did not end with a soldier's term of duty. Former soldiers carried these values into retirement, frequently in locations far from their original homes, helping to spread them through Roman society as a whole.

The leaders of the Knights Templar faced a very different organizational challenge. Cultural differences, basic military training, and conditioning were nonissues. The order's warrior recruits all derived from European nobility. They were expected to be trained in arms and ready to fight from the moment they joined.[10] In many cases, they supplied their own horses, squires, and equipment.[11] What they lacked were values, specifically, the core Christian values of meekness, obedience, charity, and self-sacrifice.[12]

The engine of their transformation from brutal, grasping, worldly men into Christian paladins was the monastic discipline of "The Primitive Rule of the Templars." When not on campaign, much of the Templars' daily routine mirrored that of civilian monks. Their dormitories were lit through the night.[13] Their drills and other military requirements were organized around monastic devotions held roughly every two to three hours from 4 a.m. to 9 p.m.[14] The rule regulated how they wore their hair (short), what they could eat and when, and even when they could speak.[15] The result of this conditioning was an awe-inspiring, supremely committed fighting force whose members subordinated personal ambition to the will of the order and rejoiced in the prospect of martyrdom.[16]

The monks of China's Shaolin Temple in Henan Province, the fabled source of Chan Buddhism and much of Chinese martial arts, observe a similarly intense routine of training, physical labor, and scheduled devotions. But their tradition turns the Templar experience on its head. The founder of Chan Buddhism, Bodhidharma, viewed structured exercise as a means to enhance the impact of devotional meditation, thereby creating better monks.[17] No one knows if he planned to turn them into fighters, but that's what happened. From the seventh through seventeenth centuries, Shaolin monks fought in numerous battles against bandits, pirates, and imperial troops, usually on the winning side.

The link between the practice of Buddhism and military prowess was even stronger in feudal Japan. The earliest dojos were attached to Buddhist shrines and temples.[18] In addition, the history of Japanese swordsmanship features several master swordsmen who developed their signature techniques only after lengthy periods of meditation and isolation.[19]

Miyamoto Musashi, possibly the greatest swordsman of all time, began practicing Zen meditation (the Japanese version of Chan meditation) early in his career.[20] Zen principles and patterns of thought suffuse *The Book of Five Rings*, his famous treatise on military strategy and the way of the sword. The *Dokkodo*, twenty-one short injunctions that effectively function as his last testament, works equally well as a Buddhist text or Yoda's lesson plan. To cite a few examples:

5. Be detached from desire your whole life long.
8. Never let yourself be saddened by a separation.
17. Do not shun death in the way.[21]

Despite this, Musashi was a total badass who fought at least sixty duels to the death before he was thirty, including one where he killed his opponent with a sword he carved from an oar.[22] After he stopped killing people for a living, he perfected the art of defeating his opponents without delivering a single blow.[23] One account suggests he moved in a kind of force field of his own making.[24] Of course, mental state plays a major role in any conflict. Those who expect to lose probably will.

They might even psych themselves into a panic attack—which calls to mind Darth Vader choking the hapless officer's life away on the Death Star. If Musashi's later victories can be attributed in part to his opponents' belief in his invincibility, what does that say about Darth Vader's so-called Jedi mind tricks? Were they mind magic or applied psychology using the terror inspired by Vader's well-earned reputation to invoke a graphic physiological response.

Either way, it still works.

Mental conditioning—minus the panic attacks—remains a potent tool in the training and development of U.S. military personnel. The United States shares the Roman values of human equality and respect for the rule of law, as well as the goal of achieving peace and stability on the world stage. As a result, the conditioning of U.S. military personnel displays many similarities with the Roman model.

Like the legions, the U.S. military is a professional, volunteer force composed of a diverse mix of citizens from all regions of the country. It transports recruits to remote induction centers, isolating them from their previous lives. Upon arriving, the recruits are issued standardized clothing and gear. They are also subjected to rigid standards of grooming to break down their sense of individuality and foster a sense of group identity. They are toughened through physical activity, drilled to distraction, and relentlessly hectored. Since the 1980s, they are no longer subject to physical assault by their drill instructors.[25] But the combination of verbal abuse, grueling exercise, fear, and exhaustion remains compelling—intentionally so. The ultimate purpose of basic training is to see which recruits crack under stress, to help the others rise above it, and to instill strong military values such as loyalty, teamwork, and valor.

As former Marine Sergeant Jon Davis wrote in a March 15, 2013, article for *Quora*,

> You have to train 18-year-olds to run to the sound of gunfire and perform under fire and the threat of death.
>
> This act defies all logic, goes against all human instinct, and takes one of the most intensive acts of psychological reprogramming to overcome. . . .
>
> . . . Normal people can't do the things warriors are asked to do. They can't imagine it and shouldn't be forced to. But there are those that do. For these people though, there must be a transition from "civilian" to "warrior." Boot camp is the means of that evolution, and every part of it is necessary.[26]

Special operations forces' training reinforces and intensifies this conditioning. The emotional identification of sniper Chris Kyle with his SEAL team approached the level of a Spartan to his dining mess. He wrote in his autobiography, *American Sniper*, "Being a SEAL wasn't just what I did, it became who I was."[27]

When after four deployments and the greatest number of confirmed sniper kills in U.S. military history, his health and his family necessitated a return to civilian life, he felt like he was running away, letting down the team: "I know it doesn't make sense. I know I had accomplished a huge amount. I needed a rest, but felt I shouldn't take one. I thought I should be stronger than was possible."[28]

The success of this mental and physical conditioning is amply demonstrated by U.S. military performance in the field. But the landscape, tactics, and technology of the modern battlefield are constantly changing. To ensure U.S. military personnel can adapt and survive what General Peter W. Chiarelli, former vice chief of staff of the U.S. Army, called "the shifting complexity of modern wars," military training and conditioning must evolve to match the challenges of the operational environment and the speed at which it changes.[29]

One of the ways the U.S. Army hopes to overcome these challenges and improve soldiers' ability to adapt and thrive is the Army Ready and Resiliency Campaign. Described by the U.S. Army as a holistic, multidisciplinary approach to physical, psychological, and emotional health, the campaign seeks to enhance individual performance and increase overall unit readiness.[30] The psychological and emotional components of the campaign encompass research and training in a number of disciplines, including mindfulness meditation.[31]

Mindfulness meditation is essentially Zen meditation stripped of religious content. It uses simple breathing exercises to relax the body and center the mind in the moment. Some have criticized elements of the U.S. Army's campaign.[32] But thanks to the Shaolin monks and Musashi, mindfulness and mindfulness meditation have an unimpeachable martial pedigree. The techniques also boast a century of successful commercial application in Japan, including in potentially high-risk occupations such as the operation of *shinkansen* bullet trains.[33] But more importantly for the soldiers and veterans in the program, mindfulness and mindfulness meditation training often shows immediate, positive results.[34]

Such mental resiliency programs could become even more important as the United States and the world venture further into the solar system. Current NASA astronaut candidates undergo extensive psychological evaluations, but the agency is updating its criteria in anticipation of much longer missions to Mars and near-space asteroids.[35] In doing so, they may find themselves borrowing a page from the U.S. Navy's submarine force, which has been evaluating the mental fitness of submariners for generations. After all, space and deep-sea operations share a lot of similarities: no personal space; no escape from workplace conflicts; no sunlight for long periods; disrupted sleep and wake cycles and sleep deprivation; excessive sea pressure (or in the case of NASA, the opposite); and socially intense, physically closed, and potentially dangerous working conditions.[36]

Sound familiar? With the exception of the psychological stress imposed by environments inherently inimical to human habitation, those living conditions display a great similarity to living conditions at the Shaolin monastery and the dormitories of the Knights Templar. Since similar conditions generally respond to similar remedies, the Jedi-like discipline of mindfulness meditation and other forms of mental resiliency training would be the logical way to address the mental component of deep-sea and deep-space operations.

But the lessons of mindfulness may ultimately play a bigger role, one vital to every aspect of future U.S. military operations. You do not need Darth Vader's sorcerer's powers to predict the progressive automation of the military battlefield. Performing in a military theater that separates the hand from the spear, a milieu that values algorithms over valor and experience, potentially augmented with implants and cybernetic prosthetics, military personnel will find themselves increasingly challenged to retain their humanity, sense of self-worth, and commitment to the common good. When warfare becomes nothing more than a video game, everyone loses. Although it uses different terminology, mindfulness meditation, like Jedi teachings about the Force, fosters a personal understanding of the inherent connection between all things—internal and external, physical and spiritual. This sense of connection, of cause and effect, of mind to fist, may be our best defense against the stormtroopers' mindless surrender to totalitarianism.

Does this mean the U.S. military can look forward to a future of flying fruit, levitating rocks, and X-wing fighters? Unlike the Imperial officer

Vader terrorized on the Death Star, I won't hold *my* breath. On the other hand, shortly after I began work on this essay, I ran across an article on the Shaolin Flying Monks Temple, a vertical wind tunnel in the center of an amphitheater recently opened on the grounds of the Shaolin Monastery.

"The concept is partially based on the phenomenon of levitation explored by the Shaolin monks for centuries," architect Austris Mailitis told Inhabitat .com. "Now they will all have an opportunity to try levitating. The idea is focused on growth, a spiritual and physical chance of making the next step towards solving the mystery of levitation."[37]

Somewhere in a galaxy far, far away, laughing, Yoda is.

Notes

1. John D. LeMothe, *Controlled Offensive Behavior—USSR (Unclassified)* (Washington DC: Defense Intelligence Agency, 1972), xi, https://www.cia.gov/library/readingroom/docs/CIA-RDP96 -00788r001300020001-6.pdf.
2. LeMothe, *Controlled Offensive Behavior*, 35–36.
3. R. Jeffrey Smith and Curt Suplee, "'Psychic Arms Race' Had Several Funding Channels," *Washington Post*, November 30, 1995.
4. Xenophon, *Constitution of the Lacedaemonians (English)*, Greek Texts and Translations (Medford MA: Perseus Project at Tufts University, 2009 release), 2.10, http://perseus.uchicago.edu /perseus-cgi/citequery3.pl?dbname=GreekFeb2011&getid=1&query=Xen. Lac. 2.
5. Xenophon, *Constitution of the Lacedaemonians*, 2.6–2.10.
6. Plutarch, *Lives of the Noble Greeks*, ed. Edmund Fuller, rev. ed. (1968; repr., New York: Dell, 1971), 68.
7. Vegetius, *Epitome of Military Science*, trans. N. P. Milner, Translated Texts for Historians 16 (Liverpool: Liverpool University Press, 1993), 5, also n3 and n5.
8. Adrian Goldsworthy, *The Complete Roman Army* (London: Thames and Hudson, 2003), 80–81.
9. Goldsworthy, *Complete Roman Army*, 101.
10. Gordon Napier, *The Rise and Fall of the Knights Templar* (Brimscombe Port Stroud, UK: History Press, 2011), Adobe digital edition, chap. 3.
11. "The Primitive Rule of the Templars," trans. Andrew Zolnai, *Projet Beaucéant*, Templiers.org, http://www.templiers.org/regle1-eng.php, para. 66.
12. Napier, *Rise and Fall of the Knights Templar*, chap. 2.
13. Napier, *Rise and Fall of the Knights Templar*, chap. 3.
14. Napier, *Rise and Fall of the Knights Templar*, chap. 3, sec. "The Initiation Rite."
15. Napier, *Rise and Fall of the Knights Templar*, chap. 3.
16. Napier, *Rise and Fall of the Knights Templar*, chap. 3, sec. "The Initiation Rite."
17. David Chow and Richard Spangler, *Kung Fu* (Orange CA: Unique Publications, 1982), 12.
18. Miyamoto Musashi, *A Book of Five Rings*, trans. Victor Harris (Woodstock NY: Overlook Press, 1974), 4.

19. Kenji Tokitsu, *Miyamoto Musashi: His Life and Writings*, trans. Sherab Chödzin Kohn (Boston: Shambala, 2004), 61, 366.

20. Tokitsu, *Miyamoto Musashi*, xxxii–xxxiii.

21. Tokitsu, *Miyamoto Musashi*, 216–17.

22. Tokitsu, *Miyamoto Musashi*, 77–80.

23. Tokitsu, *Miyamoto Musashi*, 125.

24. Tokitsu, *Miyamoto Musashi*, 110.

25. Dirk Johnson, "Means, not Goals, Shift in Basic Training," *New York Times*, August 13, 1989, http://www.nytimes.com/1989/08/13/us/means-not-goals-shift-in-basic-training.html?pagewanted=all.

26. Jon Davis, "Why Is Boot Camp So Intense?," *Quora*, March 15, 2013, http://www.slate.com/blogs/quora/2013/03/05/why_is_boot_camp_so_intense.html.

27. Chris Kyle, *American Sniper*, with Scott McEwen and Jim DeFelice (New York: William Morrow, 2012), 325.

28. Kyle, *American Sniper*, 358.

29. *The US Army Training Concept 2012–2020*, TRADOC Pam. 525-8-3 (Fort Monroe VA: U.S. Army Training and Doctrine Command, 2011), 19, 25–26.

30. Army Health Promotion, Army Reg. 600-63 (Washington DC: Headquarters, Department of the Army, 2015), 1.

31. Shannon Russ, "Mindfulness-Based Stress Reduction Finds a Place in the Military," U.S. Army, July 7, 2015, https://www.army.mil/article/151787/Mindfulness_based_stress_reduction_finds_a_place_in_the_military/.

32. Nancy Montgomery, "Army Trains Soldiers on how to Be Mentally, Emotionally Tough," *Stars and Stripes*, January 3, 2010, https://www.stripes.com/news/army-trains-soldiers-on-how-to-be-mentally-emotionally-tough-1.97711#.WRpk1mdO5jq.

33. Steve John Powell, "The Japanese Skill Copied by the World," BBC, May 9, 2017, http://www.bbc.com/travel/story/20170504-the-japanese-skill-copied-by-the-world.

34. Russ, "Mindfulness-Based Stress Reduction Finds a Place in the Military." See also Montgomery, "Army Trains Soldiers on How to Be Mentally, Emotionally Tough."

35. Tanya Lewis, "The Right (Mental) Stuff: NASA Astronaut Psychology Revealed," Space.com, August 12, 2014, http://www.space.com/26799-nasa-astronauts-psychological-evaluation.html.

36. Mark N. Bing and Commander Eisenberg, "Psychological Screening of Submariners: The Development and Validation of the Submarine Attrition Risk Scale (SARS)" (presentation, International Public Management Association for Human Resources Assessment Council, n.d.), slide 3, http://annex.ipacweb.org/library/conf/03/bing.pdf.

37. Lucy Wang, "Giant Wind Tunnel Lets Shaolin Monks Fly while Fighting in China," *Inhabitat*, March 3, 2017, http://inhabitat.com/giant-wind-tunnel-lets-shaolin-monks-fly-while-fighting-in-china/.

14

Lightsabers and Death Stars

Military-Technology Lessons from *Star Wars*

DAN WARD

In history and fiction alike, some weapons make a big splash when they first appear, blowing up entire planets or stomping loudly toward the Rebels' new secret base on a remote ice world. Despite their impressive debuts, such devices of mass destruction are inevitably revealed to have crippling flaws that significantly reduce their combat effectiveness.

Other weapons make a more understated first impression, giving little hint of their eventual impact. On the battlefield as well as on the screen, these simpler, humbler weapons tend to punch well above their weight, for reasons both artistic and scientific. In this chapter, we'll take a close look at a fictional weapon that decidedly belongs in the latter category and see why lightsabers are preferable to Death Stars.

In 1977 *Star Wars: Episode IV—A New Hope* introduced lightsabers to the world in a quietly poignant scene. Half an hour into the film, we see an old hermit named Ben Kenobi pass along an antique family heirloom to an orphan boy named Luke. Old Ben describes the weapon in downright poetic language. He wistfully explains that the obsolete artifact is "an elegant weapon, for a more civilized age," clearly implying that particular age came to an end a long time ago.

The moment Luke switched the lightsaber on and waved the glowing beam back and forth began a long-standing love affair with this simple glowing blade. A 2008 survey by 20th Century Fox (three decades after *A New Hope* was released!) selected the lightsaber as the "best weapon ever featured in a movie," beating out Dirty Harry's handgun (number 2) and Indiana Jones's bullwhip (number 3). In case you're wondering, the Death Star came in at number 9.

The thing that is so right and so appealing about the lightsaber is its simplicity. In the hands of a trained Jedi (or, frankly, a half-trained Jedi), this single beam of energy demonstrates a wide range of capabilities: deflecting blaster shots, cutting through reinforced bulkheads, and delivering some of the most dazzling swordplay ever filmed. It is a knight's weapon, graceful and sophisticated. There is something pure and good in its clean lines and unpretentious structure.

As the saga continues, viewers discover that Jedi are not the only ones in this far, far away galaxy who use such elegant weapons. Villains use them too. Throughout the original trilogy, good guys and bad guys use essentially identical lightsabers. Only the color distinguishes noble Jedi Knights (whose blades are typically blue) from malevolent Sith lords (whose blades are typically red). But in the prequel trilogy and the sequel trilogy, we begin to see design variety among these glowing, buzzing weapons. That's where things get interesting and begin to reveal something important about complexity and combat effectiveness.

When a Sith lord named Darth Maul made an appearance in *Episode I—The Phantom Menace,* he instantly captivated audiences by wielding a double-sided lightsaber. This was the first variation shown to a wide audience (not counting the various light-weapons in *Star Wars* comics or *Clone Wars* cartoons). We were all suitably impressed by the ferocity of Darth Maul's acrobatic combat skills, and there was something undeniably cool about his weapon of choice. However, he was no match for young Obi-Wan, who first sliced the weapon's hilt in half and then sliced its user in half to match. So much for double-sided sabers.

Fast-forward to *Episode VII—The Force Awakens*. When the trailer was released, fans around the world went crazy over Kylo Ren's cross-hilted lightsaber. Sure, Darth Maul used two blades at once, but this new, mysterious weapon had three! What did it mean? How would it work? Let us set aside for a moment the discussion over Darth Tantrum's emotional maturity level and dubious combat skills, or even the effectiveness of his unique weapon. Instead, take a moment to notice the pattern that is beginning to emerge: Jedi rely on elegant, single-bladed sabers, while those who follow a darker path adopt weapons of increasing complexity. Spoiler alert: the added complexity does not help. The bad guys still lose.

As further proof of the dark side's tendency to ineffectively add complexity to the elegant Jedi weapon, consider the four-armed asthmatic cyborg named General Grievous from *Episode III—Revenge of the Sith*. Naturally, he wields four lightsabers at once. Unlike the conjoined blades of Maul or Ren, each of the sabers Grievous uses is a distinct, individual weapon. However, in his metal hands they essentially become four parts of a single weapon. Big surprise, the extra blades don't help him any more than they helped Darth Maul. Obi-Wan beats him too.

We have yet to see anyone try to use five blades at once. But there are several additional movies in the works, so that might still happen. Whether or not a *Star Wars* character uses five or more blades in the future is still to be revealed (difficult to see, the future is), but I can comfortably predict that if it happens, it will be done by a villain, not a Jedi.

Something profound is happening here, an important design principle that has real-world parallels and applications. We see a tight correlation between a tendency toward evil and a preference for complexity. The upright Jedi who follow the light side of the Force are dedicated to the simplicity of a single blade. The evil Sith, in contrast, continue making things more complicated.

Darth Vader, the most fearsome of the Sith lords, is a notable exception. True to his Jedi heritage (and perhaps foreshadowing his—spoiler alert!—eventual redemption) he wields a simple, single-bladed weapon and does so to great effect. His brief fight scene in *Rogue One* is a particularly chilling demonstration of his ruthless efficiency and helped to cement his position as one of the greatest movie villains ever.

The same pattern of virtuous simplicity and evil complexity shows up in virtually every battlefield in the *Star Wars* universe. The bad guys rely on large, complicated weapons and are defeated by good guys using smaller, simpler tools.

> The first Death Star is blown up by a half-trained Jedi flying a tiny X-Wing fighter (*Episode IV*).
>
> On Hoth (*Episode V*) several of the massive All-Terrain Armored Transport (AT-AT) walkers are defeated by much smaller snowspeeders. Then Luke takes one out with a hand grenade (after using his lightsaber to cut open an access hatch).
>
> The second Death Star is destroyed by a former city administrator flying a used cargo ship (*Episode VI*).
>
> In the Battle of Endor (*Episode VI* again) the technologically advanced Imperial forces, equipped with laser weapons and gravity-defying speeder bikes, are defeated by the adorable little Ewoks using weapons made of wood, stone, and vines.
>
> Guess what happened to the even-bigger-than-the-Death-Star Starkiller Base in *Episode VII*. Yup, destroyed by a tiny team of relatively low-tech Rebels.
>
> In *Rogue One* the Rebels destroy two massive Imperial battleships *and* the shield gate all at once, using a modest-sized Hammerhead Corvette like a battering ram.

What is going on here? From a storytelling perspective, there is something appealing about situations where a small, virtuous protagonist beats a big, evil adversary. Everyone loves an underdog story, and we all cheer for the scrappy team of misfits as they bring down an oppressive opponent despite being severely overmatched.

This concept is as old as the biblical story of David and Goliath and as contemporary as Malcom Gladwell's 2013 book *David and Goliath*. But there is something even deeper and more profound happening. The idea that simplicity prevails over complexity is not just a nice romantic notion, suitable for religious history, popular social science case studies, and space operas. It is also a concept that is constantly borne out in real-world battlefields.

In a widely disseminated 2007 paper titled "Nothing's Too Good for Our Boys," military analyst Pierre Sprey famously observed, "Not all simple, low-cost weapons work. However, war-winning weapons are almost always simple." His paper went on to compare combat performance data for a wide range of weapon systems, from rifles and aircraft, tanks and missiles. In every case, there was a direct relationship between low-cost simplicity and superior performance. Sprey concluded his analysis by dividing weapons into two familiar categories: cheap winners and expensive losers. Jedi clearly prefer the former category, while Sith gravitate toward the latter.

History provides many similar examples of this dynamic in play. At the Battle of Agincourt in 1415, a numerically superior force of French knights in heavy plate armor was famously defeated by English forces led by Henry V. The muddy terrain was a significant contributor to the outcome, but the English longbow is widely credited with contributing decisively to the victory. The longbow, it should be noted, was considerably cheaper, lighter, and simpler than the crossbow favored by European armies, to say nothing of the cost and complexity of a full suit of armor. The Battle of Endor was basically a reenactment of Agincourt, in which the English were played by Stone Age teddy bears.

Other analyses, in genres far beyond military technology, have reached identical conclusions about the way complexity reduces system effectiveness. A program management research firm named the Standish Group analyzed hundreds of IT development projects and identified a stark contrast between "Winning Hand" projects (which embraced speed, thrift, and simplicity) and "Losing Hand" projects (which were deliberately slow, expensive, and complicated). They used different category labels than Sprey did, but their conclusion is essentially identical. Spending more time and money does not improve quality or boost performance. Neither does allowing complexity to rise. Instead, as the cost, schedule, and complexity of a system increases, the likelihood of catastrophic failure rises proportionally, resulting in projects that cost more, take longer, and deliver less than promised.

These data suggest that there are several reasons *Star Wars* scriptwriters and prop designers give simple weapons to the good guys and complex weapons to the bad guys. In part, this is because they want the bad guys to look imposing (see Goliath). They want to add drama to the story, and they know there is nothing more impressive and dramatic than a moon-sized battle station or a set of four lightsabers being twirled by a cyborg. But there is another, deeper reason.

The one thing these stories need more than a daunting villain is . . . a victorious protagonist. The *Star Wars* writers want the good guys to win in the end; and for their triumph to be dramatically satisfying, it must be *convincing*. Every storyteller knows that the best fiction is built on a foundation of truth; so to ensure that the good guys convincingly come out on top by act 3, the filmmakers decided to give them the most effective weapons and to stick the villains with weapons that were merely intimidating. Thus, the protagonists got single-bladed lightsabers. A bucket-of-bolts, hunk-of-junk cargo ship. Single-seat X-wing fighters. And don't forget R2-D2, a droid without a face or voice who managed to nevertheless demonstrate a genuine personality and who was once described by George Lucas as "the hero of the whole thing."

In film and on the battlefield, in fiction and in real life, the most effective designs express a clear preference for thrift and simplicity. Such weapons and technologies tend to outperform their specifications and do more than they were designed to do. Complicated and expensive designs, in contrast, contribute far less to the fight than their inventors intended. They take longer to build, cost more, and dramatically underperform.

The lesson for modern military technologists is clear: minimize complexity. Exercise restraint. Rather than trying to solve technology problems by spending more time and money, we are better off using a constrained approach. Short schedules and tight budgets help reduce the expansive growth of complexity. Huge price tags and high levels of complexity? A Jedi craves not these things.

Also, the Empire should stop building Death Stars. Those things keep getting blown up.

For all the fantastic elements inherent in science fiction, filmmakers must acknowledge certain realities if they want their stories to work. *Star Wars* can get away with claiming Han Solo did the Kessel Run in less than twelve parsecs, a dubious bit of braggadocio to be sure, but could never get away with showing highly complex weapons outperforming their simpler alternatives. Audiences would not stand for it, because deep down we know that complexity reduces effectiveness and introduces vulnerabilities that can be exploited by a womp rat–hunting farm boy.

In other words, the *Star Wars* films are not just telling a David and Goliath story because it's dramatic or entertaining. They're doing so because it is true, a lesson today's militaries would do well to remember.

PART 3
Waging a War

There are two kinds of warriors: effective and dead.

And sometimes even the dead were effective, which reveals war's inherent unfairness.

The real requirement in battle is not the raw ability to fight but to fight amid the conditions at hand. The question is less *how good you are* and more *how you are good*: Are you better than your adversary in a given environment?

This rule applies to all armies as well as all warriors. The next group of essays cover wartime effectiveness: inevitable shifts in strategy, evaluating and understanding the Battles of Hoth and Endor, preventive versus preemptive military strikes, and what future war reporting and correspondents might look like. At war, these subjects matter, today and in the far-off future.

15

Hybrid *Star Wars*

The Battle of Endor

JAMES STAVRIDIS AND COLIN STEELE

How do you defeat a Death Star when you cannot possibly afford to make one for yourself?

That is the challenge facing the Rebel Alliance throughout *Return of the Jedi* in the lead-up to the climactic Battle of Endor. Thanks to an apparent intelligence coup and a combined battle on the surface of the forest moon of Endor and in the surrounding space, the Rebels are ultimately able to destroy the second Death Star and precipitate the fall of the Galactic Empire.

That the Rebels accomplish their mission makes for great cinema, but the way in which they do it should give us pause. In the Battle of Endor, the Alliance makes a logical decision for a smaller and weaker force going all in against a much bigger and stronger opponent—they elect a strategy based on hybrid warfare.

In their respective definitions of the term, both Nadia Schadlow and Frank Hoffman emphasize that, tactically, hybrid warfare is a "blend" (Schadlow) or "tailored mix" (Hoffman) of means ranging from conventional to irregular to terrorism and criminal behavior.[1] These kinds of blended operations are perfect for smaller and weaker forces confronting much larger ones, since fighting "fair" would be suicidal. Force or no Force, the Rebels could never hope to win a fleet action in space pitting one- or two-seat fighters against entire squadrons of Star Destroyers.

Both authors also emphasize that hybrid war—like all war—is ultimately waged for political ends. When *Return of the Jedi* opens, the Alliance is still licking its wounds from the beatings they took from the Empire on Hoth and in Cloud City in *The Empire Strikes Back*. Politically, the Alliance's goal is to wrest control of the galaxy back from the Empire; therefore, their military strategy is to avoid defeat while looking for an opportunity to deal a surprise blow to their much stronger enemy.

This makes hybrid warfare a natural choice for the Rebels. Given their military objectives, hybrid tactics offer four main benefits: ambiguity, surprise, tempo, and cost efficiency. Economics alone are a strong argument for the Rebels to go hybrid; they cannot build a Death Star of their own nor fight an Imperial fleet head-to-head. Staying small, hidden, and distributed is the Rebels' best hope to stay viable and, all the while, to attempt to seize the initiative by surprise and tempo.

These two features—surprise and tempo—are the keys to the Alliance victory at Endor. When their intelligence network hits pay dirt, the Rebels commit to a knockout blow against a supposedly inoperable Death Star. Plans go awry, but the Rebels' intelligence operations and combat actions in space and on the forest moon of Endor offer rich lessons for U.S. and allied strategists who will likely face Rebel-like hybrid forces in future conflicts.

INTELLIGENCE PREPARATION OF THE BATTLESPACE

Like many hybrid battles, the Battle of Endor begins with intelligence and counterintelligence efforts by both sides. Although they are not filmed, these operations are critical in setting up the battle, and their consequences are shown directly on-screen.

The Alliance decides to seek battle in the first place on the basis of intelligence about the Death Star's whereabouts and disposition. The first famous line of the battle is Chancellor Mon Mothma's, when she tells the Rebel leadership that "many Bothans died to bring us this information."

The Bothans are a race known for their galactic spy networks, and it is through those networks that the Alliance receives the information that convinces them to cast the die with an all-out attack on the unfinished second Death Star.

Intelligence warfare ultimately boils down to judgment calls, and sometimes very high-stakes ones—as in gambling the Rebel fleet on a knockout blow against the Death Star. The Alliance leadership trusts their Bothan networks and their products enough to order the attack, but the attack force soon learns that the information gleaned by the Bothans is really counterintelligence fed to them by the Emperor. The second famous line of the battle is Admiral Ackbar's exclamation upon realizing the Death Star's shield is still up, meaning the Empire is expecting the attack: "It's a trap!"

Intelligence and counterintelligence alone do not suffice to make the Battle of Endor unique or hybrid, but they point to the shadowy elements that are frequently part of hybrid warfare, especially when used by a much smaller and weaker force whose very existence might hang on decisions about when and where to seek or avoid battle. Without the (unfilmed) intelligence battle, the space and land battles of Endor would not have happened in the first place.

HYBRID BATTLE IN SPACE

The space battle around Endor, which ends in the destruction of the second Death Star, has some striking parallels with real-world scenarios, both historical and contemporary.

The first two layers of command look thoroughly conventional, with the decision to attack taken by political leadership (Mon Mothma) and operational planning delegated to military leadership (Admiral Ackbar). One layer down, though, things start to look less regular. At the head of the Rebel attack, as Gold Leader, is self-proclaimed "galactic entrepreneur" General Lando Calrissian, flying his old freighter, the *Millennium Falcon*. Although Lando is wearing rank and uniform, he is much more like a hastily commissioned privateer than a conventional military leader.

These expediencies make a lot of sense for the Rebels, and they certainly make for great cinema. Who doesn't want to stand up and cheer for a team of scrappy underdogs who are able to take down a much larger and stronger opponent? It is tempting to see parallels to the Battle of Midway, where U.S. pilots dealt a massive strategic defeat to the Imperial Japanese Navy by sinking all four of its large carriers.[2] There is something heroic in watching a handful of pilots destroy an enormous enemy target against long odds.

Even if that is the analogy the filmmakers want us to draw, it is not fully paralleled by the Rebels at Endor. The U.S. pilots at Midway were all naval aviators—not hybrid hotshots like General Lando Calrissian, who appeared at the last moment to lead the attack. A much closer analogy would be what the Chinese appear to be doing in the South China Sea, where fishing vessels are crewed with un-uniformed members of the maritime militia and the coast guard may be coordinating or supporting the militia's actions (with even higher levels possibly involved in the planning process as well).[3] Suffice it to say, we might cheer for the on-screen General Calrissian, but hybrid warriors like him are one of the chief concerns for real-world naval officers today, who have to consider whether, for example, fishing ships are simple merchants or maritime militias.

HYBRID WARFARE ON LAND

To enable the star fleet to accomplish its objective, the Rebels first have to insert a team onto the surface of the forest moon of Endor to disable the shield protecting the Death Star from attack in space. This attack kicks off in typical hybrid manner, with Luke (taking a turn as Commander Skywalker) piloting Han (General Solo), Leia, and a team of Pathfinders (Alliance special operations forces) to the moon's surface in a captured Imperial transport.

That team is also heading into a trap, since the Emperor has deployed "an entire legion of [his] best troops" to meet them. As ever, the Rebels' plan does not survive contact. The team is allowed to land, but they are promptly discovered by Imperial scouts. And in a truly unexpected twist, Princess Leia is brought into the Ewoks' village. Han, Luke, and the droids of course cannot abide a missing princess, so they send the Pathfinders on to the shield generator and go off in search of Leia—only to fall into the Ewoks' clutches themselves. With a little assist from the Force, our heroes win the Ewoks' hearts and minds, and the Ewoks' insurgency tips the balance of the battle against the Emperor's best troops and enables the Rebels to disable the shield, thereby allowing the ultimate attack on the Death Star to proceed and win.

Even if the ground battle is more insurgency than hybrid warfare, it is nevertheless notable for a few reasons. First, the opening gambit of a special operations insertion by means of a captured enemy shuttle is a classic false-flag operation—and a real no-no for conventional militaries on earth.[4] Clandestinely inserting a single special operations team is not out of the realm of possibility, but it is easy to see how these tactics can scale. Those who have read *Ghost Fleet* will recall that novel opening with an invasion borne by commercial roll-on–roll-off ships, and what could be more ordinary than that?[5] Second, the Rebels' teaming with the Ewoks demonstrates the kind of diplomatic-military-informational blending that Schadlow describes as typical of hybrid warfare. Think of the way in which multiple countries' special operations forces have partnered with local factions in Syria to advance various agendas in that complex environment.

Finally, the Alliance's actions in the Battle of Endor may provide a glimpse of what hybrid warfare might look like in the near- to medium-term future here on Earth. To date, the world has taken notice of hybrid land warfare as practiced by Russia's "little green men" and maritime hybrid warfare as practiced by Chinese maritime militias (sometimes called "little blue men"). Like *Ghost Fleet*, the Battle of Endor provides a useful example of how hybrid war can simultaneously blend domains as well as tactics—imagine a country (or non–state actor) employing hybrid tactics simultaneously on land and sea.

IS HYBRID WARFARE A TRAP?

The Battle of Endor provides many potential lessons for the United States in evaluating hybrid-warfare strategies, of which we will highlight three.

First, there is no significant cyber component to either side's battle plan at Endor. Despite the elements of disguise and deception, both sides attempt to physically destroy the other. Today, we have to assume that critical infrastructure (like the Death Star's shield generator) would more likely be hacked than blown up. As we look at hybrid warfare on Earth, we cannot be so distracted by shooting and explosions that we neglect to look for major attacks in the cyber domain.

Second, we can and should take seriously the idea that the Alliance employed hybrid warfare "a long time ago in a galaxy far, far away." Despite all the focus on hybrid, or gray-zone, warfare in recent years, it is not some newfangled creation, nor is it employed exclusively by U.S. adversaries. As Admiral (Ret.) Stavridis has written elsewhere, "Hybrid warfare is as old as combat itself. There is nothing fundamentally new about incorporating unconventional, and unacknowledged, forces on the battlefield in surprising ways to undermine conventional forces and obscure attribution."[6] Identifying and exploiting asymmetries is the essence of strategy—war is the continuation of policy not by the enemy's chosen means but by the means most likely to damage the enemy.

The final, and most sobering, lesson follows: hybrid warfare works. And if the Empire's experience is any guide, it seems to work particularly well against vastly more powerful forces that are wedded to conventional paradigms. As much as we cheer for the Rebels when we watch *Return of the Jedi*, we should remember that the United States is much more in the business of building extremely powerful but fundamentally conventional platforms and force structures—and like the Empire, we might not have an answer for a small but scrappy opponent able to concentrate asymmetric advantages and irregular forces against us at a time and place of their choosing.

In light of all this, the biggest challenge that hybrid warfare poses to the United States is likely that of developing strategies and tactics to counter it without fully embracing the dark side. U.S. force structure and posture frankly look more similar to the Empire's than to the Alliance's, but the United States can neither build enough Death Stars to deter the entire planet nor go too far in the direction of hybrid warfare itself. There is a place for black ops in real life, but they are generally best left to video games. Even if all soldiers could be special operators (and they can't), that would be dangerously destabilizing and would cede the moral high ground the United States claims in its military operations. Remember the global opprobrium that greeted the Russian annexation of Crimea with the help of unmarked "little green men." The United States and our allies might not have an answer for little green men yet, but we cannot afford to be caught in the position of using them ourselves.

Like the Empire, the United States has—for logical and understandable reasons—focused on building bigger and more high-tech forces rather than more flexible and less conventional ones. But bigger is not always better. If the Rebels' strategic challenge was how to defeat a Death Star without being able to build one, the challenge facing the United States—if we do not wish to go the way of the Empire—is learning how to counter forces that we cannot build ourselves and that Death Stars are not designed to see or shoot.

Notes

1. Nadia Schadlow, "The Problem with Hybrid Warfare," *War on the Rocks*, April 2, 2015, https://warontherocks.com/2015/04/the-problem-with-hybrid-warfare/; Frank Hoffman, "On Not-So-New Warfare: Political Warfare vs. Hybrid Threats," *War on the Rocks*, July 28, 2014, https://warontherocks.com/2014/07/on-not-so-new-warfare-political-warfare-vs-hybrid-threats/.

2. Six months after the attack on Pearl Harbor, the Imperial Japanese Navy attempted another knockout blow against the U.S. Navy in the Pacific, this time at Midway Atoll from June 4 through June 7, 1942. The Japanese plan was to trap and destroy the U.S. carriers and take over the U.S. garrison at Midway, but (as in *Star Wars*) intelligence efforts alerted the U.S. Navy to the Japanese plan and facilitated a countertrap. In the span of about twenty-four hours, U.S. pilots managed to sink all four Japanese carriers at the battle—a loss from which Japanese naval aviation never recovered.

3. China's maritime militia is a seaborne paramilitary force that is formally organized, trained, and equipped but that largely puts to sea in civilian clothes aboard fishing vessels. Their activities range from normal fishing to harassing other countries' fishermen. For much more detailed information, see the work of Conor M. Kennedy and Andrew S. Erickson, for example, "China's Third Sea Force, the People's Armed Forces Maritime Militia: Tethered to the PLA," *China Maritime Report No. 1* (China Maritime Studies Institute at the U.S. Naval War College, Newport RI, March 2017), https://cwp.princeton.edu/news/china%E2%80%99s-third-sea-force-people%E2%80%99s-armed-forces-maritime-militia-tethered-pla-cwp-fellow-alumni.

4. A false-flag operation is one in which one military carries out an activity with the intent of making it appear as though it were carried out by another force (a third party or even the same force that is attacked). This has been expressly illegal for over a century, since The Hague

Regulations of 1899, and has been consistently reaffirmed in international law since then. The Additional Protocol I (1977) to the Geneva Conventions of August 12, 1949, states that "it is prohibited to make use of the flags or military emblems, insignia or uniforms of adverse Parties while engaging in attacks or in order to shield, favour, protect or impede military operations." See the ICRC database of customary international humanitarian law at https://ihl-databases.icrc.org/customary-ihl/eng/docs/v2_rul_rule62.

5. P. W. Singer and August Cole, *Ghost Fleet* (New York: Eamon Dolan, 2015).

6. James Stavridis, "Maritime Hybrid Warfare Is Coming," *Proceedings* 142, no. 12 (December 2016), https://www.usni.org/magazines/proceedings/2016-12-0/maritime-hybrid-warfare-coming.

16

Han, Greedo, and a Strategy of Prevention

CHUCK BIES

When states and actors try to prevent future or imminent aggression from a potential adversary, it is sometimes desirable to be the one to strike first. This is especially true when the effects of being struck first have fatal or irrecoverable political and military consequences or when the state or actor feels that they've been "backed into a corner" and have no other viable options remaining. The strategic dilemma becomes whether to employ a strategy of prevention or preemption. Though they are often used interchangeably, they are not synonymous.

One of the best ways to illustrate the difference is to examine the shoot-out at the Mos Eisley cantina from *Episode IV—A New Hope*, one of the *Star Wars* franchise's most iconic scenes. Since the mid-1990s, it's also become one of the most contentious, thanks to the remastering of the shoot-out between Han Solo and a green alien named Greedo.

In case it's been a while since you've seen the movie, after concluding an agreement with Obi-Wan Kenobi and Luke Skywalker for transport to Alderaan, a jubilant Han is getting up to follow Chewbacca to their ship when he is held up by a blaster-toting Greedo. Greedo, a bounty hunter, threatens to take Han to the local mob boss, Jabba the Hutt, so that he can collect the bounty on Han's head. Han implores Greedo to let him go so he can finish the job for Obi-Wan; if he does, he'll have the money needed to repay his debt to Jabba. Greedo rejects Han's pleas and threatens to take both his life and his ship. What happens next depends on the version of the movie you happen to be watching and spawned the "Han Shot First" meme.

THE SHOOT-OUT

The differing versions of the cantina showdown between Han and Greedo all share the same dialogue, but they differ in who pulls the trigger first. One has Greedo shooting first and missing before getting blown away (the 1997 version), another has Greedo only just barely shooting before Han (the 2004 version), and yet another has them shooting essentially simultaneously with Han barely pulling the trigger first (the 2011 version). These versions are all wrong—the one that matters the most is the 1977 original, where Han murders Greedo in cold blood before the green thug has a chance to get off a shot.[1] There's no laser blast directed at Han; he simply gets up and walks away from the alien's smoking corpse.

On the surface, this seems to clash with our collective perception of Han as a hero; after all, what kind of hero would just shoot an opponent without warning? The same can be said of governments. Throughout history, we can see numerous examples where nation-states make similar surprise attacks to varying degrees of success; there's Prussia's invasion of Silesia in 1740 (successful), Germany's invasion of France in 1914 (initially successful), Germany's invasion of Poland in 1939 (successful), Germany's invasion of the Soviet Union in 1941 (initially successful—notice a trend yet?), Japan's air raid on Pearl Harbor in 1941 (tactically successful), and the U.S. invasion of Panama in 1989 (successful), to name just a few. But remember, countries and statesmen position themselves as the "good guys" when they are making historical decisions in real time.

So what gives? What motivates otherwise "good" people (as they see themselves at the time) to use their instruments of national power to execute what is essentially a sucker punch? What about situations where the attack is a little less surprising, like the U.S. invasion of Iraq in 2003? How does that fit into all of this?

It turns out that we're talking about two things that are distinct but often confused. The former is a preemptive strike; the latter is a preventive strike. It so happens that Han's "shoot-out" with Greedo illustrates both.

HAN'S CALCULUS

Let's go back to Han and Greedo and put ourselves in Han's shoes. Han has three things to consider: who his adversary is and what Greedo's motivations are, what the short- and long-term repercussions of killing Greedo are likely to be, and what the likely cost is if he does nothing.

So what does Han know about Greedo? Well, he's a bounty hunter who works for a gigantic gangster (Jabba the Hutt) and lives in Mos Eisley, a "wretched hive of scum and villainy." Mos Eisley's a rough town, and its cantina is even rougher. Case in point, moments before the Han-Greedo conversation, Obi-Wan cut off an alien's arm, and nobody batted an eye. The only thing anybody seemed to care about was not having any droids in the establishment, which kind of makes sense (because, hey, droids don't drink). You've got to be pretty tough to be a bounty hunter in that kind of environment, and Han's been around long enough to know that Greedo is dangerous just by being willing to set foot in the cantina.

But wait, why not negotiate with Greedo? Try to talk him out of taking Han back to Jabba? First, we know that Greedo can't be compelled to change his mind. We know this because of a deleted scene from *The Phantom Menace* where we see a young Anakin beating up a young Greedo because Greedo accused him of cheating.[2] Qui-Gon breaks up the fight, Greedo flatly refuses to take back his accusation, and Qui-Gon tells Anakin, "You'll have to tolerate his opinion; fighting will not change it." Greedo's probably been like that his whole life; and knowing Greedo, Han would recognize that he has no chance of verbally or physically coercing Greedo into letting him go, even if he was not witness to the Greedo-Anakin altercation. Han has dealt with Greedo and his ilk before, so he would intuitively know the character traits that we had to see in a deleted scene from a prequel.[3]

Second, Han knows that Greedo, being a bounty hunter, is not trust-worthy. So when Greedo suggests that he "might forget he saw him" and not tell Jabba if Han pays him, there are two big problems with that claim. One, there's nothing to stop Greedo from taking the money and turning him in to Jabba anyway. Two, it doesn't solve Han's bigger problem, which is that he'd still owe Jabba a lot of money.

As far as Greedo's motivations, Han can surmise for several reasons that Greedo wants to take him in alive. First, Greedo doesn't have strength above and beyond what a human has (remember, young Anakin kicked his ass); if he kills Han at the cantina, then he'll have to carry Han's corpse out of the cantina and down a few alleys until he can get to a speeder—no easy task, especially with the added prospect of other bounty hunters potentially murdering Greedo along the way so that they can easily collect Han's corpse and bounty after Greedo just did the hard work. So why not just shoot Han in the back and take his severed head back to Jabba? This goes to the second point: *The Empire Strikes Back* and *Return of the Jedi* both demon-strate that Jabba the Hutt is vindictive and cruel and revels in the torture of his enemies.[4] Han would have dealt with Jabba enough by this point to know this, and it is probably why Greedo didn't just shoot him on sight.

Next, Han weighs what the repercussions would be if he were to shoot Greedo in the bar. The short-term consequences are negligible. There's no real law and order in Mos Eisley, with no local police or government other than the occasional Imperial patrol. Even the stormtroopers are more concerned with trying to find R2-D2 and C-3PO than with local crime; they actually were in the cantina moments before the shoot-out, where a brutal dismemberment by lightsaber had just taken place, about which their give-a-crap level was zero. Similarly, the bartender was more concerned about droids in his establishment than he was about a strange old guy busting out his laser sword and hacking off limbs. If anything, the bartender would be most concerned about cleaning up the mess, but that's from the perspec-tive of freeing up a table for additional patrons, because local sanitation inspections appear to be nonexistent.

What about long-term consequences? It's not like Han can get into *more* trouble with Jabba by shooting Greedo than he already has by owing Jabba money. Jabba isn't the kind of boss who particularly cares about his employees' welfare. Heck, he fed one of his dancing girls to a rancor just for kicks. No, Jabba only cares about his bottom line; so when Han jettisoned his cargo at the sight of an Imperial cruiser, he committed an unforgivable crime. Killing Greedo won't affect the price on his head either way. Han will still end up owing money to Jabba, but his prospects of being able to pay it back improve substantially.

At this point for Han, there isn't a whole lot of downside to simply offing Greedo. So what's the cost of doing nothing? If Han doesn't shoot Greedo, there are a few ways that the scenario could play out. First, Greedo walks Han at gunpoint to Jabba's palace, where he will be condemned to a torturously slow, agonizing death. This is the most likely outcome and is pretty bad for Han. Second, Greedo kills Han where he sits. As previously discussed, it's not Greedo's preferred choice, but it's still a possible outcome and is also unfavorable from Han's standpoint. Third, he sits in the cantina and keeps Greedo talking . . . at least for a while, but then he's looking at either outcome one or two. Fourth and most unlikely, Greedo walks him to Jabba's palace, where he is miraculously able to convince Jabba to give him more time to pay off his debt. But the delay means he loses his transport contract with Kenobi, so he's out the money he needs and is back where he started. The upside to these outcomes? Han most likely gets to spend the rest of his short and excruciatingly painful life with the satisfaction that he did the "right thing." And that's what smugglers and rogues really aspire to, right?

So to recap, Han's life is on the line with a dangerous and violent criminal whom he has almost no anticipated hope of negotiating with. If Han shoots Greedo, there are no negative consequences other than his own internal guilt (the cantina's morality-free ambiance suggests nobody will judge him), and not shooting Greedo can only result in bad things happening. The real question here isn't why Han shot Greedo; it's why he waited so long to do it.

When Han shot Greedo, he conducted a preventive strike.[5] It is so-called because Han looked at his situation and though he wasn't sure what Greedo would do, he was sure that he didn't like the threat that Greedo posed. He needed to take action to prevent Greedo from injuring or killing him or from utterly derailing his interests.

From a nation-state standpoint, this preventive strike looks like Japan bombing Pearl Harbor or the United States invading Iraq in 2003 or Israel's bombing of Iraq's Osirak nuclear plant in 1981. Though the other nation-state in question is not likely to conduct an imminent attack, the concern is that the other nation-state will eventually pose a mortal threat if not dealt with, and the cost of allowing the other side to strike first in that situation would be intolerable. This future aggression must be prevented, hence the term *preventive strike*.

So then what is a preemptive strike? To answer that we need to look at the 2011 version of the cantina scene. Like the other remastered scenes since 1997, it still has the absurd digitally enhanced head bob, where Han dodges Greedo's missed blaster shot (which is preposterous not only because Greedo missed but because it would indicate that Han has reflexes fast enough to dodge a laser beam); but unlike the 1997 and 2004 versions that have Greedo shooting first, in the 2011 version Han just barely gets his shot off before Greedo, which does a better job of explaining Greedo's laughably awful aim.

What we see in the 2011 version is a preemptive strike on Han's part. His calculus prior to pulling the trigger remains the same with one critical difference: he sees Greedo about to pull the trigger and understands that his enemy's attack is imminent. Han just needed to be quicker on the draw than his enemy. This is where preemption differs from prevention; the preventive strike aims to prevent future strategic threats from manifesting, where a preemptive strike aims to be quicker on the draw than a tactical threat that has already manifested itself.

The quintessential historical example of the preemptive strike is the Schlieffen Plan of 1914. In this case, an invasion by France was imminent, and Germany was able to strike first by virtue of being able to mobilize more rapidly than its adversaries. The Germans correctly concluded that they would lose a protracted war, so their strategy depended on being able to individually force adversaries out of the conflict as quickly as possible. A lesser-known example of the preemptive strike is Napoleon's Jena-Auerstadt campaign, in which Prussia declared war on France. Napoleon was able to mobilize his Grande Armeé faster than the Prussians could, and he was able to bring the campaign onto Prussian soil. By making the first operational move, Napoleon was able to dictate the tempo and location of the war.

So remember, if a nation-state takes action akin to Han shooting Greedo outright, like in the 1977 version of the film, then that nation is executing a preventive strike. If the situation looks more like the version of the film where Greedo is able to get a shot off, then that nation is executing a preemptive strike. Nations and actors employ these types of strikes and strategies when they feel that they are threatened and that the cost of not taking action is intolerable.

And for the record, Han shot first.

Notes

1. You can see all four versions run simultaneously at "Star Wars Greedo Scene Comparison 1977–2011," YouTube video, 0:27, posted by TheStarWarsTrilogy.com, August 21, 2014, https://youtu.be/Lv3t0Be3aHc.
2. This clip is deleted scene 6, "Anakin's Scuffle with Greedo," in the collector's edition. It is viewable at "The Phantom Menace Deleted Scene," YouTube video, 0:56, posted by CArlP-bonus95, May 14, 2008, https://youtu.be/fgyyBLrYgC0.
3. Consider that the deleted scene was written and filmed twenty years after the original film in order to show us this element of Greedo and validate Han's decision to shoot first.
4. Remember, we're talking about the original 1977 version here, so we can forget that nonsense about Han having a civil conversation with a computer-animated Jabba at the Mos Eisley hangar.
5. For a detailed explanation of preventive and preemptive war from the national strategy perspective, see Joe Barnes and Richard J. Stoll, "Preemptive and Preventive War: A Preliminary Taxonomy" (paper, Baker Institute Research Project, Rice University, Houston TX, March 2007), http://www.bakerinstitute.org/media/files/Research/50987fa2/Preemptive_and_Preventive_War-1.pdf.

17

The Logic of Strategy in Space

STEVE METZ

One of the most challenging aspects of strategy is knowing when to change it. Edward Luttwak, in his masterful *Strategy: The Logic of War and Peace*, explained that because strategy pits two or more thinking, scheming adversaries against one another, each attempting to impose its will and prevent the others from doing the same, it has a paradoxical, nonlinear logic.[1] Actions that appear to be best often are not, and what works today often will not tomorrow. A strategy, in other words, has a finite life span. When young, it competes with other strategies. Those that emerge from this competition and grow to maturity are effective for a while; then they begin to age, becoming increasingly ineffective, until they die altogether. This makes it vital to understand when to abandon a strategy on its final legs—when, in other words, to undertake a strategic shift.

Like the paradoxical logic that imbues strategy, the need for periodic strategic shifts appears obvious, yet they are devilishly difficult to do. Strategy's intricacies and complexities are camouflaged, only revealing themselves during the design and implementation of a shift. History—even mythical history like *Star Wars*—can provide illustrations, even guideposts. But ultimately a strategic shift, like the creation of strategy itself, is more art than science, demanding psychological acuity; cross-cultural perceptiveness; an ability to peer through the fog of the future; and, most of all, the boldness to abandon something that had been working and strike out into the unknown with only a blurry, prediction-dependent map.

A number of things can inspire an empire, state, or protostate to consider a strategic shift. None is more powerful than a defeat or disaster that proves that the old strategy was bankrupt and compels the boldness and risk tolerance that strategic shifts demand. Think Britain after Dunkirk or the United States after Pearl Harbor and the loss of the Philippines.[2] Samuel Johnson once said that the prospect of being hanged concentrates the mind wonderfully. So does defeat or disaster.

Even short of this, though, major change in the security situation can inspire or compel a strategic shift. Take the emergence of a new enemy. In *The Empire Strikes Back* Emperor Palpatine, recognizing that Luke Skywalker had become a Jedi under Yoda's tutelage, told Darth Vader, "We have a new enemy." He then adjusted his strategy for defeating the Rebels, adding a high-priority new objective: bringing Skywalker to the dark side. This action—encouraging part of an adversary coalition to switch sides—is a time-tested technique in strategy that has the dual benefit of both strengthening one's own side and weakening the enemy. After the defeat of the Galactic Empire, the former Rebels themselves were forced to shift their strategy to deal with the emergence of a new enemy from the dark side—the First Order, which appears in *The Force Awakens*.

Strategic shifts can also be in response to something that makes existing enemies more dangerous, such as a new capability or technology or a change in the enemy's behavior or strategy. The best example in *Star Wars* is, of course, the Death Stars—the first in *A New Hope* and the second in *Return of the Jedi*. Both force the Rebels to adopt a more aggressive strategy and take the operational offensive. Another example is when Yoda takes command of the Clone Army created by the Kaminoans in *Attack of the Clones*, thus allowing the Republic to shift toward a more aggressive and military-based strategy.

New adversary alliances can also signal a fundamental change in a conflict and compel a strategic shift, as when Count Dooku, the leader of the Confederacy of Independent Systems, built a coalition with the Corporate Alliance, the Trade Federation, the Commerce Guild, the InterGalactic Banking Clan, and the Techno Union in *Attack of the Clones*. Shifting alliances often drive strategy in classic works on statecraft, like Thucydides's *The History of the Peloponnesian War*, and remain important today, as in Richard Nixon's opening to China during the 1970s or, more recently, Russia's alliance with Iran to prop up Syrian dictator Bashar al-Assad.[3] At times, greater clarity through a better understanding of the situation can drive a strategic shift. Take, for instance, the scene in *The Force Awakens* when the leader of the First Order concluded that the Resistance would find the map leading to Luke Skywalker and potentially reconstitute the Jedi and determined that "our strategy must now change."

Often a strategic shift is shaped by altered expectations about the future, particularly the belief that some sort of window of opportunity was closing, forcing a state to seize the initiative or become more aggressive while it still had a chance to do so. Scholars have concluded that Germany escalated what could have been a controllable crisis in the summer of 1914 to major war because Berlin believed that Russian industrial growth would eventually take the chance of a quick victory off the table. For the Kaiser, it was now or never.[4] The United States invaded Iraq in 2003 in part because the George W. Bush administration knew that the post–September 11 political window of opportunity when the American public would support armed intervention was finite. There was no dramatic increase in the danger Saddam Hussein posed, but there was a limited time to address the existing threat. In *Return of the Jedi* the Rebels believed that they had to shift from defensive to offensive strategy before the new Death Star was operational, since once it was, they would have no chance of survival, much less of overthrowing the Empire and restoring the Republic. This illustrates an important point: for Rebels, separatists, and weaker nations, strategic shifts are always higher-risk ventures, since their aggregate power inferiority means that they have less of a cushion if the shift turns out to be unwise, undertaken too soon, or undertaken too late. Weaker parties must have a greater risk tolerance than stronger ones, but this makes them more susceptible to disaster.

Unsurprisingly, though, the *Star Wars* metaphor is incomplete when it comes to understanding strategic shifts. Its mythological universe is missing some of the things that can drive strategic shifts, such as the ascension to power of a new leadership cadre with different priorities, objectives, value systems, and risk-tolerance levels and domestic factors like deep social, demographic, and political change or altered economic conditions. In the real world, economics always affects politics and hence strategy, while in *Star Wars* economics are nearly irrelevant, with ideological value structures— freedom versus oppression—being all that really matter.

Star Wars also underplays the difficulty of undertaking a strategic shift. In reality, strategic shifts are like turning a large ship or, in the days of linear ground combat, reorienting a brigade or division of infantry. For even more complex strategic actors, like great powers or coalitions, shifts can be as hard as redirecting an entire fleet or army, requiring many component organizations and the public to abandon the old consensus with its constituent priorities, values, perceptions, and beliefs and adopt new ones. Like most mythological universes, the *Star Wars* one is much simpler than reality. A leader decides on a new strategy, and it happens. All subordinates immediately accept the change, and it is put in place. In reality, leaders who see the need for strategic shifts first must convince their allies, superiors, subordinates, and constituents. This can be even harder than seeing what needs to be done. And the more dispersed strategy-making authority is, the harder it is to undertake a strategic shift. For instance, Richard Nixon's bold opening to China and the beginning of detente with the Soviet Union were only possible because he had concentrated strategy-making power in his own hands and those of Henry Kissinger.

The inertia inherent in large organizations like states or empires is always an impediment to strategic shifts, at least in the absence of a major disaster or defeat. Luttwak's dictum that "what works today may not tomorrow" is difficult for political leaders and security strategists to grasp. The larger and more complex a state—the bigger the ship or fleet to redirect—the greater the tendency to stick with an existing strategy until it collapses into disaster. Hesitancy to expend resources even when evidence suggests it is necessary—simple cheapness—can also constrain and even prevent needed strategic shifts. Often, a modest shift at the right time can forestall the need for a bigger one later, but the foresight this requires is rare.

At other times, political leaders may resist a needed strategic shift out of fear that it will have unintended consequences or provoke an adversary. In *Attack of the Clones*, for instance, Senator Amidala, even though she was concerned about the growth of the Confederacy of Independent Systems, said, "If the Senate votes to create an army, I'm sure it's going to push us into a civil war." A negotiated solution would be impossible, Amidala contended, if the separatists "feel threatened." Forgoing a strategic shift, in this case, was a form of appeasement. But this may not always be a bad thing. As political scientist George Liska pointed out in his 1982 book, *Russia and the Road to Appeasement*, appeasement is a time-tested and sometimes-useful tool of statecraft discredited by Neville Chamberlin, the British prime minister, caving in to Hitler in the 1930s.[5] But it can be misguided if the adversary is committed to victory rather than seeking a negotiated settlement. This was true both of Hitler and of the Confederacy of Independent Systems. By hesitating to move to a war footing, the Republic—like Chamberlain's Britain—gave the separatists time to grow stronger and thus put itself in greater danger.

A strategic shift that requires a change in basic values or ethics is particularly difficult. Facing the growing power of the Confederacy of Independent Systems and knowing that it had a huge Clone Army available (even though by accident), the Republic resisted using this new capability until compelled to do so, even though an earlier deployment of it might have deterred or prevented the rising threat from the separatists. Major change is always difficult, and the deeper and more far-reaching it is, the harder it is.

Missing or inadequate information—intelligence shortfalls—can also impede a strategic shift. In *Attack of the Clones* the Jedi Council did not want to notify the Senate of the diminished power of the Force and the rise in the dark side, even though knowing this might have led the political leaders to consider a strategic shift, possibly preempting the conflict with the

Confederacy of Independent Systems that eventually forced the Republic to use the Clone Army. Misperception is a particular risk when adversaries do not share a culture. The ethical asymmetry between the forces of good and the forces of evil caused the Republic and the Rebels to underestimate their enemies. This problem of cross-cultural understanding hinders the United States today, since each of its likely adversaries has a very different strategic culture than the American one. Since strategy seeks both psychological and physical effects, messaging is always important. Doing this across cultural boundaries is particularly difficult.

As much as anything, though, the *Star Wars* canon, like astute studies of war from Homer to today, shows that hubris by political leaders and strategists can impede strategic shifts, or at least delay them to the point that they become more difficult or less effective. After all, a strategic shift demands that leaders admit that what they are doing is no longer effective, even wrong. It takes an intensely self-aware and confident leader or a very desperate one to do this. That war is inextricably linked to honor and fear makes the shackles of hubris even more powerful.

Even so, there are times when leaders do undertake successful strategic shifts despite all the constraints and obstacles. To do so requires a collective leadership who can grasp strategy's paradoxical logic, even if they do not articulate it with Luttwak's elegance; who can anticipate second- and third-order effects, understanding that while not everything is connected to everything else, many things are; who can comprehend their adversaries; who can build a consensus for change despite the risk; who can understand the importance of timing in strategy, knowing that even doing the right thing at the wrong time is an error; and who can institutionalize change, rather than simply design and articulate it.

Star Wars was designed explicitly to show that good triumphs over evil. Hence the strategic shifts of the Republic and the Rebels encountered initial difficulties but eventually succeeded, while those of the Empire and the First Order seemed headed toward success but ultimately failed. But at this point the *Star Wars* analogy runs out. In the real world, the aspiration is for good to triumph over evil, but it is never certain. At times, the forces of evil win, at least temporarily. In the real world, leaders sometimes undertake strategic shifts too late or not at all, whether out of fear, ignorance, or hubris. Sometimes they undertake strategic shifts that are thwarted by the enemy or are simply ineffective, often leaving their nation or organization in greater danger than it was before. Ultimately *Star Wars* shows how strategic shifts should be done; but lamentably, in the real world, nothing compels them to be done or to be done correctly.

Notes

1. The notion of strategy's paradoxical logic was introduced in Edward Luttwak, *Strategy: The Logic of War and Peace* (Cambridge MA: Harvard University Press, 2002).
2. For the United States, the attack on Pearl Harbor and the loss of the Philippines made the old strategy of deterrence through strength instantly obsolete, forcing American political leaders and military strategists to adopt a high-risk strategy based on long-range power projection and the phased conquest of the Japanese Empire.
3. Iran considered Russia a mortal enemy since the 1979 revolution that overthrew the Shah and brought a theocratic regime to power, but the two nations have become allies of convenience because both have an interest in the survival of Assad's government.
4. One of the best explanations of this is Fritz Fischer, *World Power or Decline: The Controversy over Germany's Aims in the First World War* (New York: W. W. Norton, 1974).
5. George Liska, *Russia and the Road to Appeasement: Cycles of East-West Conflict in War and Peace* (Baltimore MA: Johns Hopkins University Press, 1982).

18

Darth Vader and Mission Command

JONATHAN BRATTEN

Darth Vader is known to be many things; he is a Sith lord, a masterful war-rior, a man with complicated family issues, a skilled pilot, and a vindictive adversary. Together with the Emperor, he wielded an incredible amount of power over the galaxy. But what these descriptions miss—and what represents his greatest failure—is his role as a joint commander of Galactic Imperial operations. And his overall failure in this capacity can be attributed to his misuse of mission command.

As a commander, Vader had to oversee strategic and operational issues across the two components of the Galactic Empire's military force: the army and the navy. The Imperial Navy's fleet of ships provided transport and firepower capabilities and ranged from small TIE fighters used for pursuit and close air support all the way up to capital ships like the Imperial Star Destroyers. The navy also managed the Empire's massive Death Star battle stations. The Imperial Army was the land component, which, in part, provided security for the navy's ships, with detachments from the storm-trooper corps. The army also possessed all air-defense artillery capabilities.

The relationship between the army and the navy was rocky, to say the least, with each component vying for a greater piece of the Imperial mission. As Emperor Palpatine's emissary, Darth Vader provided—in theory—mission and direction to the army and navy commanders and was responsible for ensuring that their service squabbles did not interrupt the efficiency of galactic operations. Acting as a joint commander, Vader needed to communicate clearly, effectively, and concisely to the fleet and ground forces to coordinate their efforts to destroy the Rebellion. He needed, in short, to ably apply the tenets of mission command.

Throughout the history of warfare, commanders have sought ways to balance the need to keep track of their units in combat—what military doctrine calls "control"—with that of giving their subordinates the freedom of initiative needed to take advantage of opportunities that present themselves. The U.S. Army uses the philosophy of mission command to do this. This philosophy's central ideas were first developed by the Prussian army in the nineteenth century. Prussian strategist Helmuth von Moltke the Elder reasoned that because "victory or defeat in battle changes the situation to such a degree that no human acumen is able to see beyond the first battle," plans built on an initial situation will quickly become irrelevant.[1] In essence, no plan survives beyond the first contact with the enemy. Therefore, von Moltke concluded, "the advantage of the situation will never be fully utilized if subordinate commanders wait for orders." They should instead be given the requisite latitude to exercise initiative as opportunities emerge. This is the essence of mission command, which the U.S. Army defines as "the exercise of authority and direction by the commander using mission orders to enable disciplined initiative within the commander's intent to empower agile and adaptive leaders" in and out of combat.[2] Laborious as this doctrinal definition might be, the ideas are vital to battlefield success.

Mission command includes six key principles: build cohesive teams through mutual trust; create shared understanding; provide a clear commander's intent; exercise disciplined initiative; use mission orders; and accept prudent risk. In theory, mission command keeps commanders from micromanaging their subordinates while also developing an accurate picture of what is taking place on the battlefield. This, however, is precisely where Darth Vader failed.

Overlooking Vader's questionable formative background—it's far from clear whether he ever received training in field and staff operations as a Republic general—he comes to the fight with a host of assets common in successful senior military officers; he is aggressive and tenacious, requires excellence in his subordinates, and has a surplus of personal courage. That said, he exhibits faults that can be fatal in a joint commander.

Vader is completely unable to develop cohesive and winning teams; his method of exercising quality control over his subordinates is to Force choke those who are unable to accomplish their missions to standard. While the consequent terror he engenders ensures unwavering compliance, the fear that infects the fleet and ground forces is a poor substitute for trust. Fear also ultimately contributes to a regimented mindset among the Imperial armed forces, which reduces their initiative and fosters an unhealthy degree of risk aversion among subordinate commanders. What officer would be eager to take initiative absent direct order after witnessing Vader strangle Admiral Ozzel to death as punishment for a tactical error—bringing the Imperial fleet out of hyperspace directly above Hoth in *The Empire Strikes Back*? Why exercise independent judgment and risk suffering the fate of Captain Needa, whom Vader also killed after Needa failed to capture the *Millennium Falcon*? Officers on capital ships in the fleet naturally refused to take any initiative, choosing instead to wait for orders from Vader. The fear that grips the Imperial officer corps is made apparent when Vader intimidates the commander of the second Death Star into near paralysis. Vader responds to the commander's assurance regarding the superweapon's progress toward completion with a threat: "I hope so, Commander, for your sake. The Emperor is not as forgiving as I am." This absolute intolerance of initiative is what dooms fighting organizations facing a more mentally agile adversary, such as the Rebel Alliance.

As the joint commander of the Imperial Army and Navy, Vader has been empowered by the Emperor to oversee the destruction of the Rebel Alliance. However, as a Sith lord, he is also tasked with finding and neutralizing all remaining Jedi within the galaxy. These two competing requirements ultimately conflict with each other. By the Battle of Endor, Vader has almost lost sight of his objective of crushing the Alliance because he is so focused on Luke Skywalker. Divided between the two missions and distracted from his command role by his pursuit of Luke, Vader fails to provide a clear commander's intent or fashion a unity of purpose among those he commands.

Central to the idea of mission command is the concept not just of initiative but of *disciplined* initiative. That means pursuing opportunities as they appear but avoiding any overextension of a military force's capabilities. Vader, of course, understands his own capabilities well but fails to keep his command on track, operating effectively and within the limits of its capacity while still pursuing moments of advantage when they present themselves. During *Return of the Jedi* the Emperor orders Vader to "send the fleet to the far side of Endor. There it will stay until called for." Vader gently pushes back, citing intelligence reports of the Rebel fleet massing nearby. The Emperor brushes him off, telling him that his work here is done. Mission command would have left room for Vader to exercise judgment within a clear intent from his superior—in this case, destruction of the Rebel fleet—and should have allowed him to trust his own intelligence sources and his greater awareness of the situation in this matter. That he was neither given this latitude nor willing to take it leaves little wonder that his own subordinates would themselves act only in accordance with precise orders.

Mission orders—those that include a task and its purpose but not a micromanaged plan to fulfill the task—rarely appear in the *Star Wars* universe. When seen, they most often appear in the form of flight briefings for Rebel pilots. Throughout the series of films, Vader never once gives a mission order. He communicates only through in-person sessions, holograms, or video teleconference. This absence of written orders means that it takes time for his intent to be conveyed throughout the fleet. It also means that opportunities to inflict grave damage on the Rebel Alliance pass because subordinates have not yet received the requisite direct orders. For example, after Admiral Ozzel brings the fleet out of hyperspace directly above Hoth (and Vader disciplines him to death), Vader's instructions for *the entire operation* are, "Make ready to land our troops beyond their energy field, and deploy the fleet, so that nothing gets off the system." Concise? Yes. Clear? Sort of. Comprehensive? Not at all.

Probably the most important aspect of mission command is the need to accept prudent risk. High-payoff targets have a corresponding amount of risk associated with them. And Vader was indeed a risk taker; it was, in part, how he advanced to such a vaunted role by the time of *A New Hope*. It is in that film that we see Vader take one enormous risk, allowing Luke, Leia, Han, Chewbacca, and the droids to make their escape from the Death Star via the *Millennium Falcon*:

> GOVERNOR TARKIN: Are they away?
> DARTH VADER: They've just made the jump into hyperspace.
> GOVERNOR TARKIN: You're sure the homing beacon is secure aboard
> their ship? I'm taking an awful risk, Vader. This had better work.

It turned out that Vader's risk paid off—the Empire was able to track the *Falcon* to the Rebel base at Yavin 4. However, the Death Star's attempt to destroy their base was foiled by a group willing to take an even higher degree of risk: the Rebel pilots. Vader himself only escaped the destruction of the Death Star because he assumed the *imprudent* risk of flying attack missions against the Rebel pilots—a single well-placed shot aimed at him would have left a paralyzed officer corps without the command's only decision maker.

Vader was less successful in his pursuit of the *Millennium Falcon* in *The Empire Strikes Back*:

> ADMIRAL PIETT: Our ships have sighted the *Millennium Falcon*, Lord.
> But it has entered an asteroid field, and we cannot risk . . .
> DARTH VADER: [interrupting] Asteroids do not concern me, Admiral!
> I want that ship, not excuses!

The foray into the asteroid field did not end well. They lost sight of their quarry, and the fleet sustained damage from the asteroids. Repeatedly, Vader's risk taking placed his mission in danger, because he failed to ever demonstrate a capacity to weigh the prudence of his risks.

While Vader's personal courage was never lacking, his obsession with being on the front end of nearly every attack left other elements of the Imperial armed forces without guidance. Whether on the Rebel shuttle over Tatooine or inside Echo Base on Hoth, Vader routinely placed himself too close to the battlefield to be able to see the big picture with the clarity a commander with his overall responsibilities requires. And this is perhaps his gravest error: in his monomaniacal fixation on capturing Luke Skywalker, Vader lost sight of the entire battlefield. He allowed personal issues to cloud his judgment. This mistake—and a bit of luck—allowed the Alliance to mount a raid on Endor and an attack on the second Death Star, simultaneously. With Vader and the Emperor distracted by Luke's diversionary presence, the Rebel Alliance gained freedom of movement without having to contend with Vader's aggressiveness. And with Vader out of the fight, Imperial flag and junior officers were hesitant to act decisively for fear of fatal reprimand later. They thus lost the initiative and thereby the battle.

In the end, Vader was undone by a series of failures, all of which likely would have been avoided if he had properly executed mission command. Instead of doing so, he leaned too heavily on his own force of personality, his personal courage, and a finely developed aura of fear. And these proved to be not enough to fight and win a war on multiple fronts against a savvy, adaptive enemy.

Notes

1. Helmuth von Moltke the Elder, quoted in Milan N. Vego, *Joint Operational Warfare: Theory and Practice* (Washington DC: Government Printing Office, 2007), v–16.
2. Department of the Army, *Mission Command*, Army Doctrine Publication 6-0 (Washington DC: Government Printing Office, 2012).

19

The Battle of Hoth

A Critical Analysis

ANDREW LIPTAK

With the destruction of the Imperial Death Star during the Battle of Yavin, the Rebel Alliance established itself as a formidable opponent against the Empire. However, despite their victory, the Alliance found itself facing two major problems: a new, serious effort by the Empire to track down and eliminate the threat that the Alliance posed and an inability to stand toe-to-toe against the Empire.

The Battle of Hoth provides an excellent case from which to examine the mindset of Alliance leaders during this critical time. By examining the assault on a newly established headquarters and the reaction from Rebellion commanders, it's clear that the leadership from the Alliance commanders and the dedication of the soldiers on the battlefield are what helped keep their movement from collapsing, while they were aided by critical military errors on the part of the Empire's armed forces.

SETTING THE STAGE

Forced to abandon its central headquarters on Yavin 4, the Rebel Alliance now had to locate a suitable home base from which to plan their operations while broadly withdrawing from the center of the galaxy. With Imperial forces redoubling their efforts to locate the Alliance command structure, Rebellion commanders had to contend with inhospitable choices.

Alliance commanders selected a planet in the Anoat sector, Hoth. Because of the planet's inhospitably cold temperatures and massive asteroid belt, they believed that the largely uninhabited planet would likely be overlooked by Imperial surveillance.

> With all the meteor activity in this system, it's going to be difficult to spot approaching ships.
>
> General Rieekan

The Rebellion tasked the construction of their new headquarters to General Rieekan. Under his watch, soldiers used native tauntauns to patrol the surrounding areas and to set up a sensor system to detect Imperial equipment. To further bolster the base's defenses, they also installed a costly V-150 Planet Defender surface-to-orbit ion cannon, which would allow the base to defend itself from direct orbital attacks. To complement their defenses, a small squadron of modified T-47 airspeeders was assigned to the base.

As the Rebel Alliance worked to reestablish their headquarters, Darth Vader and the Imperial forces under his command began a massive search to locate the Rebellion's core leadership. The task force was commanded from Vader's own Super Star Destroyer by Admiral Kendal Ozzel. To aid their search, they began deploying thousands of Viper probe droids, which would autonomously search planets and report back their findings to Vader's task force. One such probe was deployed to the Hoth system, where it began to seek out any signs of the Alliance.

Prior to the Battle of Hoth, a key figure in the Rebellion, Luke Skywalker, went missing, attacked by a native life-form. The disappearance forced Rebellion technicians to accelerate the efforts to adapt the T-47s for flight, allowing them to join the search-and-rescue operations the next morning and giving the pilots a chance to test out the aircraft.

Echo Base's control crew picked up movement on the new sensor system and quickly ruled out native life-forms and Rebellion personnel before identifying it as an Imperial probe droid, which then self-destructed.

The information was received aboard the *Executor* and reviewed by Captain Firmus Piett and General Maximillian Veers, each of whom believed the information was a solid lead in their search.

> We have thousands of probe droids searching the galaxy. I want proof, not leads.
>
> Admiral Kendal Ozzel

Piett noted that the Hoth system was supposed to be devoid of human life. Vader, upon seeing the information, ordered the task force to deploy to the Hoth system and ordered Veers to begin preparing his units for an assault.

This appears to be a critical moment for the failure of the Imperial forces to ultimately stop the Rebellion at this point in the war. With the self-destruction of their probe—the Empire's only intelligence asset on the planet—the Empire was now limited in the amount of information that they had from the planet. Rather than deploy further intelligence assets to the planet, Vader ordered an immediate deployment of the task force to Hoth.

Following the discovery of Echo Base, the Rebel Alliance began their evacuation, anticipating the imminent arrival of the Empire's forces. The base had a small fleet of GR-75 medium transports at their disposal for transporting equipment and personnel, along with a squadron of Incom T-65B X-wing starfighters for escort duty. Due to the short amount of time available to evacuate, the Alliance had to come to terms with abandoning much of the heavy equipment installed on the base.

Rieekan's decision to abandon the newly established base was met with some skepticism—the base had only just been completed, with a considerable amount of equipment installed. Ultimately, his caution proved to be the deciding factor in the survival of the Alliance.

With the arrival of the Imperial task force, Rieekan ordered the activation of the base's energy shield. With the forces arrayed overhead unable to bombard the base, he was able to effectively dictate the course of the battle by forcing the Imperial Military to fight on the ground, without air support from TIE fighters or bombers. This not only allowed him to task his X-wing fighters for escort duty but also bought him time to continue the evacuation.

The Imperial task force (which included the *Executor*, the *Tyrant*, the *Devastator*, and the *Avenger*) dropped out of hyperspace in close orbit over the planet Hoth. As Vader had ordered an immediate redeployment, Ozzel followed his orders, assuming that the Rebel forces would be quick targets from orbit.

However, the lack of information about the disposition of the Rebels foiled these plans. Echo Base had already anticipated the arrival of the Imperial task force and prevented them from carrying out a routine orbital bombardment. It was at this point that the Empire lost the ability to effectively end the Rebellion. Ozzel was executed for his error, thus depriving the task force of its most senior flag officer.

Despite the setback, Vader's task force had been designed specifically for the actions that followed in orbit. The smaller Imperial II–class destroyers' maneuverability would allow the Imperial forces not only to capture escaping vessels but to contend with any additional armed threat that the Alliance might field.

As it turns out, Rebel forces were woefully understaffed for such an escape; troop transports would be escorted by a single pair of X-wing fighters tasked with running interference with Imperial fighters.

Despite the disparity in force projection on the battlefield, the Alliance base did have an asset that they could use to aid their escape: the V-150 ground-to-orbit ion canon. Due to the Empire's rush to arrive at Hoth, their knowledge of Rebellion assets was next to nothing, and they arrived at the battlefield not knowing the state and disposition of Rebellion fighters. Their lack of knowledge about the Alliance's ground-to-orbit assets became a critical weakness for the task force.

The first transport lifted off from the planet's surface, followed by a pair of salvos from the V-150. The blasts targeted the *Tyrant*, the Star Destroyer covering the ship's escape vector, disabling it and leaving a hole in the Imperial blockade. Rebel troopers cheered as they learned of their comrades' escape, which provided a major morale boost to the soldiers on the ground.

The lack of knowledge about the Alliance forces on the ground likewise led General Veers to certain tactical decisions. His primary target was to destroy the base's power generators, which in turn would eliminate the shield protecting the base. To this end, he landed a squadron of All-Terrain Attack Transports, along with an All-Terrain Scout Transport, beyond the shield. With the shield up, it is clear that he only anticipated meeting resistance from ground troopers, as fighter assets would be utilized for escort duty. Additionally, the planet's climate made fielding aircraft difficult— something that the Rebellion had only accomplished in the rush to locate a missing pilot.

Rieekan had already identified the power generators as a primary target and deployed his forces accordingly: Rebel soldiers from the 61st Mobile Infantry's Twilight Company manned hastily prepared trenches, backed by heavy stationary weapons.

On the ground, Veers's armored forces attacked Rieekan's ground troopers, targeting the heavy guns between them and the power generator. As they approached, Rieekan scrambled his T-47 squadron to provide air support for the 61st Mobile Infantry. Despite the heavy armor protecting the AT-AT walkers, Rogue Squadron was able to exploit a critical weakness; using tow cables, they undermined the legs of at least one walker, while another was destroyed by a pilot who had been shot down. Despite their innovative use of equipment, the squadron was quickly depleted.

> Yes, Lord Vader, I've reached the main power generators. The shield will be down in moments. You may start your landing.
>
> General Veers

The Rebels' combined use of ground and air power, coupled with the lack of battlefield intelligence, was not enough to stop Veers from advancing and ultimately destroying Echo Base's power station, but that wasn't their primary objective.

What the members of Rogue Squadron and the 61st Mobile Infantry were able to accomplish was to slow the incoming armored forces enough to allow the rest of the Rebellion forces to escape into orbit. As Veers deployed his snowtroopers, Organa issued the order for the remaining ground forces and base personnel to board the last transport.

AFTERMATH

While Veers was ultimately able to destroy the power generator and occupy the base, he did so at great cost; he lost several of his heavy walkers before reaching the Rebellion's lines and took further casualties as he entered the base. Furthermore, the task force itself suffered from major losses in orbit; the loss of one Star Destroyer at the onset of the battle demonstrated the cost of Imperial confidence in their tactics, while another Destroyer was heavily damaged in the pursuit of the remaining Rebel commanders in the asteroid belt.

Despite the high cost to the Imperial forces, the cost to the Alliance was equally high, but not catastrophic; while they took numerous casualties on the battlefield (in both personnel and equipment), they were able to escape with their command structure largely intact. What could have been a major blow to the Rebellion became a mere battlefield loss.

The loss of a permanent headquarters meant a setback in the Alliance's ability to command their forces on the battlefield and to plan a larger strategy for winning their fight against the Empire. Additionally, the loss of critical weapons, equipment, and personnel would further impact the ability of the Rebellion to continue its military operations in the short and long terms.

It was the work of the commanders on the ground on Hoth, as well as errors by Imperial commanders, that prevented the loss from ending the Rebellion completely. Rieekan's prudent measures to abandon the newly completed base saved numerous lives and preserved what equipment could be evacuated from the base. Admiral Ozzel's decision to drop his task force near the planet within sensor range allowed the Rebellion not only to push forward their evacuation plans but to devise a quick defensive plan that helped hold off Imperial ground forces to evacuate the remaining personnel from the planet and regroup with the rest of the Alliance fleet, where they began to plan their next moves.

20

Why Military Forces Adapt, Even in a Galaxy Far, Far Away

CHUCK BIES

If you don't like change, you'll like irrelevance even less. This applies to tactical warfare as well; except, when it comes to fighting, being irrelevant usually means that you'll soon be dead. With stakes so high, it doesn't seem like changing would be all that difficult, especially when your own survival is on the line. And yet, time and again, the sides that failed to adapt at the tactical level in the Clone Wars, the Galactic Civil War, and the First Order's Uprising ended up being relegated to the dustbin of history in a galaxy far, far away.

So why do soldiers, commanders, and armies fail to adapt in the face of death? This chapter will explain why some sides do or don't adapt, using four *Star Wars* conflicts, big and small: a skirmish between the Trade Federation droids and the Gungans during the Naboo Blockade Crisis; the titanic battles between the Republic Clone Army and the secessionists' droid armies during the Clone Wars; the battles fought between Imperial stormtroopers and Rebellion soldiers; and the First Order stormtroopers' raids against pretty much everybody. In the end, an army's willingness and capacity to embrace tactical adaptation is rooted in troop scarcity and time available to change.

THE NABOO BLOCKADE CRISIS

The two major sides that were still standing by the end of the Naboo Blockade Crisis consisted of the Gungans, a race of failed comic-relief CGI rabbits with subtly racist Caribbean overtones, and the Trade Federation, an interstellar conglomerate run by a race of overtly racist Asian caricatures called the Neimoidians in an equally overt jab against *Star Trek*. The Naboo defensive force was all but wiped out by the Trade Federation's massive droid army, and the Gungans, the sentient race native to Naboo (but, curiously enough, not called "Nabooians"), avoided conflict until the Federation threatened to destroy their native habitat. If this seems stupid, it is, because *Phantom Menace*.

The Federation's droid army consisted of two main types of battle droid. The standard battle droid was humanoid, said "Roger, Roger," and carried a blaster rifle. It was also a multipurpose droid and laborer. It did not have an integral weapon system, so it was able to use its hands to manipulate tools, control panels, and armored vehicles. It didn't have shields or armor, and its joints were unprotected and visible. One blaster hit could take them down. It received its controls and orders from a centralized Federation control ship, because it did not have its own artificial intelligence. It communicated to other battle droids verbally, which is kind of impractical when you consider that a droid could have transmitted volumes of dense and complex data to another droid in the same amount of time it took to say, "Roger, Roger," but hey, *Phantom Menace*. They were cheap to produce in huge numbers and easy to replace.

The second type of droid was the droideka, or destroyer droid. It made its appearance early on in *Phantom Menace* after Obi-Wan and Qui-Gon escaped from the ambush in the meeting room and attempted to force their way into the ship's control bridge. Unlike the standard droid, it was more insectoid than humanoid and moved by rolling up into a fast-moving ball.

When it deployed out of the ball, it used its two autocannon arms to lay down a heavy base of fire and employ a deflector shield to protect its front from blaster fire. It had a very rudimentary AI that boiled down to, "Face toward enemy, deploy shield, and don't stop shooting until it's dead." It was fast when moving in ball form, but it was immobile and highly vulnerable to attack from the rear once it deployed out of its ball. It was an impractical method of locomotion and an unnecessary trade-off in capabilities, because *Phantom Menace*. Where the standard battle droid could be considered multipurpose, the droideka's design and blaster arms reduced its utility to being a marginally mobile pillbox. The droideka's cost per unit to manufacture was higher than that of the standard droid. While replaceable, because they cost more to replace, they weren't seen in the same numbers as the standard droids.

Unsurprisingly, the Gungan army consisted of Gungans. They employed active protection measures in the form of individually carried energy shields, as well as energy shields that could be deployed to cover a larger area. Despite this incredible technology and being able to build submersibles capable of traveling through the planet's watery core, they didn't have vehicles or lasers; instead they rode animals, carried spears, and hurled blue energy balls with slings and catapults, because *Phantom Menace*. They existed in large numbers (unfortunately), but they couldn't quickly replenish their numbers, because they had to procreate and grow to adulthood and because they were only found on Naboo (thankfully).

There are a few points to note about the Battle for Naboo. The battle took place on an open plain with no natural cover or concealment, nor was there any key terrain for either side to rally toward. The Gungan army approached Naboo City, compelling the droids to sally forth and deploy against the Gungans. Initial bombardments failed against the Gungan shields, so the droids were forced to take the tactical offensive. The droids suffered heavy losses but succeeded in forcing the Gungans to surrender, and they would have won it for good if Anakin Skywalker hadn't destroyed the orbital droid control ship, a deus ex machina that had nothing to do with the Gungan battle performance, because *Phantom Menace*. Though the droids sustained heavy losses, the Gungans did not, and Gungan resolve broke before their numbers did. Few Gungan bodies lay on the battlefield as the droids began rounding up Gungan prisoners of war, though the ground was littered with the shattered and broken remnants of countless droids.

So which side really won? Because the Gungans certainly didn't defeat the droids; if anything, the droid-Gungan battle didn't really matter. From the standpoint of adaptation, neither side was adaptive. The droids didn't try anything particularly new: go find the enemy, start shooting at them, and keep shooting until they either are dead or give up. What the Gungans did, as the underdog, was pretty stupid. They were riding animals and hurling blue balls. The droids had friggin' tanks! So faced with an enemy that outnumbered them; outgunned them; and, thanks to its command and control network, was capable of perfect coordination, the Gungans, armed with spears, chose to meet them in battle on a plain with nothing resembling cover. They could have drawn the droids into a forest or into a narrow pass to negate their numbers and firepower—as was done at Thermopylae.[1] Instead they stuck with what they'd always done, and it nearly cost them everything.

THE CLONE WARS

The Clone Wars were fought between the Galactic Republic and the secessionist star systems, sometimes referred to as the Confederacy of Independent Systems (CIS). The CIS, which included the Trade Federation, fought primarily with droid armies, while the Galactic Republic fought primarily with armies made of "human" clones.

The droids used by the CIS were essentially the same as those seen during the Naboo Blockade Crisis, with two key differences. The first difference was that the standard battle droids were no longer dependent on an orbital control ship; the Geonosian manufacturers realized the folly of not building each droid with its own control AI and added AI into their droids. The second was the introduction of a third type of droid, the super battle droid. Larger than the standard droid but still humanoid, the super battle droid had a laser blaster built into the tops of its hands, allowing it to manipulate vehicles and control panels while still having an internal weapon system. They didn't have shields, but they had more armor (not that it mattered against lightsabers or lasers), so they were more expensive to produce. But because they were new, they were not fielded in nearly the numbers that standard droids were.

The Republican clones were people in the sense that they could think for themselves and required food, air, and other essentials to life. However, they were raised from birth in isolation from other nonclones on Kamino and had their physical growth accelerated, and as a result of the cloners reducing their source material's propensity for independence, they didn't have their own personalities. If they were people, they were disposable people. Like the stormtroopers that followed, their armor let them survive in different environments but offered no protection from lasers or blunt impact. Usually their armor was white, though on occasion they camouflaged their armor with paint, as they did during the Kashyyyk campaign—but then they sort of just stood in the open while Wookiees got behind cover. Because they had been created on Kamino over the course of many years and their growth was sped up, there was a substantial stock of clone troopers ready for combat, with more in the pipeline.[2] Replacing battalions in large numbers would require time—not as much time as a human battalion would have taken but still more time than it took to roll a droid off a production line.

In battle, both sides suffered astronomical casualties, but man-for-man the clones killed droids at a higher rate. The clones won the Battle of Geonosis, but they suffered heavy casualties in the process.[3] They lost multiple transport aircraft but didn't seem to really pay much attention to those losses as they happened. Similarly, during General Grievous's raid on Coruscant, the Republic fleet lost dozens of capital ships and countless starfighters, but no priority was ever given to assist individual clone pilots in distress.[4] Though the clones were people, they seemed to mind their own losses as much as the droids did, which is not at all.

In the end, the clones won most of their battles. However, the war was won not on the battlefield but in Anakin's murder of the CIS leadership on the Mustafar system. Neither side was particularly adaptive during the war. When either was on the attack, they massed their numbers, advanced in lines, and poured on as much laser fire as they could. When either was on the defensive, they massed their numbers, stood in lines, and poured on as much laser fire as they could. Both sides were set on employing an attritional strategy against an opponent that had limitless manpower.

THE GALACTIC CIVIL WAR

In this true David-versus-Goliath matchup, the Rebel Alliance fought for both victory and survival against the evil Galactic Empire. The Rebel Alliance consisted mostly of human systems with the support of a few alien races, but Rebel soldiers were human.[5] The Empire also fought with mostly human troops and leaders, but it is widely believed that a significant portion of the rank-and-file stormtroopers were leftovers of the Republic's Clone Army. This is attributed to the stormtroopers across all three movies in the original trilogy having similar-sounding voices, being of the same height and build (prompting Leia to ask Luke, "Aren't you a little short for a stormtrooper?"), and displaying similar levels of precision with their weapons and to the near certainty that the Empire had nothing even remotely resembling a Department of Veterans Affairs or a jobs program for billions of laboratory-grown people who were created and trained from birth for the sole purpose of combat.[6] The Empire's officer corps was almost completely human, and apparently "British accent" was the only real requirement for becoming an officer.

Pitched battles between the Empire and the Rebels were a rarity, and the few that did occur were dwarfed in scale by the titanic battles of the Clone Wars. At the strategic and operational levels of interstellar warfare, the Rebels sought to avoid contact with strong Imperial forces whenever possible; they did this by keeping their bases hidden, as they did on Yavin 4, or by evacuating their strongholds upon discovery by the Empire, as we saw during the Battle of Hoth. When the Rebels did fight, they attempted to do so either as a delaying action to buy time for their forces to withdraw, as part of a surprise attack such as at Endor, or when the Empire forced them into a situation where retreat was not practicable and fighting meant survival, as seen during the raids on each of the Death Stars.

Tactically and on the ground, Rebel forces took pains to increase their survivability. Knowing that all the available body armor was pretty much worthless against lasers, even military-grade stormtrooper body armor, they discarded body armor completely so that their individual mobility was maximized; the only armor typically worn was helmets to protect against blunt-force impacts. They wore camouflage suited to their environment, from woodland on Endor to snow-white on Hoth. As we saw on Hoth, they dug trenches to increase their survivability, and they used vehicles and beasts of burden suitable to the climates they operated in.

The Empire, on the other hand, didn't care much for individual survivability. The stormtroopers tended to stand in the open and in large clusters, even though cover was readily available nearby. They wore armor that didn't protect against laser blasts or against blunt force (as we saw on Endor); and regardless of the environment, that armor came in one color: white. The opening scene of *A New Hope* is particularly informative as to how the stormtroopers fought: they simply flooded the area in question with troops, put up a wall of blaster fire, and maintained forward pressure against their enemy until one side or the other was dead. For every stormtrooper who died, two more would come forward, step over the corpse, and maintain the advance, until the side that actually cared about casualties broke. We saw similar tactics on Hoth and on Endor; they made no attempt to seek cover and ignored their own casualties as they pressed the attack. Yes, they took losses, but those losses were easily replaced.

In the end, the Empire lost, but not because its pool of stormtroopers was exhausted. The Empire was defeated because its head was decapitated, not because its back was broken. Though the Imperial Army paid heavily in blood for its victories, it was still winning victories, and given its nearly inexhaustible resources, there was no compelling reason to change how it fought. The Rebels, on the other hand, constantly shifted their tactics, uniforms, and equipment to suit the environments that they fought in to compensate for the Empire's numbers. The Rebel strategy was to survive and inflict heavy damage with precision strikes, and the Rebels were continually victorious in their engagements against the Empire. These small battlefield victories—even Hoth, since the Rebels escaped annihilation on that planet—made little difference. Until the Rebellion was able to assassinate Palpatine and destroy the second Death Star, the Empire had enough stormtroopers to keep fighting and winning as it had been.

THE FIRST ORDER UPRISING

Out of the ashes of the Galactic Empire, the First Order rose to power. Its main adversary was the Resistance, which was the military force that fought for but did not belong to the newly constituted New Republic. It's a bizarre arrangement of forces and structures, so stay with me on this.

The First Order was essentially the remnants of the old Galactic Empire. They had starships similar to Star Destroyers, their starfighters were basically TIE fighters with a few cosmetic and technical upgrades, and their soldiers still wore white stormtrooper armor. Though the First Order had considerable resources, enough to convert a planet into a world-destroying battle station, its resources were still dwarfed in comparison to the Galactic Empire's. Being a rogue government, they didn't have countless recruiting worlds at their disposal, their manufacturing base was limited, and their resources were not disposable. Decades after the events of *Return of the Jedi*, the First Order had no clones in its formations. Instead, the First Order stole its soldiers as children and raised child soldiers to become stormtroopers.

As a result, we see very different behaviors in First Order stormtroopers than we did in Imperial stormtroopers. Despite the white armor, individual soldiers moved to and from positions of cover against incoming blaster fire. Stormtroopers maneuvered in teams instead of advancing as a human wave. When their comrades were killed, they noticed, and First Order commanders had to monitor discipline and retrain noncompliant soldiers in a way that Imperial commanders did not. If Imperial stormtroopers fought in a 1914 World War I style, First Order stormtroopers fought in a style more akin to 2004 Operation Enduring Freedom. The trade-off, though, is that it takes more training to achieve this level of performance, which means it takes longer to field new troops.[7]

What of the Resistance? Though they fought for the New Republic and received tacit support, the Resistance was a private military force headed by General Leia Organa for the express purpose of *resisting* (see what they did there?) the power and threat of the First Order. Any financial or materiel support received from the Republic was done under the table. This meant that, like the First Order, though they were able to field a capable force, it was small. But unlike the First Order, the Resistance did not exploit child soldiers or consider the use of clones, so its losses were even less readily replaceable. The Resistance relied on quality over quantity.

As a result of this and the fact that the plot to *The Force Awakens* is almost a complete mirror of *A New Hope,* the Resistance fights in a manner similar to the Rebel Alliance of old; they are sensitive to casualties, avoid ground engagements whenever possible, and engage in starship combat only when the situation is dire enough to demand it.

Time will tell how or whether the Resistance prevails over the First Order, because this is the first war where both sides displayed a capacity for tactical adaptation. In the previous wars, only the Rebel Alliance demonstrated any willingness or ability to adapt to the enemy. This means that any First Order or Resistance victory will be hard-won.

WHAT DRIVES TACTICAL ADAPTATION?

So what's so special about the Resistance, the First Order, and the Rebellion that they were able to adapt? Adaptability comes down to two key factors: sensitivity to casualties and availability of time.

The armies of the Federation, the Republic, and the Empire didn't adapt because they didn't have to. Lose a battalion of clones? Order up another from Kamino—there's more in the hopper. Lose a legion because your Death Star got blown up? Increase recruiting quotas and shift a few Star Destroyers full of stormtroopers to the sector. Lose entire armies of droids to a Republic offensive? Have the manufacturer fire up another production line and send in some more droids faster than Amazon Prime.

They weren't asking their troops to do anything particularly difficult either. How long does it take to install a droid's AI chip or train a trooper to walk straight ahead while shooting nonstop? Not very long. If your soldiers are literally disposable or you don't care about them on an individual level or there's no limit to your ability to replace them, there's really no incentive to adapt to anything your opponent does as long as you can grind the other side down until they quit.

Consider the Rebellion, the Resistance, and the First Order. Every soldier they lose is a significant cost in time and resources, both to produce in the first place and to replace. They can't just order up more battalions, which means they have to train individual soldiers to take independent action to survive. Every soldier lost also creates a public relations problem that makes it more difficult for them to attract willing recruits. Their combat power isn't a one-time purchase; it's an investment.

"Wait a minute," you say, "what about the Gungans? They didn't have limitless numbers that required minimal training!" You'd be right, which leads to the second key factor: time to adapt. The Gungans didn't have time to study their enemy, figure out how to adapt, and behave accordingly. The Naboo defense forces got beaten and rounded up into camps so quickly that the Gungans couldn't get out from under their lake to see what had happened. Further, they only faced the Federation in battle once, before someone else took care of their droid problem for them.

The other wars we've looked at were slow burning in comparison. The Clone Wars lasted long enough for Anakin to grow his hair out, the Galactic Civil War began immediately afterward and carried on for about eighteen years, and the conflict between the Resistance and First Order had been going on for the seventeen years or so after the Galactic Civil War ended. We're talking about thirty-plus years of open conflict here, which is why the First Order, the Resistance, and the Rebellion have had plenty of time to analyze and adapt.

Armies are generally conservative organizations, even armies made up of CGI rabbits. They don't change unless they have to, and even then they won't turn on a dime. An army's capacity for tactical adaptation can be predicted based on its sensitivity to casualties and the time available for it to change.[8]

Notes

1. At the Battle of Thermopylae, the Greeks were heavily outnumbered by an invading Persian army. The Greeks chose to make their stand at Thermopylae, a narrow defile that offered the Persians no bypasses and forced them to reduce their frontage to fit into the defile. Instead of being confronted with a larger Persian front that would have been able to flank and ultimately envelop the Greek defenders, the constricting terrain allowed the front ranks of the Greeks to meet the front ranks of the Persians on equal terms, partially nullifying the Persian numerical superiority.

2. At the beginning of the Clone Wars, two hundred thousand were ready, with one million more nearing completion. These estimates are based on Obi-Wan's conversation with the cloners in *Episode II*, though there is some debate over whether the cloners were referring to "units" as individual soldiers or battle formations. For the purposes of this essay, the aforementioned figures work.

3. See *Star Wars: Episode II—Attack of the Clones*.

4. These events took place following the opening crawl of *Star Wars: Episode III—Revenge of the Sith*.

5. This term loosely applies to anything not resembling a human. This all took place in a galaxy far, far away; so strictly speaking, all the characters are alien.

6. Of note, none of the original trilogy films show Clone War veterans as being amputees, despite the colossal scale of those battles. This suggests that very few clone troopers survived their wounds, making the toll on life even more appalling.

7. As wars became more technical, the demands placed on soldiers and commanders by their states grew commensurately. Consider an army from 1714 or 1814; soldiers needed to know how to march in formation, load their muskets correctly, and fire three rounds a minute without breaking. The technical-training portion of marching, loading, and firing was relatively brief and compliance focused since troops could not stray from their formations. Without getting into too many details, commanders needed to know how to best position their lines of troops on terrain to gain a position of advantage and keep their troops, horses, and guns provisioned. Battlefields were relatively small and constrained. By 1914, muskets had given way to rifles with cartridge ammunition. Soldiers were expected to move with more initiative in smaller teams and groups, using the terrain for cover as they saw necessary, and dig individual fighting positions and trenches for protection from artillery. The sheer mass of troops required made it difficult for these more independently operating soldiers to be truly autonomous. Artillerists began to shift from aiming their cannons directly at troop formations to firing indirectly by adjusting azimuth and elevation given map coordinates. Battlefields grew to the point where they spanned the continent of Europe, requiring field commanders to communicate via telegraph. Coal-powered ships and trains allowed commanders to plan around more-predictable logistics. Increased complexity required more time in training. By 2014 the common infantry soldier was expected not only to control more-powerful individual weapons, advanced optics and goggles, and unmanned aerial vehicles but also to drive utility vehicles; call for strikes, not just from artillery but from helicopters and aircraft; be able to hand out textbooks to schoolchildren; and communicate with foreign people, using pocket reference guides. Commanders were expected to maintain fleets of vehicles, move supplies

across oceans and continents, and translate vague government policy into military action. As the scope of global engagement and individual lethality grew, formations and overall troop levels decreased. Training demanded not just compliance but understanding and internalization, so that soldiers were intrinsically motivated to stand and fight as opposed to extrinsically motivated as in previous generations. As war "progressed," so did the expectations of performance placed on the soldiers who fought in them, creating a necessary increase in the time required to train and prepare soldiers for battle.

8. For more reading on adaptation and change in military formations, three books must be recommended. First is a historiographical collection of readings edited by Clifford J. Rogers on whether or not so-called military revolutions actually exist given the context of military change in early modern Europe, titled *The Military Revolution Debate: Readings on the Military Transformation of Early Modern Europe* (Boulder CO: Westview Press, 1995). The next book, MacGregor Knox and Williamson Murray's *The Dynamics of Military Revolution, 1300–2050* (Cambridge: Cambridge University Press, 2001), concedes that military revolution took place and expands the aperture to the twentieth century. Finally, for a discussion of the expansion of battlefield sizes and the burdens placed on soldiers and commanders over time, see John Keegan's *The Face of Battle: A Study of Agincourt, Waterloo, and the Somme* (New York: Viking Press, 1976).

21

Dispatch from Hoth

When the Blood Runs Cold

AUGUST COLE

The following dispatch is from C3U2, an Industrial Automaton anthrocomm droid, writing as Wilt Nassaug, who regularly chronicled exploits for readers and holoviewers on Alliance-affiliated worlds. This column was received via latent burst transmission from the sixth planet of the Hoth system to the final Alliance transport ship to flee the Imperial forces following the surprise takeover of that frozen body. A veteran correspondent of armed engagements over nearly two centuries, C3U2 possessed a unique understanding of the nature of warfare and the importance of narrative in the contest between the Alliance and Imperial powers. Because of that, it was unsparing in its vivid and often-grim accounting of war, knowing that to offer anything less than the uncomfortable truth would ultimately harm the Alliance's bid to thwart tyranny. After the retreat, C3U2 remained behind on the planet surface in anticipation of the return of Rebel scouts; however, the droid has yet to be recovered.

SIXTH PLANET, HOTH SYSTEM—The tauntaun ran screaming across the crevasses and zigzag trenches dug into the Nev Ice Flow, its fur singed black and gold and slathered in crimson. A tauntaun doesn't bleed red though. Rebel infantry does.

Unlike the rest of the 61st Mobile Infantry, the crazed, riderless creature charged brazenly toward the approaching Imperial armor and occasionally tripped on its entrails before a direct shot from a chin gun finally killed the beast. Was that mercy? Or luck?

On this day, the last that the Alliance forces would ever spend on the sixth planet of the Hoth system, the Rebels lacked both.

It's funny how fast we can get into a fight. Lightspeed drops, right under the enemy's nose, can put the galaxy's deadliest fighters almost within a blade's reach of their targets. Retreating, though, is another matter. An attack is plans and vigor; a retreat is chaos and smoke and desperation.

At Echo Base there was plenty of all that to go around.

I watched the final Alliance vessel lift off from the planet's unforgiving surface in a halo of vaporized snow and ice. It was just one of the many troop ships jammed into precious gaps in the Rebel shield defenses, holding out for the chance that nothing more than a pair of fighter escorts and some danger-close ion cannon fire might be enough to cheat the odds for an escape. How many of them ultimately made it free I could not tell from my perch planet-side.

Going back to the beginning of the rout, there was a moment when it was clear what needed to be done. Two years of work to construct Echo Base, the heart of the Rebellion hidden inside a forgotten frozen body. Another year of construction could have given the base the defenses it—and the Alliance—deserved, but when has time favored a just cause? In victory and loss we see our true nature, and this time was no different in revealing the pulse of the Rebellion. Once again the movement owes its survival to the galaxy's mystics and outlaws. It is ironic that the cover for Echo Base and its outsized shield generator was as a smuggler's redoubt and fitting that it was the legendary Han Solo who first confirmed the presence of Imperial probe droids on the planet surface. The black-painted forms of the Vipers stood out against the snow, better for the entire galaxy to see the Empire's unrelenting hunt for the Rebel leadership.

The retreat began in an orderly manner. I saw the order given in the low-ceilinged operations center by a gloved commander whose urgent breath gathered in clouds with each directive he gave to the evacuating units. There was an accommodation for stay-behind forces who would sneak off the planet at the last moment. But it was all too orderly, building only in urgency and intensity when the Rebel corpses began to stack up on the fighting trench floors.

The Imperial forces emerged from hyperspace with little care for stealth or concealment. The unimaginable darkness masquerading as order again marshaled its forces in full view to brazenly attempt to snuff out the light of the rebellion. Would it succeed? Yes, of course. The Imperial officer cadre knew it. Even I knew it. But I had to see for myself, not to wonder from the comfort of a transport's hold, safe in the beautiful fold of lightspeed, whether the ember of the Rebellion would burn on. That would be revealed not in the earnest faces of those leaders who fled but by standing alongside those soldiers who stayed to die.

Beneath a sky of that special blue an ice planet often sees before battle, steady hands gripped cold metal carbines. Stocks tucked tightly into padded shoulders as the 61st Mobile Infantry held their weapons close to keep them warm and better conserve their power charges. Against Imperial armor, what defenses could Echo Base's northern approach offer? Its best hope against a ground assault was that the treacherous crevasses and ice caves would take a toll on an approaching adversary until they got into range of the dug-in fighting positions. Yet a defensive trench network dug only weeks before, just after the completion of Echo Base, would be shown to be little more than theater. The heaviest weapons were tower laser cannons jutted at regular intervals, manned by the bravest Rebel gunners of all. These weapons—which the Alliance knew to be ineffective against AT-AT armor—would be the first targeted.

"We will hold our fire, until the last minute, to ensure maximum effect for the tower cannon," said Gigg Rathkins, a sergeant in the 61st and a veteran of the Yavin campaign. Rathkins led a weapons squad, Tango. Tango Squad was made up of a good-humored, two-person tower cannon crew who seemed to cherish the thermal benefit of manning the imposing weapons system; three surly heavy-weapons gunners; and four carbine-armed brothers from Tatooine whose teeth chattered so fiercely it was impossible to understand their names.

When the first AT-AT crested the switchbacks from the Kerane Valley, it was Rathkins who spotted it. We counted down the moments until it was in range, studying crystals in the frozen snow, using the frozen trench as a latrine one last time before the onslaught. Some soldiers pestered comrades to see if anybody had any extra water to cope with the profound thirst caused by the dry air and the coming combat.

There was silence; then, in an instant, death. The battle's first blast killed Rathkins, a direct hit on Tango's tower cannon. I had watched Rathkins take his men sledding three days earlier. They used man-sized pieces of spare orbital thermal shielding, with the underside coated with X-wing actuator lubricant stolen from the mech bay. They spent over an hour racing up and down the valley's steep walls like children. It was on one of those improvised sleds that the brothers from Tatooine lay Rathkins's unconscious and battered body when two of them sprinted off, dragging him into the north entrance's still-open shield doors. That was the kind of combat leader he was, teaching them how to improvise under fire without them even realizing it.

The fusillade of returning fire lacked power but made up for it in ferocity. The Rebels, cornered, fought with no expectation of survival. They were to buy time for a retreat. If they were lucky, it would succeed, and the Alliance would know of their sacrifice. One by one the approaching AT-ATs shot their way closer and closer to and then through the Rebel lines, with AT-STs skittering alongside to mop up survivors and the wounded.

Still, the snowspeeder pilots flew as if they expected to survive, at least at first. In my experience, that is often the conceit of those in the cockpit.

But once these brave pilots realized how ineffective their weapons were against the AT-ATs, apparently a new up-armored variant, they boldly changed tactics after one pilot used his craft's tow hook to trip up one of the four-legged monsters the way you lasso a shaak on Naboo. This put the snowspeeders perilously close to the AT-ATs close-range weapons, which chewed through the Rebels' two-seaters—but not all of them. Two of the AT-ATs fell heavily, leading to a hoarse cheer from the bloodied defenders. Nobody talked of the cold once the fighting began, warmed by steaming barrels and pounding pulses.

For all the rush of this small success, few of the infantry charged directly at that moment. To do so was to invite a quicker death. But the changing snowspeeder tactics emboldened a half-dozen Rebels riding tauntauns. Their heaviest weapons? Bandoliers of grappling hooks and breaching charges. They tried a flanking maneuver, following a shallow depression, but were cut down by an AT-ST hidden by a small ridge. The fusillade thrashed rider and beast, leaving only one tauntaun, which dragged its headless rider toward the Imperial armor.

Moments later the blast wave from Echo Base's blown generator rocked the valley, shaking loose seracs and sending the remaining infantry in full flight toward the north entrance. No retreat order was needed. The concussion of orbital covering fire from the base's ion cannon on the other side of the ridge could be heard in the distance, a drumlike sound that resonated in the heaving lungs of the retreating Rebels.

Inside Echo Base, in the icy tunnels that once echoed with jocular laughter, floors were slick with blood, and the air thick with vaporized water from blaster fire. The dreaded Imperial 501st Legion advanced on foot from the Rebel trenches to the tunnel entrance far faster than seemed possible. They deployed from the remaining AT-ATs to the battle fresh, and it showed. One moment they were clambering up the icy slope to the base's hangar doors, and the next they were clearing the living quarters as though they had done it a hundred times before. Or maybe it was the presence of the Sith lord Darth Vader.

My own path took me to the lower levels, to avoid a detachment of four legionnaires sweeping toward me. They caught up with me as I entered the medical bay. The med droids were gone; valuable as they were, I was sure they would already be aboard a transport. Unarmed, as is my code, I accepted that I could stand and die at the hands of the Imperial forces or lie down amid the bloody bandages and amputated limbs now frozen to the ice floor. Mercifully, the lights failed at the very moment the Imperial troops ran by without a word, clearly unconcerned by yet another motionless form on the ground. I know precisely how long I waited before moving, but the amount of time does not matter, because I marked it in blasts, not minutes. It was an eternity, for me and for the Alliance, which had spirited its high command to safety by the time the last Rebel was executed.

When I got to my feet, the base was dark; the room was mostly quiet, except for the burbling of a bacta tank. I activated my light to scan my surroundings, unsure if I would be able to find a clear route back to the surface. I turned toward the sound of the tank. There, suspended in the fluid and still attached to the tank's healing apparatus, was the lifeless body of Gigg Rathkins, the forgotten hero of the Battle of Hoth. Rathkins. The one Rebel whose blood never ran cold.

PART 4

Assessment of War

Strategic reflection. Critical analysis. Monday-morning quarterbacking.

It's all pretty much the same—a search for the broadest explanation of strategic success versus failure, a task best accomplished while gazing backward. Often painful, this process asks, Did we do the right things? Did we do these things better than the enemy? In what ways can we improve for the next conflict?

These are the lessons of "big strategy," an attempt to get beyond "specialized and self-contained" segments of analysis to grasp strategy "as a whole."[1] This matters most in multigenerational wars, because today's tactical defeat can sow the seeds of tomorrow's strategic victory.

Notes

1. See "Big History Project," a web-based effort to broaden the study of history with a more "multi-disciplinary approach" (https://www.bighistoryproject.com/home).

22

Darth Vader's Failed Counterinsurgency Strategy

LIAM COLLINS

Sitting around a conference table on board the second Death Star, orbiting the forest moon of Endor, a number of Darth Vader's senior officers are discussing the Empire's current strategy to defeat the Rebel Alliance. Admiral Piett, the commander of the Super Star Destroyer the *Executor*, is leading the discussion.

"How can our strategy possibly fail?" Piett asks. "In major engagements, like the battle on Hoth, Rebel casualties outnumber ours by more than ten to one. And each time, they lose valuable leaders and equipment that cannot be replaced. With the exception of Yavin, we have never lost a battle. While the unfortunate loss of the Death Star was significant, that was due to a deliberately designed engineering flaw by the traitor Galen Erso, combined with a lucky shot. Without that weakness, this Death Star will be unstoppable, and we can systematically hunt down and destroy the Rebel Alliance. For worlds that resist, we will use the power of this battle station to intimidate and, if necessary, eliminate."

"Sir," answers Captain Foley, an Imperial Navy strategist assigned to the Death Star, "I've been studying counterinsurgency theory, and I believe that if we continue to follow an enemy-centric strategy, we may lose this fight. We can't just focus solely on hunting down and destroying the Rebel fleet. We must address some of the underlying grievances that are driving people to join the Rebellion. We must adopt a population-centric strategy to win their 'hearts and minds.' If not, I fear no matter how many Rebels we kill, the Rebellion will reconstitute itself and only grow stronger."[1]

"Admiral," counters Commander Gherant, a bridge officer on the *Executor*, "we need to cut the head from the snake. If we can eliminate Skywalker and Leia, the Rebellion will crumble. Intelligence indicated that the Rebellion nearly disintegrated prior to the Battle of Scarif and would have, had it not be for an emotional plea by Jyn Erso. After seeing the Death Star destroy Despayre, the various Rebel factions had decided to break apart, but somehow held together when Admiral Raddus brought the Rebel fleet to Scarif to destroy the shield gate. If we eliminate its leaders, the Rebellion will surely disintegrate this time."[2]

"Commander Gherant," counters Captain Foley, "of course some rebellions are fueled by the strong cult of personality of their leaders, but that isn't the case here. We must understand the social and political drivers of the conflict to develop an appropriate strategy. Our sponsorship of unpopular economic and social programs; repression, exclusion, and a lack of an adequate voice in government following the disillusion of the Senate; and our indiscriminate use of violence against these groups—look what we did to Alderaan and Despayre—this is what drives the Rebellion. It's not some charismatic leader. If Skywalker and Leia are killed, someone else will merely take their place, because these structural conditions remain. Remember, the Rebellion started long before Skywalker and Leia took the helm."[3]

"Structural conditions didn't create the Rebellion—people and ideas did," argues Commander Gherant. "Captain Foley would have you believe that 'revolutions are not made; they come' due to our policies that establish conditions that drive people to rebel, and it's not a matter of if, but when, the rebellion will start. As usual, Captain Foley is wrong. Thus, we need to focus on—"[4]

"Wrong!" Captain Foley interrupts. "I was one of the few officers who believed the Rebels had the ability to destroy the Death Star and was smart enough to depart before it was destroyed. I was right then, and I'm right now."

"'Fleeing' would be more appropriate to describe your actions," retorts Commander Gherant. "As I was saying, revolutions do not come; they are made. It's not the structural conditions that drives the revolution—it's political entrepreneurs. Structural conditions do not dictate what people will do, they only limit options. These political entrepreneurs must organize the population and articulate a vision for them to rally around. This leadership, or agency, combined with cultures that have histories and compelling stories that drive people to act and risk certain death, is what drives the Rebellion. How else can you explain why the Rebellion takes hold in some areas but not others? Eliminate these charismatic leaders, and there is no one to organize it and keep it going."[5]

"I'm not concerned with the cause of the Rebellion," quips Admiral Piett. "I only care about how we can end it."

"But if we don't know the cause of the conflict, how do we know our strategy isn't counterproductive?" replies Captain Foley. "It would be like trying to hit a target with a blaster while wearing a helmet with the blast shield down. Basically shooting blind."

"I said, *Enough!*" barks Admiral Piett. "Let's get back to the discussion of our current strategy."

"Admiral," replies Captain Sarkli, an Imperial spy and nephew of Admiral Piett, "the strategy is simple. We need to continue with our enemy-centric strategy to hunt down the Rebel Alliance and destroy its fleet. Once we get this Death Star operational, we simply destroy any space station, moon, or planet that puts up even minimal resistance. Soon it will be clear that resistance is futile. No one will join, and there will be nothing left to join. Given our superior technological advantage, our Imperial probe droids will eventually find every vehicle in the Rebel fleet. Just as you found the Rebel base on Hoth, our technology will allow us to find their remaining bases. All we need to do is double down on our current strategy."

"Admiral," counters Commander Gherant. "Captain Sarkli is correct. We should continue our current strategy of hunting the enemy—but not the Rebel fleet. We need to focus our human and technical intelligence on finding its leaders. If we can kill them, the Rebellion will crumble. Rebels will flee, and those who remain will be in pockets that are so small, they can be easily destroyed. We need to increase the price on their heads so Dengar, Bossk, IG-88, 4-LOM, Zuckuss, and every other bounty hunter goes back to hunting them. A decapitation strategy is the only way."

"Admiral, as I've already argued, neither of these strategies gets at the root cause of the conflict. We need to develop a counterinsurgency strategy to destroy the Rebellion," argues Captain Foley.

"All right, Captain Foley," replies Admiral Piett. "Humor us and tell us what this counterinsurgency strategy would look like."

"What we must do is separate the Rebels from the population," answers Foley. "The population provides support and intelligence that is critical to the Rebellion's survival. We must break this link. If we can separate the active Rebels from the population, the Rebellion will wither."[6]

"I agree with Captain Foley," replies Colonel Dyer, an officer in the Imperial Army who is responsible for the defense of the shield generator on Endor. "But I would also add that we must create a specific force to deal with this insurgency. Our force is made to defeat Rebel fleets and more conventional militaries. It is ill suited for dealing with location populations. Our stormtroopers are effective at what they do, but their random searches and other restrictive measures only aggravate the population and make the situation worse."[7]

"Are you serious?" questions Captain Sarkli. "Do you really believe our stormtroopers can't handle a few Rebels and some poorly behaved civilians? Our troops are the most effective fighting force in the galaxy. If they're able to fight in high-intensity conflict, they can easily handle a ragtag bunch of insurgents. But if we start designing units for low-intensity conflicts, what happens when a real war comes? They'll be entirely ill equipped for the fights that pose the real threat to the Empire."

"Captain Sarkli, you are mistaken," replies Captain Foley. "Counterinsurgencies are much more complicated—not some sort of 'lesser' mission as you say. And they pose just as much of a risk—maybe more—to the Empire than any conventional force. Our stormtroopers currently lack the ability to conduct counterinsurgency operations, at least without adequate doctrine. They give the appearance of maintaining law and order, but their presence throughout the galaxy only seems to grow underground resistance that will eventually explode."

"Admiral Piett," states Colonel Dyer, "I agree with Captain Foley. Direct action against the Rebel fleet is only one part of a larger strategy, and right now that is the Empire's only strategy. In addition to targeting the Rebel Alliance, we must increase our own legitimacy and control of the local population where the Rebel Alliance resides to cut off its support, and do the same on planets and systems where the Rebels aren't present to keep them from gaining support there. There should be five parts to our strategy: increase our control, disrupt Rebel support, directly attack the Rebel fleet, disrupt external support for the Rebellion, and gain external support for the Empire."[8]

"Admiral Piett," replies Captain Sarkli, "once again Captain Foley and his lackeys would have you believe that we should divert our forces against the main threat, which is the Rebel fleet. As I have argued, me must double down and commit our forces to destroying the fleet, not waste time worrying about legitimacy. How long would they have this war continue? And they talk of control, but we control the galaxy!"

"We only have the appearance of control, Captain Sarkli," remarks Lieutenant Grond, an aide to Colonel Dyer. "Think about the Rebellion as a system. There are inputs—the fighters, food, material, information, and intelligence. And there are outputs—things like attacks by the Rebel Alliance against the Empire. And there are conversion mechanisms that turn these inputs into the outputs—like training, which turns a moisture farmer into a pilot, or Rebel bases, which turn raw materials into starships. Right now, we are solely focused on the output—the Rebel fleet itself. We need to think more broadly. We should focus more on reducing their resources and impeding their conversion mechanisms. Isn't it better to stop people from supporting and joining the Rebel Alliance than fighting them after they are trained and armed?"[9]

"Enough!" Admiral Piett interjects. "You keep telling me that we must stop the support for the Rebellion, but you don't offer any real solutions on how to do this. I still say fear of this battle station is enough to keep local systems in line. What does your counterinsurgency strategy have to say, Captain Foley?"

Before Captain Foley can answer, the door slides open, and Darth Vader enters the conference room. "The Rebellion will soon be eliminated," states Darth Vader. "We destroyed the remnants of the Rebel base on Yavin 4 and their base on the desolate planet of Hoth. Between my power with the Force and the Empire's technological dominance, there is nowhere they can hide that we cannot find them. The loss of the first Death Star was a setback. The destruction of Alderaan eliminated nearly all support for the Rebel Alliance, but support has increased following the Death Star's destruction. However, it was only a minor setback. Once this Death Star is operational, all support will cease. Without the support of the population, the Rebellion will soon fall, and we can easily root out the remnants. We must continue to hunt down and destroy the Rebel Alliance.

"My power with the Force tells me the Battle for Endor will soon be at hand," continues Darth Vader. "Skywalker is on his way here now, and I'm sure the rest of the Rebel fleet is not far behind. Admiral Piett, return to your ship. Commander Sarkli, you return to Endor to guard the shield bunker. Now, if any of you still have doubts about our current strategy, speak."

"Lord Vader," answers Captain Foley, "if we continue to execute this strategy, we are doomed to fail. Our repressive policies have created structural conditions that almost guarantee rebellion. If we destroy the current Rebel force, another will simply replace it. We need to address some of these underlying grievances and develop a counterinsurgency doctrine, or this war will never end. In addition to targeting the Rebel fleet, we must—"

Captain Foley's words are interrupted by his gasps for air. "I find your lack of faith disturbing," Vader tells him as he applies his Force choke.

"Who else thinks we need to change our strategy?" asks Vader. Only silence follows, and with the decision made, the Empire's destiny is sealed. Soon, Darth Vader will be mortally wounded by the Emperor on the second Death Star. Admiral Piett and Commander Gherant will be killed when an A-wing crashes into the *Executor*'s bridge. Commander Sarkli will meet his fate in a blaster duel with Han Solo at the shield bunker on Endor, where Colonel Dyer and Lieutenant Grond will also be killed. Their deaths will inevitably be followed by that of the Empire.

Notes

1. There has been much debate as to whether an enemy-centric or population-centric strategy is better; Jardine and Palamar make the case that a population-centric strategy was more effective for the Canadians in Afghanistan. See Eric Jardine and Simon Palamar, "From Medusa Past Kantolo: Testing the Effectiveness of Canada's Enemy-Centric and Population-Centric Counterinsurgency Operational Strategies," *Studies in Conflict and Terrorism* 36, no. 7 (2013): 588–608.
2. There is also debate as to the effectiveness of targeting enemy leaders; Johnston argues that while targeting enemy leadership is not a silver bullet, targeting insurgent leadership does increase the probability of success. See Patrick B. Johnston, "Does Decapitation Work? Assessing the Effectiveness of Leadership Targeting in Counterinsurgency Campaigns," *International Security* 36, no 4 (2012): 47–79.
3. Jeff Goodwin, *No Other Way Out: States and Revolutionary Movements, 1945–1991* (Cambridge: Cambridge University Press, 2001), 35–64.
4. Eric Selbin, "Revolution in the Real World: Bringing Agency Back In," in *Theorizing Revolutions*, ed. John Foran (New York: Routledge, 1997), 118–32.
5. Selbin, "Revolution in the Real World."
6. This was one of the many recommendations made by early counterinsurgency theorist David Galula. See David Galula, *Counterinsurgency Warfare: Theory and Practice* (Westport CT: Praeger Security International, 2006).
7. See Steven P. Basilici and Jeremy Simmons, *Transformation: A Bold Case for Unconventional Warfare* (Monterey CA: Naval Postgraduate School, 2004). They argue that the Department of Defense needs to create a new organization focused on unconventional warfare as opposed to modifying the conventional force or delegating the mission to current special operations forces.
8. For more on the "Diamond Insurgent / COIN model," see Eric P. Wendt, "Strategic Counterinsurgency Modeling," *Special Warfare* 18, no. 2 (2005): 2–13.
9. To better understand an insurgency as a system, see Nathan Constantin Leites and Charles Wolf, *Rebellion and Authority: An Analytic Essay on Insurgent Conflicts* (Santa Monica CA: RAND, 1970).

23

Why the Jedi Won Fights, Not Wars

JOHN SPENCER

The term "Jedi" is loaded with connotations of reverence and respect. Seen as the greatest warriors in the galaxy, even the mention of a Jedi knight put fear in the hearts of the rank and file of the Empire's forces. The Jedi Knights of a galaxy far, far away sit in a timeless, intergalactic pantheon of esteemed warriors, alongside the medieval knights, samurais, and Spartans of our own planet's history. But while the Jedi are worthy of such praise—for their superiority in individual combat and their clandestine capabilities, for example—they arguably fall short in key areas that define true martial prowess. In fact, they lacked the training, skills, and critical abilities necessary to represent mastery of the military profession.

At the height of their power, the Jedi Knights served as the guardians of peace and justice in the galaxy. One of the earliest missions viewers see the Jedi execute is during *Episode I—The Phantom Menace*. Jedi Master Qui-Gon Jinn and his padawan, Obi-Wan Kenobi, are sent as ambassadors of the Galactic Senate to mediate a dispute arising from Trade Federation ships' practice of stopping all shipments to the planet Naboo in an outlying sector of the Galactic Republic. This diplomatic mission—on a different scale than, but remarkably similar to, tasks undertaken by even junior officers on real-world battlefields—is of critical importance. But the two Jedi fail and are forced to flee after facing two destroyer droids.

Later in the same film, the Jedi turn from diplomacy to a range of other operations. First, they conduct a clandestine mission similar to those conducted by U.S. Army Special Forces today, linking up with a local guerrilla force on Naboo, the Gungans, in an attempt to gain the Gungans' support in resisting the Trade Federation's invasion of the planet. Next, they mount a successful search-and-rescue mission to free Queen Amidala from her captors. Finally, the Jedi are assigned by the Jedi Council to serve as a Personal Security Detachment, tasked with escorting Queen Amidala back to Naboo, where they subsequently find themselves engaged in hand-to-hand combat against the Sith lord Darth Maul.

Each of these missions showed off the individual skills emphasized by the Jedi Knights. Jedi are trained in the ability to move silently, employ visual and mental deception, and eventually become masters of individual combat using their primary weapon—the lightsaber. These missions are what they prepared for and why they were successful after failing at the initial diplomatic tasks for which they were unprepared. But whether for Jedi or for soldiers on the contemporary battlefield, it is a fatal mistake to assume that the skills of an individual warrior are transferable to the wider range of capabilities intrinsic to warfighting and military leadership.

In *Episode II—Attack of the Clones* we see the errors inherent in seeking to utilize Jedi—unmatched in individual combat—as leaders of a military campaign. Ten years after the Battle of Naboo, what started as a Trade Federation disagreement had evolved into a full-scale rebellion that brought the galaxy to the brink of civil war, as thousands of systems sought to break away from the Republic. The separatist movement, with a droid army as its warfighting organization, was led by Jedi Master Count Dooku. After seizing power through political means—disguising his machinations as an attempt to save the Republic—Sheev Palpatine, as the newly elected supreme chancellor, ordered the Grand Army of the Republic, made up of clones, to deploy into combat to destroy the separatists' droid army. He commissioned the Jedi as generals in command of the Clone Army units.

Put as simply as possible, the Jedi Knights lacked the skills necessary to be effective commanders in an army at war. Today, the U.S. Army requires military officers to develop expert knowledge in four fields: military-technical, moral-ethical, political-cultural, and leader–human development.[1] Assessing the newly minted Jedi generals against these fields of expertise reveals their shortcomings as leaders of warfighters.

The military-technical field represented their largest deficiency. This category includes the knowledge and application of military formations, force generation, and the effective use of ground forces. It also includes the integration of technology and weapons in the conduct of military operations.

The Jedi Knights, however, did not receive the military education or training necessary to develop this knowledge, much less to serve as leaders of combat formations in battle. They were not educated in either the theory or practice of military science. Jedi students were schooled in individual combat skills during their training at the Jedi academy. When they were later paired with Jedi masters, becoming padawans, they learned the ways of the Force and the Jedi Code. Throughout their training, they focused on mastering the Force, honing precision skills with their lightsabers, and readying themselves for solo or two-man missions that often culminated in intense, one-on-one close combat. And the result was impressive—but wholly insufficient to prepare them to lead others in battle.

Jedi lacked knowledge of even the simplest warfighting tactics. This failing was made manifest during the Battle of Geonosis, when the Jedi Knights led the Clone Army in frontal assaults. These attacks are historically among the worst tactics to employ, unless the force conducting them enjoys overwhelming numerical superiority (which the Clone Army did not), because they typically result in massive casualties. The more preferred attack tactic would have included one formation establishing a base of fire while another maneuvered to the enemy's flank. The heavy fire from the frontal unit allows the maneuvering unit to move with less danger of receiving effective incoming fire from the defender and creates a vulnerable flank for the enemy forces, who must return fire to their front. This is one of the most basic but fundamental tactics of warfare.

One of the greatest military theorists of all time, Carl von Clausewitz, wrote, "Tactics teaches the use of armed forces in the engagement; strategy, the use of engagements for the object of the war."[2] Clausewitz believed military officers needed extensive firsthand experience to truly gain an understanding of the tactical waging of war. In the training of Jedi padawans, Clausewitz would have told the Jedi High Council to include years of critical analysis of historical battles and campaigns through which he believed a synthetic experience could be achieved. These experiences arm warfighters with a deep appreciation of the patterns, principles, and fundamentals of warfare, which can then be applied to future wars, in which the weapons and environments may change but the enduring character of war—along with many of the most successful tactics—remains the same. This critical analysis also provides professional military leaders with the mental flexibility to adapt to the specifics of the war they encounter. This has been the proven path of successful military commanders, from Sun Tzu and Caesar through Napoleon and Eisenhower.

The integration of technology is also included in the military-technical field of expertise, because the science of warfighting relies heavily on incorporating the most advanced weaponry and equipment. The pursuit of the next game-changing weapon, revolutionary armor, or innovative vehicle has historically been as important to the evolution of warfighting as tactics. The development of new weapons and equipment—black powder, machine guns, tanks, and airplanes, among other innovations—has provided armies with marked advantage over enemies that persisted in clinging to older tools of warfare.

Jedi, however, resist technology. They stubbornly adhere to their ascetic lifestyle and a single, simple weapon, while the weapons of the galaxy evolve around them. They are easily neutralized with the very technologies they reject. They run from destroyer droids and get captured by force field traps. Armed with advanced technologies and not powers of the Force, the bounty hunter Jango Fett nearly defeats Jedi Master Obi-Wan Kenobi. A formation of droids comes within minutes of eliminating a large group of Jedi who are only saved by reinforcements at the Battle of Geonosis.

The moral-ethical field of military expertise frames the application of lethal power within the expectations and values of the society the military professionals represent. It reflects a set of shared beliefs, rules, and standards that guide soldiers in the conduct of military operations and their performance of duty and are passed along from generation to generation as the accepted norms of the professional warfighter.[3]

The Jedi Knights, though, lacked a strong moral or ethical system, and to the extent they did have such a system, it was not one shared by the society they served. Their behavior was guided by the Jedi Code, but there is little evidence that adherence to the code actually fostered an internalized value system, shared by all Jedi, to govern moral and ethical considerations in the execution of lethal force. This was evident in the repeated deaths of unarmed people at the hands of Anakin Skywalker, along with several other Jedi who turned to the dark side. He beheaded Count Dooku after first cutting off his hands and massacred an entire group of Tusken Raiders—men, women, and children—on the planet of Tatooine after learning that his mother had been tortured. The emotionally traumatized Anakin eventually turned to the dark side. Count Dooku leaves the Jedi Order himself, actively plotting against the Republic. In neither case did the code enable them to overcome emotion and resist the dark side, nor did it equip them with an ethical guidance system that ensured their actions in combat matched the values of the society they, as Jedi, ostensibly represented.

In military formations, commanders serve as the moral compass for those they lead. They provide the backbone ensuring that the implementation of force is in accordance with a recognized code and that the rules of engagement align with that code, despite the fog, friction, emotions, and ethical dilemmas that always arise in battle. The ability to serve as this moral compass in combat is not an inborn gift. It takes learning and the internalization of a taught value system. The Jedi's individually focused training produced superior combatants, but not ones equipped to be moral leaders of other men and women warriors.

Expertise in the political-cultural field requires an understanding of how military professionals and their organizations interact with external actors— partner government organizations and civilian populations, both foreign and domestic.[4] It also includes practical knowledge about the military's role within the civil-military relationship; in the United States this means subordination of the military to civilian leadership and the military's execution of missions given to it by these civilian leaders in order to support and defend national interests. In the first of these two components, the Jedi Knights measured up well. They demonstrated an adeptness in interacting with external organizations—fighting alongside Wookiee, Ewok, and Gungan tribes, for instance. But they struggled to act appropriately within the bounds of effective civil-military relationships.

Officers in the U.S. Army today receive a professional military education that emphasizes the concept of civilian oversight and the civilian authority's ultimate responsibility for national strategy and policy.[5] They learn the unique and limited role of general officers: to provide expert military advice to civilian decision makers without attempting to influence, shape, or make national policy. Without a similar education, Jedi struggled to maintain an apolitical identity as military commanders. In *Episode III—Revenge of the Sith* Jedi Master Obi-Wan told Jedi-in-training Anakin Skywalker that the Jedi Council wanted him to report on the actions of Chancellor Palpatine after he was given special emergency powers by the Senate. The Jedi Council may have had altruistic reasons for their concerns about the Senate, but spying on a senior civilian authority represented an incredible breach of norms within an appropriate civil-military balance of powers.

Finally, leader–human development expertise informs a range of interactions between a military force and others, including both the citizenry it serves (e.g., how the military profession inspires citizens to accept a calling to honorable service) and adversarial forces (e.g., how military professionals understand the enemy).[6] In this regard, the power of the Force gave the Jedi Knights a distinct advantage—namely, the ability to essentially search the thoughts of others. A military commander's requirement to assess subordinate troops' morale and foster maximum unit cohesion would naturally be greatly enhanced by the Force.

Similarly, applying the Force in order to understand the enemy also lent Jedi a considerable advantage in the leader–human development field. Clausewitz famously wrote that "war is an act of force to compel our enemy to do our will."[7] By understanding the thoughts, feelings, and vulnerabilities of their adversaries, Jedi were in an immensely advantageous position to do just this.

Taken as a whole, though, the Jedi's expertise in the field of leader–human development was not nearly enough to surmount their shortcomings in the previous three fields or to equip these supremely skilled combatants to lead others with nearly the same degree of effectiveness.

At the end of *Episode II*, Chancellor Palpatine issued the infamous Order 66, directing the Clone Army soldiers to assassinate their Jedi commanders. The loyal clones implemented Order 66 without hesitation. The Jedi were eliminated by the very soldiers they had commanded. It may have always been Chancellor Palpatine's master plan to put the Jedi in charge of the Clone Army solely for this reason, so that he could eliminate the only threat to his growing power. But the Senate's agreement to the proposal that the Jedi should command the army that would protect the Republic was also a mistake. It reflected an erroneous impression that the unique skills of the Jedi would translate naturally to military leadership. This mistake would prove to have disastrous consequences.

The Jedi were in fact the greatest warriors the galaxy had ever seen. But they were ill equipped to succeed as combat leaders.

Notes

1. See Center for the Army Profession and Ethic, *Army Doctrinal Reference Publication (ADRP) 1—The Army Profession* (Washington DC: Department of the Army, 2015), p. 5-1.
2. Carl von Clausewitz, *On War*, indexed edition, ed. and trans. Michael Howard and Peter Paret, with Bernard Brodie (Princeton NJ: Princeton University Press, 1984), 128.
3. See Center for the Army Profession and Ethic, *Army Doctrinal Reference Publication (ADRP) 1—The Army Profession*, p. 5-1.
4. See Center for the Army Profession and Ethic, *Army Doctrinal Reference Publication (ADRP) 1—The Army Profession*, p. 5-1.
5. See Center for the Army Profession and Ethic, *Army Doctrinal Reference Publication (ADRP) 1—The Army Profession*, p. 6-3.
6. See Center for the Army Profession and Ethic, *Army Doctrinal Reference Publication (ADRP) 1—The Army Profession*, p. 5-1.
7. Clausewitz, *On War*, 75.

24

Why the Galactic Republic Fell

An Imperial-Network Perspective

VAN JACKSON

The emergence of the Galactic Empire from the rubble of the millennia-old Republic represents the most dramatic political transition in the *Star Wars* universe and perhaps in all of science fiction. But how did it happen? The obvious answer—the plotting and opportunism of Darth Sidious—is also the least insightful. Pointing to the misdeeds of a conspirator and his minions tells us little about how the collapse of the Galactic Republic might have been prevented; nor does it help us identify what aspects of the Republic-to-Empire transition process might be generalized across space and time. Can a deeper examination yield lessons for our real world? Could a fate comparable to that of the Republic await today's liberal democracies?

The Galactic Republic's inadvertent facilitation of the rise of the dark side can largely be attributed to the structure of relationships within the Republic. Three particular features of Republic political relations converged to create a window for dark-side opportunism: deep antagonism between a "Galactic Core" and a "Galactic Periphery"; highly differentiated rights and obligations for different political actors throughout the Republic; and a sparse, forward-stationed military presence in the Periphery.[1]

The Republic, in other words, consisted of contradictory characteristics and impulses. On the one hand, it was made up of colonies, patterns of deep inequality, and an inconsistency in the application of the rule of law across polities that is typical of empires; on the other hand, the Republic had a military and rule-enforcement system wholly inadequate to the problems of empire. The tension between these practices made it vulnerable to well-positioned demagogues like Darth Sidious. The irony is that the Republic might have been more resilient had it recognized its own imperial tendencies and either curbed them or taken the military requirements of political stability within an empire more seriously.

THE PUZZLE

The popular narrative of how the Galactic Empire arose focuses on the actions of several well-known bad actors. Count Dooku lent charismatic voice to the grievances of the Periphery and helped broker the political connections across planetary systems that would become the galactic separatist movement. The Trade Federation invaded Naboo, precipitating the Galactic Senate's political crisis that led to the ouster of Supreme Chancellor Finis Valorum and to his replacement by Senator Palpatine.[2] The Separatist Council, which included the Trade Federation, provided the financial backing necessary to convert the loose separatist movement into the formal Confederacy of Independent Systems, which would wage war against the Republic. Anakin Skywalker prevented Jedi Master Mace Windu from arresting Palpatine when it was discovered Palpatine was secretly a Sith lord. And the Sith secretly programmed the Grand Army of the Republic with Order 66, which, when activated, would nearly exterminate the Jedi. All these actions were orchestrated by Darth Sidious and were crucial steps for him to take power and establish the Galactic Empire.

This may be an accurate description of events, but politics is always full of schemers and demagogues. So why was Darth Sidious so successful? What factors were most decisive in bringing about the Galactic Republic's death? And what might *Star Wars* historiography tell us about the ability for a real-world Darth Sidious to pull off a similar feat of regime change? For those answers, we must transcend situation-specific accounts.

International-relations scholars have written extensively on the unique "network structure" of empires—that is, the durable patterns of political interaction that make up empires.[3] In contrast with other types of political arrangements, empires usually consist of relationships between a privileged core and an only weakly connected periphery.[4] In such an arrangement, peripheral actors have much stronger, closer ties to the core than they do to others in the periphery. This relative isolation makes the periphery vulnerable to dependency on the core and leads to distinct patterns of interaction that advantage the core and disadvantage the periphery.[5]

Viewing the Galactic Republic through this lens of an imperial network—relating different parts of the Republic to one another—helps explain how it was more than possible for the dark side to bring an end to democracy in the *Star Wars* galaxy. The Republic was not an empire, but greater self-awareness about the markers of empire within the Republic might have made it either more sensitive to systemic injustices or more willing to embrace the general best practices of political stability within empires. In either case, the Republic would have been less vulnerable to overthrow.

GALACTIC CORE VERSUS GALACTIC PERIPHERY

The most significant background condition contributing to the Republic's vulnerability was the de facto system of differences perpetuated between "Core Worlds" and "Peripheral Worlds."[6] At the time of the Republic's founding, more than a thousand years prior to the Clone Wars, the natural astrography of the galaxy favored a spatial division between Core and Periphery planetary systems, but the distinctions compounded over time to produce a social rift and antagonistic identities between them.

Some of the advantages of Core over Periphery were formal determinations, like the center of the Core becoming the capital of the Galactic Republic—based on the planet Coruscant—as well as home to the Senate, the Supreme Court, and the Jedi Council. On galaxy maps, the coordinates for Coruscant were 0-0-0, symbolically reinforcing that the Core was really the uncontested center of the universe.[7] In general the Periphery also suffered from a "resource curse," allowing the exports of natural resources to Core Worlds to become the basis of political dependencies on the Core.[8]

Still other distinctions were informal but undeniable. Because the Republic's governmental functions were densely collocated within the Core, and largely on Coruscant, proximity and access translated into unique opportunities for political influence that continued to favor Core prerogatives. Proximity as political advantage would probably be true of any social or political system, but it was especially so in the Galactic Republic, because most political issues were discussed and settled outside the Senate Chamber.[9] Following the Trade Federation's invasion of Naboo, for instance, Palpatine, who was then a senator, was able to persuade other senators to elect him supreme chancellor behind closed doors prior to meeting in the Senate Chamber, and he did the same in convincing Queen Amidala to ultimately cast the vote of no confidence against Supreme Chancellor Valorum that allowed Palpatine to be voted in as replacement.

Differences like these reflect the widespread perception that the Periphery was deprived of advantages and opportunities offered in the Core and that while the Core viewed the Periphery as fundamentally inferior, the Periphery viewed the Core as fundamentally elitist. In short, the social, political, and economic practices that distinguished the Core from the Periphery were perceived as rampantly unjust and the cause of growing political grievances—the very grievances that Count Dooku exploited to foment collective resistance against the Republic by bridging together Peripheral Worlds previously only weakly connected to one another. Thus, the only common denominator across the separatist movement was shared identification as a Periphery receiving unfair treatment from the Republic; without that binding sentiment, there would have been no unified basis for the Clone Wars.

POLITICAL UNREPRESENTATION

The hostility between Core and Periphery could have been ameliorated through political processes that preserved the Republic's legitimacy outside the Core. Preventing the creation of the Confederacy of Independent Systems required that aggrieved planets and social groups in the Periphery believed their stake in the Republic gave them the means to actually redress their grievances, not just express them.[10] A properly representative Galactic Senate and judiciary could have served as a kind of social pressure valve that made voice in existing institutions more appealing to the aggrieved than the option of exit from the Republic altogether.[11] In practice, by contrast, rights and obligations across the Republic—especially in the Senate—were inegalitarian and highly unrepresentative in numerous ways.

First, the Republic routinely granted Core "pioneers" rights to "procure and settle new territories, either by cutting deals with indigenous populations or simply by overrunning them, and finally to establish trading colonies capable of furnishing the Core with much needed resources."[12] The Galactic Senate repeatedly made decisions to not simply tolerate the widespread practice of colonization but to endorse and enable it. Second, membership in the Senate was essential to having a planet's interests represented in Republic decision making, but Core World senators deliberately stalled, and often rejected, entry from applicants located outside the Core World. This despite the claim that the scope of the Republic's laws spanned the galaxy, which meant a planet could be subject to Republic rules even if it had no say in establishing them.

Third, while being a planetary system was no guarantee of representation in the Senate, neither was it necessary. Over time, corporations, guilds, and various moneyed interests—including the Trade Federation—had direct, formal representation in the Senate, while many planets and territories still did not. Finally, judicials—the Republic's law enforcement officers—"were often withheld from intervening in [Periphery] disputes . . . as punishment for refusing to provide the Core Worlds with profitable deals."[13] In practice, this meant that territories subject to Republic taxation could not even depend on the Republic for their security. As an alternative, many planetary systems formed local security forces that sometimes grew into largely autonomous military powers, like the Outland Regions Security Force created to counter the organized piracy that was rampant in the Outer Rim.[14]

Political rights and obligations were highly unrepresentative in the various ways specified above. Consequently, the Republic was unable to adequately address the problems that arose from the Core-Periphery divide; the Republic's institutions and rule-making and rule-enforcement mechanisms not only deprived the Periphery of adequate voice in the existing system but also inflamed rather than dampened long-standing feelings of injustice. Although the Republic did not seem to acknowledge it, these practices—of leveraging superior position with individual Peripheral actors to strike lopsided bargains favoring the Core (even to the point of outright exploitation)—are common in empires generally.[15] Keeping such an uneven system running without challenge depended on keeping the Periphery fractured, which in turn required political and bureaucratic institutions that the Periphery viewed as legitimate.

SPARSE, FORWARD MILITARY PRESENCE

To safeguard political stability from challengers like Darth Sidious and Count Dooku, the Republic would have ideally sought to shrink the Core-Periphery divide by constructing inclusive political processes representative of constituent interests. Absent that, the Republic needed the ability to detect mounting political opposition in the Periphery, put down localized rebellions before they grew, and respond quickly and decisively when major challenges to the political order did emerge.

A sustained, forward military presence in the Periphery could have accomplished each of these essential tasks for preserving the Republic. But because the Republic lacked a forward-deployed military (or a military at all), it lacked the means to cope with a classical threat to empires throughout history: *collective* resistance of the Periphery against the Core.[16]

The Republic had little capacity to enforce order across the galaxy. The Jedi numbered only around ten thousand at the start of the Clone Wars, which is a pittance for a galaxy that included thousands of solar systems.[17] And even though the Jedi were highly skilled warriors, neither they nor the judicials had training or experience in military campaigns. A Republic military presence in the Periphery would have helped rectify the warfighting imbalance between the Republic and the Confederacy; it also would have afforded the Republic other advantages in service of political stability.

The Sith, for example, were only able to implant Order 66 in the clone troopers being clandestinely built on Kamino *because* they were being clandestinely built, in a hidden location far away from the prying eyes of government accountability. If transparent budgeting and authorization processes were used to build the Grand Army of the Republic, the Sith would have struggled to infiltrate and turn the clones against the Jedi. The absence of a military, and the seeming taboo against fielding one prior to the Clone Wars, indirectly facilitated the Jedi-extermination part of Darth Sidious's plan.

Maintaining a local military presence in the Periphery would have also helped bolster friendly Periphery governments and proactively counter misinformation campaigns. Count Dooku successfully rallied the Periphery to a common cause by more than charismatic speeches alone. He also conspired with local groups to overthrow status quo governments outside the Core, "backing coups on Ryloth, meddling in the affairs of Kashyyyk, Sullust, Onderon, and many other worlds," all for the purpose of installing Periphery governments more likely to secede from the Republic.[18] Peripheral governments could have been girded against Dooku's attempts at destabilization if they had support from Republic forces to maintain order, especially because one of the chief complaints from secessionists was the failure of Republic-aligned governments to provide security against marauding space pirates and criminal gangs.[19]

Finally, the lack of a forward military meant the Republic was unable to respond to military challenges quickly enough to prevent small threats from becoming major ones. In essence, the Republic maintained its Jedi and judicials in an "offshore-balancing" posture, keeping its limited capacity in reserve, in the Core, deploying it to the Periphery only as the pressing need arose.[20] But as scholars of grand strategy have often identified, offshore-balancing postures are based on a dangerous assumption—namely, that time and distance will not undermine the relevance of your power.[21] The Republic's implicit offshore-balancing posture meant it could not build and deploy forces quickly enough to contain threats from the Periphery.

The Separatist Crisis snowballed into attacks against Core Worlds and eventually the Clone Wars, precisely because the Republic was ill prepared to defend forward positions and strategic locations.[22] The best of many examples of this is the Republic's inability to defend the Nexus Route that provided the most direct transport link from Core to Periphery, which the latter used to repeatedly assault Coruscant and other Core Worlds.[23] This onslaught of Confederacy attacks on the Core brought the Republic to the edge of defeat, helping justify emergency powers and the imperial ascension of Darth Sidious.

LEARNING FROM THE GALACTIC REPUBLIC'S FALL

The deeds of Darth Sidious and his various agents were central to the plot of *Star Wars*, but we should not succumb to the science fiction equivalent of historical determinism—that the rise of the Galactic Empire and the fall of the Republic was somehow inevitable. It was not. Only through a convergence of several unfavorable circumstances was it possible for Darth Sidious to pull off regime change: a long-standing rift between the Galactic Core and Galactic Periphery; recurring practices of unfair and inconsistent political representation throughout the galaxy; and an approach to Republic security that was woefully unprepared for any serious challenge to the existing political order. Remedying just one of these factors might have been sufficient to frustrate Darth Sidious's schemes.

What lessons, then, does science fiction's greatest political transition hold for the real world? First, the duration of time that a democracy has existed is not itself a reliable indicator of its durability. Democratic institutions in the *Star Wars* galaxy seemed durable—until their legitimacy was challenged. Too often Core World politicians, and even the Jedi, spoke of the thousand-year reign of democracy in the galaxy as if they had achieved the best of all possible worlds. This hubris blinded them to the extreme degree to which the Republic served elite interests and was perceived as disenfranchising the Periphery.

Second, operating a political system with imperial traits creates the need to be attentive to the vulnerabilities that empires face—especially if you claim to be something other than an empire. Different types of political arrangements have different types of strengths and weaknesses; an accurate perception of the kind of polity you are in practice is essential to managing your vulnerabilities.

Third, and related to the second lesson, idealist political rhetoric should not blind policy makers to the requirements of security, which often has a logic all its own. There is nothing wrong with lofty national security rhetoric that seeks to inspire a world built on something more enlightened than the will of the strong. But it is foolhardy to allow your aspirations to substitute for defense planning based on logic and evidence. As Niccolo Machiavelli observed in *The Prince*, "any one who would act up to a perfect standard of goodness in everything, must be ruined among so many who are not good."[24] Failure to make military preparations for plausible threats because it would be inconsistent with your ideals is a smooth path to destruction.

The Galactic Republic was founded on democratic principles, and the rhetoric of the Republic venerated high-minded democratic traditions. But Core Worlds had overwhelming control of the institutions of government, and their relations with the Peripheral Worlds were quasi-imperial in practice, meaning that it courted some of the governance and security challenges of empires. Seeing the Republic for what it was and either amending it or embracing it would have been its best protection from the dark side. Hopefully, real-world republics can learn to preserve what the *Star Wars* galaxy failed to.

Notes

1. Some have offered single-factor explanations—like the lack of a standing army or meaningful minority parties—to account for the fall of the Republic, but as Patrick Jackson and Daniel Nexon point out, these fail to explain the timing of regime change or why the Republic could exist for so long despite such problems. See Patrick Thaddeus Jackson and Daniel Nexon, "There's a Moral Order Baked into That 'Star Wars' Galaxy That's Far, Far Away," *Washington Post*, November 26, 2015, https://www.washingtonpost.com/news/monkey-cage/wp/2015/11/26/theres-a-moral-order-baked-into-that-star-wars-galaxy-thats-far-far-away/?utm_term=.4a67d94ec130.

2. It was revealed early in the *Star Wars* saga that Sheev Palpatine was actually Darth Sidious, the Sith lord who would destroy the Jedi Order and become emperor.

3. See, for example, Daniel H. Nexon and Thomas Wright, "What's at Stake in the American Empire Debate," *American Political Science Review* 101, no. 2 (2007): 253–71; Paul K. MacDonald, "Those Who Forget Historiography Are Doomed to Republish It: Empire, Imperialism and Contemporary Debates about American Power," *Review of International Studies*, 2009, 45–67; Paul K. MacDonald, *Networks of Domination: The Social Foundations of Peripheral Conquest in International Politics* (Oxford: Oxford University Press, 2014); Jason C. Sharman, "International Hierarchies and Contemporary Imperial Governance: A Tale of Three Kingdoms," *European Journal of International Relations* 19, no. 2 (2013): 189–207.

4. Nexon and Wright, "What's at Stake in the American Empire Debate?"

5. Nexon and Wright, "What's at Stake in the American Empire Debate?"

6. The Peripheral Worlds, as I refer to them here, include the Colonies, the Inner Rim, the Expansion Region, the Mid Rim, and the Outer Rim territories. All are consistently referenced as falling outside the Core throughout the *Star Wars* saga.

7. Erin Neidigh, *5,100-Question Mega-Ultimate Star Wars Quiz Book* (Pittsburgh PA: Dorrance, 2013), 458.

8. For developing economies, large endowments of natural resources can handicap political development and create structural dependencies on foreign-consumption markets. See, for example, Macartan Humphreys, Jeffrey Sachs, and Joseph E. Stiglitz, *Escaping the Resource Curse* (New York: Columbia University Press, 2007).

9. Some scholars have shown how spatial relations affect political outcomes. See, for example, Roger Gould, "Multiple Networks and Mobilization in the Paris Commune, 1871," *American Sociological Review* 56, no. 6 (1991): 716–29.

10. The Galactic Senate allowed the presence of junior representatives, who gave voice to minority populations and dissenting opinions from their appointed senators, but they were not granted any voting or agenda-setting rights.

11. Consumers or members of a system facing declining quality or benefits have three options: break from the arrangement (exit), try to remedy it (voice), or adapt to the status quo and hope things will change (loyalty). This canonical work in economics was later expanded to choices facing all manner of declining organizations and polities. See Albert O. Hirschman, *Exit, Voice, and Loyalty: Responses to Decline in Firms, Organizations, and States* (Cambridge MA: Harvard University Press, 1970).

12. James Luceno, *Star Wars: Tarkin* (New York: Del Rey, 2014), chap. 4.

13. Luceno, *Star Wars: Tarkin*, 48. There was a status and responsibility distinction between the judicials and the Jedi. The former were seen as pedestrian and the Jedi were seen as elite; formally the former were responsible for law enforcement and the latter for peacekeeping.

14. Jason Fry and Paul Urquhart, *The Essential Guide to Warfare: Star Wars* (New York: Del Rey, 2012), 54–55; Luceno, *Star Wars: Tarkin*, 48.

15. Nexon and Wright, "What's at Stake in the American Empire Debate?"; MacDonald, *Networks of Domination*.

16. Nexon and Wright, "What's at Stake in the American Empire Debate?"; Daniel H. Nexon, *The Struggle for Power in Early Modern Europe: Religious Conflict, Dynastic Empires, and International Change* (Princeton NJ: Princeton University Press, 2009).

17. Luceno, *Star Wars: Tarkin*, 99.

18. Luceno, *Star Wars: Tarkin*, 97.

19. Luceno, *Star Wars: Tarkin*, 48, 59–60. As Senator Palpatine rhetorically asked Wilhuff Tarkin long before the Clone Wars began, "The Jedi haven't provided any support in dealing with the pirates that continue to plague the Seswanna?" Tarkin replied, "They've ignored our requests for intervention. Apparently the Seswanna doesn't rate highly enough on their list of priorities."

20. Offshore balancing is an ideal-type grand strategy premised on defensive realist assumptions. It seeks to preserve military power by restraining its use and only generating and deploying forces when existential threats emerge. For a full description of offshore balancing and competing grand strategies, see Barry R. Posen and Andrew L. Ross, "Competing Visions for U.S. Grand Strategy," *International Security* 21, no. 3 (1996–97): 5–53.

21. More specifically, the assumption offshore balancers make is that the time it takes to generate adequate forces and the distance they have to travel in order to be useful will not prevent them from serving their purpose. For an argument in favor of this position, see John J. Mearsheimer and Stephen M. Walt, "The Case for Offshore Balancing," *Foreign Affairs*, July/August 2016, https://www.foreignaffairs.com/articles/united-states/2016-06-13/case-offshore-balancing. For an argument claiming it as utterly unrealistic, see Hal Brands, "Fools Rush Out? The Flawed Logic of Offshore Balancing," *Washington Quarterly* 38, no. 2 (2015): 7–28.

22. In *Episode II*, for example, Chancellor Palpatine told Jedi Master Mace Windu, "More and more star systems are joining the separatists. . . . I will not let that happen!" To which Windu replied, "But if they do, you must realize there aren't enough Jedi to protect the Republic."

23. Matt Michnovetz, "The Citadel," *Star Wars: The Clone Wars*, season 3, episode 18, directed by Kyle Dunlevy, aired February 18, 2011 (Atlanta GA: Cartoon Network).

24. Niccolo Machiavelli, "Of the Qualities in Respect of Which Men, and Most of All Princes, Are Praised or Blamed," chap. 15 in *The Prince*, trans. N. H. Thompson (New York: Dover, 1992), 40.

25

Why the Empire Failed

THERESA HITCHENS

The central theme of the *Star Wars* saga posits war on a galactic scale and casts the conflict in a morality tale that when viewed strategically, pits centralized control against that of distributed power. The Empire seeks order through a top-down hierarchy, whereas the Rebellion functions as a bottom-up organization. The Empire has an overwhelming edge in both technology and force size, yet it is repeatedly defeated by the Rebel forces and continues to fail in its end goal of an ordered Galactic system.

The Empire's failure to quell the Rebellion can be largely attributed to three elements of the Empire's leadership structure and strategy:

1. Its top-down decision-making process and leadership structure, where power is concentrated in a handful of insulated, micromanaging, and competitive elite;
2. Its failure to see the value of diplomacy as a strategic tool;
3. Its reliance on technology, especially legacy technology, as a central pillar of its warfighting strategy.

Thus, *Star Wars* provides a fictional example of how a larger, more sophisticated military force can lose in an asymmetric war due to internal dysfunction.

TOXIC LEADERSHIP, MICROMANAGEMENT, AND MISJUDGMENT

The U.S. Army's 2012 leadership manual, *Army Doctrine Publication 6-22*, gives the following definition of toxic leadership:

> Toxic leadership is a combination of self-centered attitudes, motivations, and behaviors that have adverse effects on subordinates, the organization, and mission performance. This leader lacks concern for others and the climate of the organization, which leads to short- and long-term negative effects. The toxic leader operates with an inflated sense of self-worth and from acute self-interest. Toxic leaders consistently use dysfunctional behaviors to deceive, intimidate, coerce, or unfairly punish others to get what they want for themselves. The negative leader completes short-term requirements by operating at the bottom of the continuum of commitment, where followers respond to the positional power of their leader to fulfill requests. This may achieve results in the short term, but ignores the other leader competency categories of *leads* and *develops*. Prolonged use of negative leadership to influence followers undermines the followers' will, initiative, and potential and destroys unit morale.[1]

One can see the outlines of the leadership problem early in the saga, beginning with *Star Wars: Episode II—Attack of the Clones*, the second prequel film in the story's time line and the fifth episode released in theaters. The film presages the Empire's leadership style, as based on the strict top-down organization of the Sith. The concentration of power to one man—Palpatine, the former senator who takes control of the Senate as supreme chancellor in *Attack of the Clones* and who is secretly a Sith lord—is finalized when Palpatine declares himself Emperor in *Star Wars: Episode III—Revenge of the Sith*.

Of course, Darth Vader could be said to be the cinematic embodiment of toxic leadership, micromanagement and fanatic devotion to the Empire and the Force, which he sees as the foundation of the Empire's power. This is demonstrated in his original appearance in *A New Hope*, where he uses the Force to choke an Imperial commander for his overenthusiasm in technology and lack of faith in the Force.[2] In the subsequent film, *The Empire Strikes Back*, Vader kills a senior admiral for his incompetence when undertaking a surprise attack on the Rebels on the planet Hoth that backfires by serving to warn the Rebels of the incoming assault. It is interesting to note that Vader punishes the admiral at the word of the general in charge of ground forces, who obviously does not want to take the blame for the failure of the assault. This move, which Vader also broadcasts, reinforces to other Imperial military leaders that making individual decisions without specific orders from above is a life-threatening mistake. Vader also inexplicably decides to land on Hoth, rather than letting the general in charge of the ground forces conduct the battle. Just as inexplicably, that commanding general ends up on the ground leading a team of walkers, rather than directing the overall battle. This dual bit of micromanagement makes little sense. In particular, it would have been strategically prudent for Vader to stay in orbit around the planet in case some Rebels managed to escape (as the key protagonists, Han Solo, Princess Leia Organa, and Luke Skywalker do).

Throughout the film series, the Empire's style of top-down leadership, which brooks no questioning or innovation from below, results in a number of problems that ultimately lead to failure in achieving its mission. At the top of the military command are officers who, often guilty of micromanagement, compete fiercely for the Emperor's favor and position in the inner circle. Even those who have demonstrated their competence continually find themselves required to prove their worth and loyalty to their commanding officers. Subordinates are motivated chiefly by fear and thus often respond with tactical hesitation when the chain of command is slow to respond in the heat of battle. Thus, the culture of the Empire's military as a whole has become dysfunctional and prone to strategic and tactical errors.

Military strategists may want to ponder the differences between this model and the largely successful command style of the U.S. Marine Corps, which is often emulated in the civilian world and fosters individual decision making, innovation, and responsibility at the earliest stages in training. In addition, the U.S. Marines make it a practice that even senior leaders are required to step away from their career billets to serve as trainers to both officers and enlisted personnel.[3] In addition, enlisted personnel also serve as trainers to young officers—something that also happens in the U.S. Army but not in the U.S. Air Force.[4] It can be argued that leadership philosophy is more integrated in the Marine Corps than in the other services, perhaps by necessity given the smaller force size and the structure of Marine Corps units.

THE DOWNFALLS OF IGNORING DIPLOMACY

One of the other striking strategic errors evident in the *Star Wars* saga is a complete failure on the part of the Empire's leadership to appreciate the benefits of diplomacy in gaining their stated goal of peace, security, and order in the galaxy. Perhaps this is due to the fact that the saga is essentially a morality tale, where strategic nuance is relatively less important to the story. Nonetheless, the Empire misses out early in its ascension to command diplomatic tools for establishing the order they seek and ensuring against the strengthening of the Rebellion. Instead, the overreliance on military power—and the belief that rule by fear is sufficient—lends fuel to the Rebel Alliance's growth.

The first example of this disregard for diplomacy appears in *The Phantom Menace*, which centers on the trade dispute between the Galactic Republic and the Trade Federation, one of the many business cartels in the Republic. The Trade Federation has blockaded the planet Naboo, seeking to establish a trade accord with better terms. This raises the question of why the Trade Federation, which is secretly being advised by the Sith lord Darth Sidious (later revealed as Palpatine), did not simply go to the Senate, the Republic's governing body, to resolve the issues, rather than instigating a blockade. Darth Sidious's instructions to the Trade Federation to kill the two Jedi knights deployed by the Republic to help negotiate and ease tensions presages disdain by the future leadership of the Empire for diplomatic solutions. Indeed, the Emperor is secretly pushing the parties toward war, which the Trade Federation loses in the subsequent prequel, *Attack of the Clones*. But diplomacy could have resolved the Trade Federation's problem and, if played correctly by Palpatine, could have forwarded his own ambitions as a strong and wise leader who could bring order to a fractious system.

That said, the war does lead to Palpatine's personal goal of becoming supreme chancellor, effective ruler of the Senate, and eventually Emperor. An interesting aside at this juncture is that neither the other Sith nor the Galactic Senate have cottoned on to the fact that Palpatine is playing both sides in order to gain ultimate control. One could make the conclusion that the Sith are blinded by their hierarchical structure, whereas the Galactic Senate is too fractured to share information that might have led to Palpatine's outing as a Sith lord.

The Empire's imperviousness to diplomacy also leads the leadership to renounce even the trappings of the Republic. Palpatine declares the Jedi Order (the peacekeeping and negotiating force of the Republic) an enemy of the Empire when they discover his treachery and later turns the Senate into a rubber stamp for his diktats rather than a representative body that functions through diplomacy (and sometimes corrupt political maneuvering, to be fair) among the various planetary and business blocs. He eventually dismantles it entirely. Grand Moff Tarkin, in *A New Hope*, announces this dissolvement of what is then the Imperial Senate, saying that power will be reallocated to regional governors and the people will be controlled by fear. But it is precisely the Empire's heavy hand and refusal to work with, rather than simply dominate, local governments that lead to the growth in support for the Rebel Alliance and to the Empire's eventual fall. In *A New Hope*, rather than contact the local government on Tatooine and offer a reward for the capture of R2-D2 and C-3PO, Darth Vader sends a swarm of stormtroopers to execute a scorched-earth search for the droids. With this decision, which leads directly to the killing of Luke Skywalker's aunt and uncle, Vader inadvertently creates his worst enemy and ensures his own downfall.

Classic military strategy, dating from the time of Sun Tzu, puts a value on diplomatic tools. After all, the first goal of strategy is to avoid war if at all possible—but also to be prepared to win. To quote Sun Tzu, "To subdue the enemy without fighting is the acme of skill."[5] Deterrence, as well as it can be described, is an outgrowth of both diplomacy and military strength. Diplomacy can also avoid war by bringing parties together to find modus vivendi (i.e., an ability to live and let live) status and mutual interests that can keep both the national and international peace and stability required for economic success. The *Star Wars* universe should give pause to any in leadership positions who are tempted to forget or downplay diplomatic approaches to security problems.

LEGACY TECHNOLOGY AND FIGHTING THE LAST WAR

Many *Star Wars* fans have certainly asked themselves two questions about the Empire's reliance on the Death Star:

1. Why, if the Empire's leadership knew, or even just suspected, that the Death Star plans captured by the Rebels revealed a security flaw, did they continue with their all-out assault against the Rebels by relying on the weapon rather than pulling back to assess any defensive weaknesses and rectify them?
2. Why would the Empire rebuild the Death Star, which must have been an enormous economic burden, rather than seek other ways, perhaps through more distributed assets, to counter the insurgency?[6]

While the first question is somewhat vexing, the apparent answer is that the small opening in the ventilation shaft that could allow penetration of the reactor core by a missile was considered too inconsequential to be taken seriously. A Rebel assault that resulted in such a lucky shot would be a black swan (i.e., a highly unlikely event, but one with a highly negative impact) of epic proportions; therefore, the possibility was written off. This is understandable. Governments and militaries generally find it difficult to appreciate black swan risks and to prepare adequately against them. One reason is budget constraints—not, however, that such constraints seem to have been an issue for the Empire in this instance. Weighing the potential for black swan events, however, is increasingly seen as necessary for both military strategists and economists, as technological innovation continues to outpace humankind's ability to understand it. For example, one could argue that the U.S. military's decades-long and successful efforts to integrate space capabilities into warfighting operations and power projection has resulted in unforeseen vulnerabilities as technology has proliferated, especially to the civil sector, and become less expensive. The interconnectivity of today's world also plays a part in the growing necessity to identify potential black swan events and assess their potential impacts. There is also a question of why the Empire leadership did not consider the possibility of sabotage by Rebel special operations forces infiltrating the gigantic Death Star or by a disaffected insider.[7] Perhaps these potential scenarios were also considered as easily dismissed black swans. Of course, *Rogue One* shows what damage one rogue Imperial scientist (as well as one rogue pilot) could do—that is, successfully incorporating the Death Star's fatal flaw into its design and subsequently providing the blueprints to the Rebels.

In *Return of the Jedi* Darth Vader and Emperor Palpatine command the construction of a new, improved Death Star with a more powerful laser that could fire more often and destroy several targets at once—think MIRV (multiple independently targeted reentry vehicle) nuclear missiles. They also decide to lure the Rebels into a trap by broadcasting false information that the new Death Star, under construction in orbit around the second moon of the planet Endor, has not yet reached operational capability. This leads to the Rebels sending a force led by Han Solo to the forest moon of Endor, home of the Ewoks, who help destroy the Death Star's ground station, which provides power for the Death Star's shielding.[8] This, in turn, leads to Rebel pilots (including loveable rogue Lando Calrissian) successfully targeting the Death Star's reactor core and blowing it up (again).

The second question of why the Empire decided to redesign and rebuild the Death Star—which even in its more powerful version still seems to have a problem with an exposed reactor core—is more complicated. At its heart, the answer involves a two-pronged, and common, weakness for national security leaders: the tendency to rely on evolutionary development of legacy technology and to fight the last war. While it is important that military commanders learn from the past, "fighting the last war" means applying a strategy that worked in the past but is no longer appropriate in the current situation. A historical example often cited is the French building of the Maginot Line before World War II. Weapons systems that made sense in the past don't necessarily make sense for the future. But given the long lead times for weapons development and internal and external pressures to upgrade legacy systems—from costs to turf to institutional pride to the interests of big defense contractors and congressional representatives with jobs to protect—this is a mistake that is easy to make and hard to avoid.

Indeed, in *A New Hope* Darth Vader quite forcefully (pun fully intended) makes a point about the dangers of overreliance on technological prowess. But by *Return of the Jedi* he seems to have forgotten his own warning. Vader and the Empire's leadership seem to be irresistibly drawn to the awesome power represented by the Death Star and its potential to hold the galaxy at risk. They also seem to be unable to realistically rethink their tactics in fighting the Rebellion—perhaps a result of insular and hierarchical leadership where subordinates are actively, and sometimes viciously, discouraged from innovating or even proposing alternative paths.

The tendency to fall back on updating weapons systems, rather than spending effort and money on development of radically new or innovative ones, stems from familiar bureaucratic and economic drivers. Fighter jets are an example; for many years, the single-minded devotion of the U.S. Air Force to development of ever more sophisticated, but also ever more expensive, manned airplanes actually impeded the development of cheaper, similarly capable unmanned drones. Putting fighter pilots out of jobs, especially given that U.S. Air Force leadership has been controlled by the oft-noted "fighter mafia," was simply not a good career move for either innovative U.S. Air Force officers or defense contractors seeking U.S. Air Force funding. And the temptation to fight the last war can be seen in the difficulties the U.S. military has faced over the past few decades in redesigning its force structure, weapons systems, and doctrine for urban warfare and fighting terrorist insurgencies. Again, the *Star Wars* saga can provide a cautionary tale to future military thinkers on these strategic traps.

CONCLUSION

Star Wars is of course fictional. But fiction can elucidate modern problems and potential solutions. Indeed, science fiction has always been a vector for consideration of human concerns unfettered from the constraints of everyday thinking and even current politics—whether these be concerns about human nature, societal problems, or even military strategy. Studying the Empire's strategic failings does have lessons to teach military strategists, policy makers, and leaders. Besides, it's fun.

Notes

1. Department of the Army, *Army Doctrine Paper 6-22: Army Leadership* (Washington DC: Department of the Army, 2012), 3, http://cape.army.mil/repository/doctrine/adp6-22.pdf.
2. This is the scene in which Darth Vader utters perhaps the most famous quote from the *Star Wars* saga: "Don't be too proud of this technological terror you've constructed. The ability to destroy a planet is insignificant next to the power of the Force. . . . I find your lack of faith disturbing."
3. Patrick Lefler, "Leadership Lessons from the Marine Corps," Academy Leadership, May 2011, http://www.academyleadership.com/news%5C201105.asp.
4. George R. Mastroianni, "Occupations, Cultures, and Leadership in the Army and Air Force," *Parameters*, Winter 2005–6, 80, www.dtic.mil/get-tr-doc/pdf?AD=ADA485668.
5. Sun Tzu, *The Art of War*, trans. Samuel B. Griffith (New York: Oxford University Press, 1971), 77.
6. For a slightly tongue-in-cheek look at the costs of the original Death Star, see Carol Pinchefsky, "How Much Would It Cost to Build the Death Star from Star Wars?," *Forbes*, February 21, 2012, http://www.forbes.com/sites/carolpinchefsky/2012/02/21/how-much-would-it-cost-to-build-the-death-star-from-star-wars/#38cd29c8779f; David Z. Morris, "The Death Star Would Cost $7.8 Octillion a Day to Run," *Fortune*, December 3, 2016, http://fortune.com/2016/12/03/death-star-operating-costs/.
7. Although there are a number of different estimates of crew size, with the highest showing some 2.5 million personnel, the star base is clearly large enough for Rebel infiltrators to be able to maneuver inside. See Claudia Gray, *Lost Stars* (Los Angeles CA: Disney–Lucasfilm Press, 2015); Adam Bray et al., *Star Wars: Absolutely Everything You Need to Know* (London: Dorling Kindersley, 2015); Pablo Hidalgo, *Star Wars: Rogue One; The Ultimate Visual Guide* (London: Dorling Kindersley, 2016).
8. The Ewoks are cuddly, teddy-bear-like creatures that many hard-core *Star Wars* fans love to hate.

26

Star Wars, Cyclical History, and Implications for Strategy

KATHLEEN J. MCINNIS

Mark Twain once supposedly said that "history doesn't repeat itself, but it often rhymes." It is a sentiment that has gained particular resonance since the end of the Cold War and the prosecution of the U.S.-led global war on terror. Any number of strategic and tactical-level practitioners have sought to decipher the pasts of the peoples in whose countries we have intervened, trying to find ways to move beyond those pasts in order to settle grievances, build stability, and improve global security. Beginning at least with the interventions in the Balkans and continuing into Iraq and Afghanistan, helping these peoples escape their histories has for better or worse become a key objective of successive U.S. administrations. As the logic goes, winning hearts and minds, reducing the possibility of ethnic cleansing, or building the capacity of other states means, at an abstract level, breaking history's rhymes and replacing them with a different narrative largely based on humanist values and individual liberties.

Yet our track record on being able to actually break these narratives is mixed. Tensions still seethe in the Balkans, and the interventions in Iraq and Afghanistan have failed to deliver conclusive, stable results. Indeed, the U.S.-led coalition's performance in Afghanistan triggered significant concerns as to whether the United States was repeating Russian missteps in that country, while ethnic tensions have begun to rise once again in Kosovo. And despite the fact that the collapse of the USSR marked for many a decisive "end of history," post-Soviet Russia has had its own back-to-the-future moment in an effort to position itself for competition with the United States in Europe and beyond. As Yogi Berra put it, "It's déjà vu all over again."

Charles Hill reminds us that great fiction and literature provides a creative, methodologically unbound way to contemplate our circumstances, including statecraft.[1] *Star Wars* is no exception. Many, of course, maintain that the *Star Wars* movies are merely a lengthy space opera with the occasional camp line thrown in for good measure. This is true, but they are also so much more. The movies represent a way to reflect on history as a series of cycles to find individual agency within those cycles. In other words, the *Star Wars* movies are an elegant, if somewhat lengthy, exploration of history's inherent rhymes—and what can be done about them.

PHILOSOPHIES OF HISTORY

Although today it is a dominant assumption in Western philosophy and culture, the notion that history is a linear chronology that points us inexorably toward a future end is a relatively new one. As Europe progressed from the Middle Ages, through the Renaissance, and into the Enlightenment, scholars became increasingly aware of the centrality of the individual to the ordering of society. The fates of men were no longer necessarily dependent on the whims of the divine; rather, through reason and learning, men could chart their own paths and build their own societies. It was a radical notion that found its expression in a variety of places and manners. In the Americas, for example, the constitutional convention to design the government of the new United States sought to learn from prior historical examples and mitigate the risk of its becoming a tyrannical dictatorship. Past became prologue rather than a guide to repeat itself.

Georg Wilhelm Fredreich Hegel brought form and intellectual coherence to this idea of historical progress.[2] Roughly speaking, history, according to

Hegel, is a series of struggles between a thesis and its antithesis; the outcome of the resulting clash (or dialectic) propels the spirit of history (or "geist") toward a better understanding of itself and its freedom. Geist, in the form of humanity, moves forward to new heights as a result of improved learning. Numerous other scholars detail Hegel's philosophy in more detail, but for our purposes it is enough to note that in part because of Hegel's writings, the notion of history as linear became a core component of Western thought and statecraft. It is also a philosophical and conceptual underpinning of much contemporary literature, art, and movies.

By contrast, the ancients long held the view that human experience is better conceived of as a cycle. Birth is followed by growth, which is followed by death, and the cycle repeats. Golden ages are followed by dark ones, over and over again. Aristotle, applying this concept to his philosophies on politics, argued that forms of governance evolve through stages comprising a cycle: monarchy becomes perverted and turns into tyranny and is eventually replaced by aristocracy—the rule of a few wise, privileged individuals.[3] Yet aristocracy eventually becomes corrupted and turns into the rule by the few rich and powerful—an oligarchy—which is itself overthrown and replaced by a polity, the rule of the people. Yet even polities become corrupted and are replaced by democracy. Democracy is eventually replaced when a demagogue begins to control the masses, and in this way, the cycle begins to repeat itself.[4] Polybius, building on his Greek intellectual forebears and reflecting on the Roman Empire, gave further form to this notion of political cycles in *The Histories*.[5] Islamic scholar Ibn Khaldun echoed this concept; he wrote about political cycles in terms of dynasties, which typically last around three generations.[6] As decadence sets in and unity among followers erodes, the dynasty becomes vulnerable and is eventually overthrown by another regime that is less corrupt and more ideologically unified. Rinse, repeat.

In an essay titled, "The Return of Marco Polo's World," Robert Kaplan reminds us that cyclical history is very much alive in eastern Europe and central Asia. Even as our present cultural and societal norms fade in the normal ebb and flow of ethnic and social cross-pollination, the legacies of national imperial pasts still loom large for some. Turkey, he argues, is remembering—and trying to reinvent—aspects of its Ottoman Empire; the same could arguably be said of Russia and China. Their form and reach will likely differ from their historical antecedents, but their respective impulses and ambitions, heavily influenced by geopolitics, are quite similar.[7]

Critically, this notion of history as a cycle was reflected in early epic mythical and religious narratives around the world. Mary Douglas eloquently demonstrates how these stories with a ring construction can be found in texts around the world and across centuries, from ancient China to the biblical Old Testament to the work of the famed thirteenth-century poet Rumi.[8] The basic notion is that such texts parallel and mirror each other, as the story evolves in a manner where the end meets the beginning. To those unacquainted with this type of story structure, the results can seem repetitive and disjointed—if not downright frustrating. Yet, properly understood, it is also a form of storytelling that reflects on, and helps make sense of, the repeating patterns of individual and historical experience.

STAR WARS AND RING NARRATIVES

Interestingly, *Star Wars*, and the prequel trilogy in particular, has also been derided as frustrating, repetitive, and at times disjointed. Some even go so far as to argue that *The Phantom Menace* is a fairly pointless waste of audience time and cinematic energy. Yet there is a compelling case, made well by Mike Klimo, that the *Star Wars* cycle is actually an example of ring composition, hearkening back to cyclical conceptions of history.[9] Scenes and events and struggles parallel each other across the episodes, all creating an interlocking and circular narrative whole.[10] According to ring-narrative designs, the end has to meet the beginning, and the real crux of the cycle is its middle components. Applied to the *Star Wars* trilogies, this means that fully understanding the narrative's synchronicity requires comparing the movies in like pairs:

Episode I and *Episode VI* (beginning/end)
Episode II and *Episode V* (middle builds)
Episode III and *Episode IV* (central story climax)

Events in each movie refer to and reflect the other. Thus, as we follow the Skywalkers across generations, we begin to see symbols hinting that a part of the *Star Wars* story design is the notion of history repeating. *Episodes I* and *VI* both end with father figures—one light, one dark—burning on a funeral pyre. Both explore duality. In *Episode I* it is between the populations of Naboo as Palpatine conspires to become emperor. In *Episode VI* the duality is represented most clearly at the final battle, as both Luke and Anakin Skywalker struggle between the light and the dark and eventually cause the Emperor's demise.

Episodes II and *V* feature chases involving bounty hunters; both Anakin and Luke lose their hands toward the end of each. But while Anakin is ruled by his feelings and succumbs to the dark side by slaughtering the Sand People, Luke finds a way to control his emotions while in the swamps of Dagobah. And of course, *Episode III* and *Episode IV* are the key points around which the entire cycle turns. Both feature battles between Obi-Wan Kenobi and Darth Vader. Anakin takes the final steps to the dark side, becoming Darth Vader; Luke begins his quest to understand the light.

Beyond the ring-narrative structure, the parallels in the stories of both Luke and Anakin are also unmistakable. Both start as innocents living on Tatooine that happen to be excellent mechanics and pilots. Both take down massive enemy ships on their first adventures. Both have to confront the possibility of losing the ones they love most. And while Anakin loses his mother and his wife, which drives him to the dark side, Luke ends up saving his sister, friends, and eventually his father.

And this leads us to one of the important points *Star Wars* raises. Namely, in spite of the cyclical, rhyming nature of history, humans do have agency over their circumstances. Indeed, despite the overwhelming similarities between Luke and his father and despite the structurally cyclical nature of the circumstances in which Luke finds himself, the younger Skywalker manages to choose a path different from that of Anakin. He follows neither the advice of Obi-Wan nor that of the Emperor, both of whom advise Luke to kill his father. Instead, through an act of self-sacrifice, he manages to destroy the Emperor once and for all. This suggests that moments of agency—escaping the cycles of history—are ones that also involve extreme tests of principles and values. And they are fleeting moments that are perhaps fewer and further between than we might hope. Applied to statecraft, this suggests that leaders must be careful to discern, and take advantage of, those rare moments when a new course of action can have meaningful, positive impact on the global system and the ability to advance national interests.

The American democratic experiment itself may be one such instance. Indeed, George Washington's repeated insistence on adhering to the rule of law during his tenure as president and his refusal to allow himself to become a king-like ruler of the United States were two key demonstrations of agency in the face of history in the early days of the American Republic.

It is interesting to note that this sense of agency—charting a truly new path—was only realized by Anakin's successor generation. Their father's example underscores to both Luke and Leia that the dark side, and the empire that it has given rise to, was an oppressive order they could not support. In the final battle, Luke becomes truly conscious of the costs of killing Vader and instead chooses to trust that there is something good in his father that is worth respecting rather than exterminating. In terms of parallels with the real world, this calls to mind post–World War II Europe. Rather than once again repressing Germany as a penalty for its wartime aggression and atrocities, the United States and Europe determined it would be better instead to rebuild and reintegrate Germany into a broader project of European integration. This, of course, had the added benefit of creating a bulwark against the Soviet Union. Since the end of the Cold War, however, it is not clear that the United States has had such a unity of purpose. Along these lines, it is interesting to contemplate whether the post-9/11 interventions—all in the name of eliminating terrorist safe havens and keeping U.S. and allied homelands safe—may have represented a moment of historical agency that has been squandered. Are U.S. missteps in these far-flung places around the globe a historical reflection of similar missteps by the British empire? Or the Dutch before them?

Indeed, the first three episodes of *Star Wars* can also be construed as a meditation on the consequences of an inability to forge deeper purpose against a looming enemy. The movies are plagued by character missteps and betrayals of the values that undergird the peaceful and democratic Galactic Republic. During the first three episodes, all the characters of Anakin's generation blindly charge into Palpatine's traps, often sacrificing their values and principles in the process. Queen Amidala, at first a pacifist, eventually decides to wage a war against the Trade Federation in order to take back her planet. Master Windu, a high-level Jedi, at first claims that Jedi are not soldiers yet subsequently brings himself and a number of other Jedi to the front lines of the first battle in the Clone Wars. Anakin becomes convinced by Palpatine's interpretation of the Force, surrendering himself to the greed he was innocent of when we met him in *The Phantom Menace*.

And all the while, they were ultimately ignorant of the true enemy: Palpatine, an *actual* Sith lord who manages to become the ruler of the galaxy, largely with our protagonists' endorsements along the way. They are so focused on winning the close fight that they unwittingly lose the game in the first act of the saga when Palpatine is elected chancellor (at Queen Amidala's suggestion). At an abstract level, it is a situation that recalls the "tyranny of the inbox" in contemporary policy making—a Washington euphemistic slogan for how the urgent becomes prioritized over the important. Key policy makers are often inundated by small details as the bureaucratic stovepipe in which they work increasingly narrows the scope of their perspective, making it even more difficult to orchestrate interagency and multilateral operations. The upshot is that, much like our tragic heroes in the *Star Wars* saga, their actions are tactical, uncoordinated, and often amount to less than the sum of their parts.

The strategic consequences of the protagonists' blind action and insufficient intelligence are catastrophic. Due to their missteps—their own narrow conception of interests and how to advance them—the democratic Galactic Republic dies and is replaced by a tyrannical imperial order. And this brings us to the ancients' conceptions of cyclical political orders. Echoing the ancient Greeks, George Lucas himself notes,

> All democracies turn into dictatorships—but not by coup. The people give their democracy to a dictator, whether it's Julius Caesar or Napoleon or Adolf Hitler. Ultimately, the general population goes along with the idea. . . . What kinds of things push people and institutions into this direction? . . . That's the issue that I've been exploring: How did the Republic turn into the Empire? That's paralleled with: How did Anakin turn into Darth Vader? How does a good person go bad, and how does a democracy become a dictatorship? It isn't that the Empire conquered the Republic, it's that the Empire is the Republic.[11]

It is the task of Anakin's children to reverse their parents' misdeeds. And it is a task, we see at the outset of *Episode VII*, that they have only partially accomplished. The Emperor is dead, but others have filled the vacuum—in this case, the First Order.

THE IMPLICATIONS OF CYCLICAL HISTORY FOR STRATEGY

The first six episodes of *Star Wars* invite us to consider whether history itself rhymes. Through an almost cartoonish degree of parallels and mirrors across the cycle—and across generations of Skywalkers—the audience is invited to contemplate a nonlinear conception of human evolution and history itself.

This is an extremely important point for students of international relations and strategy for two reasons. First, many of the countries in which we intervene have conceptions of history that are more likely cyclical rather than linear. The Kosovo war in the 1990s, for example, had at its core a historical grievance dating from the thirteenth century.[12] Many observers at the time concluded that this was mere populist posturing. *Star Wars* helps us understand that the truth of that old grievance—and its implications—is probably more complex than mere populism. As such, rather than history being something to surmount or dismiss, history informs and shapes present options as the cycle repeats.

This is a concept that is probably easier to abstractly appreciate than apply to contemporary operations. The American people, at least, tend to have a linear conception of history and an anything-is-possible attitude to learning from and surmounting past challenges. We define end states for our military campaigns and measure progress with milestones. But in the parts of the world where history is a more cyclical concept, and therefore always in danger of repetition, people may not always be receptive to our attempts to move them out of their history. How can we better tailor our strategies and policies—not to mention our public diplomacy efforts—to better account for these fundamental differences in perspective? What does it mean to analyze policy options and develop strategies in areas where history isn't always linear?

This leads to the second reason that *Star Wars* is an important tool for scholars and practitioners of strategy. What are the analytic and strategic implications of a world in which the cycle of history may once again be turning? Any number of Washington think tank gatherings consider the future of warfare. Often these turn into conversations on emerging technologies, climate change, resource scarcity, and likely future battlespaces. These are, of course, important discussions. But perhaps we need to consider the extent to which historical experiences and legacies can inform what the likely future strategic environment might look like. What can the rise and fall of the Ottoman Empire tell us about dynamics in the Middle East? What elements might the current Turkish government be able to resurrect? Might the Hanseatic League tell us something about the future of relations between major European cities? These are but a few questions to which no fully satisfying answer has emerged. But it seems like they are worth exploring, if only to discover the uses and limits of historical analogies.

And indeed, there are limitations. Ultimately, *Star Wars* tells us that there are some problems that cannot be solved, and there are others that, in the "solving," make things much worse. It is our characters blindly charging forward, trying to do what is right without a true appreciation for the real dangers in their midst, that eventually leads to the collapse of the Republic. And screwups as big as those in *Episodes I–III* require generations—as we see in *Episodes IV–VI*—to repair and resolve. But *Star Wars* also tells us, through the similarities and differences between Anakin's and Luke's choices, that while history doesn't repeat itself, it sure does rhyme.

Notes

1. Charles Hill, *Grand Strategies: Literature, Statecraft, and World Order* (New Haven CT: Yale University Press, 2010).
2. Georg Wilhelm Friedrich Hegel, *Lectures on the Philosophy of World History* (Cambridge: Cambridge University Press, 1975).
3. Benjamin Jowett, ed., *The Politics of Aristotle*, vol. 1 (Oxford, UK: Clarendon Press, 1885), see in particular bk. 3, pt. 15.
4. Jowett, *Politics of Aristotle*, vol. 1, bk. 5.
5. Polybius, *The Histories: Book Six* (Cambridge MA: Harvard University Press, 1922).
6. Ibn Khaldun, *The Muqaddimah: An Introduction to History* (Princeton NJ: Princeton University Press, 1989), 136.
7. Robert D. Kaplan, "The Return of Marco Polo's World and the U.S. Military Response," Center for a New American Security, May 12, 2017, http://stories.cnas.org/the-return-of-marco-polos-world-and-the-u-s-military-response.
8. Mary Douglas, *Thinking in Circles: An Essay on Ring Composition*, Terry Lecture Series (New Haven CT: Yale University Press, 2007).
9. Mike Klimo, "Ring Theory: The Hidden Artistry of the Star Wars Prequels," Star Wars Ring Theory, October 31, 2014, https://web.archive.org/web/20170629231517/http://www.starwarsringtheory.com/.
10. The actual construction of a ring narrative is highly complex; it is beyond the scope of this article to lay out its aspects in detail. Instead, for our purposes, it is sufficient to simply note that there are cinematic, technical, and plot elements that suggest that the movies are to be treated as a cycle.
11. George Lucas, as quoted in "Star Wars: Attack of the Clones," *Time*, April 21, 2002.
12. Robert Bideleux, "Kosovo's Conflict," *History Today* 48, no. 11 (November 1998), https://web.archive.org/web/20170629231152/http://www.historytoday.com/robert-bideleux/kosovos-conflict.

27

Suffer, the Weak Must

A History of the Galactic Civil War

CRAIG WHITESIDE

[Archive note: Amity Document NRGMD-23-614405 is a series of selections culled from journals written by former Imperial Staff Colonel Norunda between 19 BBY and 5 ABY (GSC).[1] Colonel Norunda is currently under quarters quarantine as part of the New Republic's "Phuk Ayn" Inquiry into the development of the Empire's illegal weapons program. While investigators compiled this Amity Document for the purposes of prosecuting the former Imperial officer for war crimes, it also lends insight into the strategic failures of Imperial generalship, as they relentlessly pursued a technological solution to a largely political problem.]

[PAGE 1]

Book 1

Introduction

This is the history of the war fought between the Empire and the Rebels, written by Norunda of Eriadu.

I knew from the very beginning, from the first skirmish, that it would be the most momentous of any conflict that I had seen or studied. At first, I thought that the Rebels could not withstand the growing power of the Empire, but my firsthand observations of the spread of Rebel power prompted me to revise this opinion. In the end, the powerful were brought down by the weak. Simply put, nothing like this war has ever happened in this galaxy.

The story of the Galactic Civil War, as some people call it, has already been told many times. As a participant, though, I can tell you that many of the accounts are wrong about the details—both large and small. I am not a poet intending to glorify this war, nor am I some kind of popular writer looking for sat-blast views. I am simply telling the true story of it, as best I can, and I do not exaggerate when I say that the war between the Alliance and the Empire is the greatest of them all.

You might ask how I arrived at such a perspective. I was a dedicated staff aide to both of the Tarkin brothers over a long period of time that included service in the wars of the Republic and later the Empire and, as such, have not only seen many events myself but also heard about them from eyewitnesses on both sides. My time spent interviewing Rebel prisoners was also an important way for me to clarify—and even dispute—accounts that I believed previously. The goal has always been to establish the truth and to write something that is lasting in importance about this cataclysmic conflict that affected so many lives.

The war started slowly, with acts of resistance (or terrorism, depending on your perspective) against the New Order, which Emperor Palpatine formed after the vote to dissolve the allegedly corrupt Galactic Republic. Although each side had its own story about how and why the insurgency started, these details would confuse us and disguise the truth. What made the war possible was the growth of the Emperor's power and the fear this caused the members of the Rebel Alliance.

We now come to the actual outbreak of war between the Rebels and the Empire of the New Order, which happened in the seventeenth year of the Empire. The Empire's continual efforts to suppress a wide range of dissidents gave the impression of steady progress, with leaders of the Rebellion being killed or captured in ever-increasing numbers. Nonetheless, due to either insufficient intelligence or an underestimation of the actual size of the Rebels, not only were Rebel attacks increasing, but Imperial intelligence reports documented a steady uniting of disparate opposition groups into a larger Alliance. According to galactic media polling, people's feelings were generally very much on the side of the Alliance, especially as they proclaimed that their aim was the liberation of the galaxy. In an effort to deter groups from joining the budding resistance movement, Grand Moff Tarkin, an Imperial admiral, had long advocated employing a doctrine of overwhelming force— one that would be enforced by the final development of a superweapon first called the Expeditionary Battle Planetoid and later the Death Star.[2] While this view—called the Third Offset Strategy—was supported by a minority among the Imperial staff, it was one growing in popularity due to the demonstrated lack of success in extirpating the Rebellion.[3]

After years of cost overruns, failed trials, labor unrest, even sabotage, Tarkin was beginning to fear that the weapon so critical to the culmination of his well-traveled doctrine might not work. According to his notes, what was needed was a proof of concept. In briefing the Emperor on the force planning considerations needed to develop such a capability, Tarkin made the following comment: "The average citizen deals in symbols, not rational analysis. If we present the citizen with a weapon so powerful, so immense as to defy all conceivable attack against it, a weapon invulnerable and invincible in battle, that shall become the symbol for the Empire. We may need only a handful, perhaps only one of these weapons to subjugate thousands upon thousands of worlds containing millions upon millions of beings."[4]

After listening to this short speech, the Emperor asked his military commander Vader to visit with Tarkin and tour the construction site. Upon arrival with other members of the Emperor's military council, Lord Darth Vader and Grand Moff Tarkin led a formal discussion of the merits of the weapons program and its impact on the Empire's strategy to defeat the long-running Rebellion, now in its second decade.

This discussion is of such importance that I quote liberally from the meeting, in the manner that I have throughout this history. At the outset of the assembly, the council listened with great patience to what Grand Moff Tarkin had to say. While the report was encouraging as to the progress of the weapon system, much of it was untrue, particularly on the cost details and production schedule. Based on this mistaken belief, there was a general consensus among the officers present to continue with the program and associated investments from the treasury. Grand Moff Tarkin asked if Lord Vader wanted to be more involved and possibly help with the human resource problems that seemed to plague this particular project. The normally taciturn Vader spoke, for the first time in the meeting, about his reservations:

> It is true that this assembly was called to deal with the preparations of the Death Star, as it is called by some. Yet I still think this is a question that requires further thought. What I say is this: in continuing this program, we are focusing great resources on a weapon that is not developed to destroy our enemies but to make new ones in different places of the Galaxy. It will not stop our enemies from attacking us, and this considerable investment prevents us from going on the offensive or strengthening our defenses in places the enemy is sure to attack next. Every day the Rebellion gets stronger, and new enemies join the Alliance. Our efforts to keep this program a secret are not as good as we think. Soon, people that normally avoid dealing with the Rebels could decide that this development is significant enough to make war on the Empire. All these points are to be considered; we have not yet come safely into harbor, and this is no time for running risks or for grasping at a new empire before we have secured the one we have already. These Rebels, once crushed, could be kept down. This weapon system, if successfully developed, would create more enemies than we already have.[5]

Grand Moff Tarkin thought about this for a bit, as the other committee members began, after a short pause, to again speak in favor of the project, having already committed to this position. They were not about to look foolish in changing their minds in such a short period of time, despite the logic in Vader's remarks or his reputation. While no one liked opposing Vader in these matters, he was, in reality, an outsider with a tenuous spot in the hierarchy. After a short period of listening, the eyes of the committee drifted toward Tarkin, known to be a carefully calculating character. His reputation had long been tied to this project, one that had the Emperor's interest. Finally, he spoke:

> Since Lord Vader makes a valid criticism of the project, let me respond. I have developed a doctrine that has become very popular among members of this council and certainly among the members of the Imperial Senate. I am telling you, from my vast personal experience in fighting—first in the Clone Wars and now in this iterant, never-ending battle against the so-called Rebels—that this program is essential to the execution of what some people are calling the Tarkin Doctrine. Do not change your minds about this project. The people that join the Rebellion are opportunists and criminals, not Imperial citizens that we should be concerned with wooing or entertaining. Their numbers are frequently embellished by their own partisans and our more timid staff intelligence officers, who often see monsters inside every asteroid. This weapon system is a game changer. The power of it cannot be rivaled, and in our hands it will force the systems across the galaxy to finally recognize the impossibility of resisting the Empire and its enlightened leadership. There seems to be, therefore, no reasonable argument to induce us to hold back ourselves or to justify any excuse for not developing this weapon. We cannot remain at rest and simply deal with the annoyances that come with Rebel attacks. It is in our nature for action.[6]

Vader sat quietly, as he often did. He seemed to sense that Tarkin would not back down, nor would the officers around him. He changed tack. Standing and pacing quietly behind the chairs of the members seated near him, he slowly turned and spoke:

> I see that you are quite determined to continue with his project, and I hope it turns out as we all wish. I have little use for doctrine and even less for the type of technology that is so attractive to my colleagues. We are dealing with a stubborn group of people, ones who are not persuaded much by promises or appeals to good governance. I found in my interrogations of their prisoners that they are very unlikely, in fact, to give up their cause, in order to be ruled by us. To deal with an enemy of this kind, we will need these special weapons and more stormtrooper armies, but also people . . . the very type of people we killed as part of the Emperor's Order 66. These types of people will be very hard to find but can match the strength of our adversaries. I can find them, and I can train them to be our special weapon against the Rebels. At the minimum, it can augment the power of this special weapon you are determined to proceed with.[7]

When the committee heard this, they immediately agreed that Grand Moff Tarkin should be allocated more resources for the plan, with fewer restrictions than before, and to authorize him to act as he saw fit for this project. After this, preparations were made, instructions for the increase of the armies were sent out, and Lord Vader was entrusted with the mission of recruiting the few remaining (and possibly future) Jedi for the New Sith. This force, although small, would be entrusted with penetrating the resistance and forcing it to collapse from within. So the meeting ended, in the seventeenth year of the war recorded by Norunda.

[PAGE 460]

The Battle of Yavin was the greatest we know of in history—to the victors the most brilliant of successes, to the vanquished the most calamitous of defeats. The Empire was utterly defeated; their sufferings were enormous; their losses were, as they say, total; army, navy, everything destroyed, and out of many, few returned. So ended the events in Yavin.[8]

When the news of the destruction of the expedition to Yavin reached Coruscant, many thought it was a new propaganda ploy by the increasingly active Rebels.[9] When reality set in, the blame was placed squarely on those who had advocated for the Death Star as the primary element of the Imperial strategy to defeat the Rebel Alliance. Tarkin was dead, and the thought of all the dead officers, pilots, and workers was hard to accept for the people, who had forgotten that they were once for this effort.

The chaos that spread through the ranks was short lived, especially since the Emperor, with Lord Vader's considerable assistance, was able to stabilize the political situation on Coruscant while new commanders consolidated the Imperial fleet for future action. Despite the Empire's now-obvious weakness, it still had its large bureaucracy to support it in regenerating the structure needed to fight on.

Because of my long service and association with both Tarkins (now deceased), I was appointed to be a member of the investigation team that followed the loss of the first Death Star. Specifically, the Emperor tasked us with identifying the intelligence failures that led to the loss of the plans for the weapon, as well as a strategy review for a new effort to defeat the Rebellion. The investigation has never been publicly released, but I distinctly remember this speech by Staff Colonel Monru, the chief of the team based in Coruscant. He said these words at the official close of the investigation, to the Emperor himself:

> In analyzing the long and costly Imperial entanglement with the Rebel Alliance, with its many consequences, some of them tragic, it is important to look at performance as well as policy. Whatever the wisdom of putting the majority of our resources into the Death Star, the immense disparity in strength and resources between the antagonists would have suggested a more favorable and conclusive outcome. Yet why has a cumulatively enormous Imperial contribution had such a limited impact for so long? Why, almost regardless of the ultimate outcome, have Imperial efforts entailed such disproportionate costs and side effects? The reasons are many, complex, and interrelated. They include the unique and unfamiliar

conflict environment in which we became enmeshed. Particularly constraining has been the sharp contrast between the adversary we combat and the allies we back—a motivated ideological insurgency led by former Republican patricians and various half-formed and seriously flawed regimes in many parts of the galaxy. Another constraint was implicit in the incremental nature of our response, for the most part doing only what we believed was minimally necessary at each stage.

But even these reasons are insufficient to explain why we did so poorly. The record shows that we thought we recognized the nature of the operational problems we confronted in fighting the Rebels and that our policy was designed to overcome them. And whatever the gradualism of our response, we ended up making a cumulatively massive investment of blood and treasure in the attempt to achieve a satisfactory outcome. Yet the Empire grossly misjudged what it could actually accomplish with the effort it eventually made. In this sense, at least, the Empire did stumble into a quagmire at Yavin and other places.

What must be added is how another set of real-life constraints—largely inherent in the typical behavior patterns of Imperial institutions involved in the conflict—made it difficult to cope with an unfamiliar conflict environment and greatly influenced what we could and could not, or would and would not, do to win the war against the Rebel Alliance.[10]

This investigation did not alter the war effort, even though Colonel Monru argued convincingly that the Imperial staff and its associated institutions had overseen the evolution of a flawed strategy and seemed powerless to change it in any remarkable way. What he meant by that was that the key actors simply did what they were always going to do. The scientists built powerful weapons; the Sith sought out more Sith to improve their numbers for some independent, cosmic war none of us can comprehend; and the stormtrooper legions occupied with efficiency and lethality. In fact, I thought it was clear from the very beginning of the war that Tarkin had a mistaken idea of how to defeat the Rebels, but he was given the preponderance of the resources despite the significant vulnerabilities of the associated levels of risk of the Death Star project. Vader had a better idea of how to defeat the Rebels but never could produce anywhere near the means necessary to achieve anything of value—itself a path with significant risk of mission failure. Finally, the bureaucracy supported these parallel efforts in an almost admirable manner, despite their strategic shortcomings. In the end, any attempt to get these factions to do otherwise, to follow a coherent and integrated strategy that achieved the defeat of the Rebel Alliance, was probably always a fruitless endeavor.

The end of the war did not come swiftly enough for those of us watching, with the exception, of course, for those of us who did the dying.

Notes

1. BBY is before the Battle of Yavin, and ABY is after the Battle of Yavin, according to the Galactic Standard Calendar (GSC). Daniel Wallace, *The New Essential Chronology* (New York: Del Ray, 2005).
2. Greg Bear, *Rogue Planet* (New York: Del Rey, 2000).
3. "Third Offset" refers to the stages of development of this particular weapons program and was more of a staff nickname than the official name of the program. Some staff officers called it the Third Off-Ramp Strategy due to its decades-long struggles to produce little of value at great cost.
4. Greg Gordon, *Imperial Sourcebook* (Honesdale PA: West End Games, 1989).
5. Vader's speech echoes the speech of Nicias to the Athenians about the Sicilian Expedition; see Thucydides, *History of the Peloponnesian War*, trans. Rex Warner (London: Penguin Classics, 1974), 414–18.
6. I used Alcibiades's speech as a framework for Tarkin's words. Thucydides, *History of the Peloponnesian War*, bk. 6, 419–22.
7. This was modeled after Nicias's rebuttal to Alcibiades. Thucydides, *History of the Peloponnesian War*, bk. 6, 424–26.
8. This speech is modified from the speech in the final paragraph of "Destruction of the Athenian Expedition 413." Thucydides, *History of the Peloponnesian War*, bk. 7, 536–37.
9. Coruscant was the seat of the Republic and later the Empire, while it lasted.
10. This quote was scarcely modified from Robert Komer's words in his after-action review of the pacification efforts in Vietnam, in *Bureaucracy Does Its Thing: Institutional Constraints on US-GVN Performance* (Santa Monica CA: RAND, 1972), v–vi. The idea to use this came from Todd Greentree, who used this very quote and technique in his analysis of the U.S. whole-of-government approach in Afghanistan; Todd Greentree, "Bureaucracy Does Its Thing: U.S. Performance and the Institutional Dimension of Strategy in Afghanistan," *Journal of Strategic Studies* 36, no. 3 (2013): 327.

28

A Strategist, Yoda Was Not

ML CAVANAUGH

Yoda wasn't a strategist. Wise sage? Yes. Fierce warrior? Sure. But undoubtedly, Yoda was an inferior strategist whose actions led directly to the Jedi's
catastrophic loss and the collapse of the Republic he was sworn to defend.

Yet the popular view of Yoda remains reverential. The U.S. Army School
for Advanced Military Studies, an elite military graduate school that conveys
institutional gravitas, lovingly refers to graduates as Jedi Knights, evoking
the luster gained by having trained under Yoda's learned tutelage.[1] The U.S.
Department of Defense's internal, long-look strategic think tank, the Office of
Net Assessment, was run for nearly four decades by a man, Andrew Marshall,
so esteemed that he was honored with a special nickname: Yoda.[2] Indeed,
the Yoda label has become synonymous with strategic acumen, strategic
excellence, and strategic vision. The perception is clear—Yoda was a great
strategic oracle that never failed to point the way to victory.

But fail he did. The myth of Yoda has departed from the reality of Yoda.
His track record during the first three *Star Wars* films (*Episodes I, II, and III*)
sharply contrasts from the public conception of the little green warrior. B.
H. Liddell Hart once noted that broad audiences are apt to confuse military

genius with fame, and perhaps through all the movie hoopla, many have missed just how flawed a strategist Yoda really was.[3] It's easy to get carried away by Yoda's celebrity, as he trained several exceptional Jedi, and he himself was tactically brilliant in a way that was truly breathtaking—evident in his brave, gymnastic fights against powerful opponents like Count Dooku in *Episode II* and Darth Sidious in *Episode III*. Whatever the reason, there can be little doubt that it's time to puncture this hot air–filled fable. Allowing it to persist would enable a flawed understanding of the strategist's craft and doom budding padawan strategists not to the dark side or the light side but to the wrong side.

Let's start with the basics. Eminent strategic thinker Colin Gray considers a strategist the individual with responsibility for a community's protection plan and the authority to determine "how the enemy is to be defeated" through a "theory of military victory."[4] Yoda was the Jedi Council's leader, and the Jedi proclaimed themselves in *Episode III* the "guardians of peace and justice in the galaxy" as the sworn servant-defenders of the Republic. So Yoda was a strategist. As such, his standard was to be "good enough" to engage and defeat rivals as a "dueling competitor."[5] Strategy's one-on-one nature means that measurement is always relative to the opponent and that superiority, therefore, matters more than simple objective calculations like "good" or "bad."[6] And as we all know, Yoda had one opponent: Sheev Palpatine (later revealed as Darth Sidious in hiding, later still to become the Emperor).

The arc of Yoda's strategic competition with Palpatine went badly. At the beginning of *Episode I—The Phantom Menace*, the Republic ruled the galaxy, and the Jedi secured this position. Yet by the end of *Episode III—Revenge of the Sith*, the Republic had fallen and was replaced by the First Galactic Empire. Perhaps most important, nearly all the Jedi were eliminated. Only Yoda and Obi-Wan Kenobi survived the Jedi extermination, which might as well have been complete annihilation, as both went into extended periods of exile on planets as remote and inconsequential as Napoleon's final island prison on Saint Helena. This hermitic exile lasted until *Episode IV—A New Hope* for Obi-Wan Kenobi and until *Episode V—The Empire Strikes Back* for

Yoda. Yoda's situation on Dagobah might also be compared with the distant strategic leadership of Osama bin Laden. Both were confined to austere, remote locations. Both were religiously inspired and guided distant proxies with strategic consequences. Both suffered long periods of obscurity. And yet bin Laden's al-Qaeda organization survived conflict somewhat intact, while the Jedi were almost entirely eviscerated.

How did this come to pass? How did the Republic and Jedi fall so steeply, so sharply, and so suddenly? In investigating this disaster, it's impossible to avoid the role Yoda played as a strategist, invested with the judgment authority and responsibility to protect both the Republic and the Jedi.

Clausewitz arms us with the means of critical analysis.[7] As we've established the final facts of the case—the Republic and Jedi were wiped out, with Yoda bearing blame as senior strategist for the state's security—we can now assess a cause for this result. The hypothesis is that if Yoda had performed relatively better than Palpatine as a strategist, then the Jedi and Republic would have at least survived and not fallen to the Empire.

To evaluate Yoda's strategic performance, we'll appraise Yoda according to the strategist's core competencies, which are to anticipate, design, and facilitate security decisions.[8] These are the things strategists actually *do*. Each core competency provides a way of explaining how and why events turned out as they did.

Because strategy is concerned with constraint and choice, strategists aid in making important decisions at war. Strategists *anticipate*, employ foresight, see ahead, and visualize the problems that are most likely to fill the bleakest and blankest sheets of paper. And when strategists define disparate problems and *design* responses to complex challenges, they create intellectual order from physical chaos, sizing up dynamic, multifaceted sets of facts and assumptions to impose some necessary structure to enable decisions or solutions. Strategists also *facilitate* judgments by using interpersonal skills, leading and supporting diverse, multidisciplinary groups and staffs and leveraging broad networks of people and information to bring out the best available option. Typically, that's where the strategist's decision support ends and senior leaders' decision making begins. However, senior as Yoda was, he actually was the decision maker for the Jedi Council—so, additionally, we must scrutinize his *judgment*.

What was it about Yoda's actions as a strategist that led to the downfall of the Republic and the Jedi? How did Yoda perform at these core competencies?

FALSE ANTICIPATION

Even armed with his powerful Jedi sense, Yoda failed to foresee the emerging threat to the Republic. While there had not been a single war since the Republic was founded, this is hardly an excuse for total military unpreparedness. The planet Naboo, for example, in *Episode I—The Phantom Menace*, was revealed to be an entirely disarmed society guarded by "security volunteers." When the Trade Federation blockaded and assaulted Naboo, they easily cordoned off the planet and landed wholly unopposed. This left Naboo's Queen Amidala no choice but to negotiate under duress, because her society was entirely at the Trade Federation's mercy, and she was unable to "support [any] action that would lead to war." Granted, this failure may have been abetted by a populace reluctant to pay the sometimes high cost of military insurance (perhaps their social conventions were antiwar)—but even that is no reason to abdicate responsibility to take at least some minimally credible advance security preparations. As G. K. Chesterton wrote, "War is not the best way of settling differences; it is the only way of preventing their being settled for you."[9] Toward the end of *Episode I* the Naboo relied on the frog-like Gungan warrior nation to make an amphibious assault to reclaim their capital, but this alliance was not formed until the damage had been done—the capital having already been lost and the entire population held hostage. It was too late. Yoda should have anticipated such a potentially calamitous weak point.

Yoda's crisis response also demonstrates his lack of readiness. When Naboo was attacked, Yoda dispatched two Jedi knights, Qui-Gon Jinn and Obi-Wan Kenobi, a choice that revealed the stunning inadequacy of the Jedi as an intergalactic Task Force Smith barely able to protect a few high-value assets and fundamentally too few in number to fight a war for Naboo.[10] So limited was Yoda's foresight that the Jedi he sent were quickly outnumbered.

Embarrassing as this incident was on Naboo, Yoda then had roughly a decade to prepare his defenses and avoid another surprise in the next engagement—yet he did not. When this next threat emerged in *Episode II*, it catalyzed the still-defenseless Queen Amidala to support the Military Creation Act in the Galactic Republic's Senate to rapidly build a clone army. This was necessary because the Jedi were losing everywhere. Even Palpatine's henchman, Count Dooku, assessed that the Jedi were so "overwhelmed" that the Republic "must agree to [the Emperor's] demands." These significant force shortages also propelled Jar Jar Binks, as Naboo's Senate representative, to vote to extend emergency powers to Chancellor Palpatine (again, the hidden Darth Sidious) to create a clone Grand Army of the Republic to counter the droid threat. This parliamentary move supercharged Palpatine's viselike grip on the Republic by putting an enormous clone army at his disposal. Disastrous as this vote's impact was, it must also be seen as a vote of no confidence in the Jedi.

Yoda's bloodiest cardinal sin just might be that his espoused Jedi philosophy actively shunned and minimized the value of concentrated thought on the future.[11] As a result, Yoda failed to foresee the threat and take appropriate measures against the Trade Federation's droid fighters even after many years, which ultimately forced the Republic into a hasty buildup of a clone army of dubious loyalty that gave Palpatine overwhelming military power. One of the strategist's "most important duties" is to "think clearly about the problem of future armed conflict."[12] Yoda did not fulfill this duty, leaving his numerically inferior Jedi and the entire Republic to the mercy of a much larger (and eviler) force. Yoda's mistake gave Palpatine a quantitative advantage, which made the difference in the long run. And the qualitative story isn't any better.

FLAWED DESIGN

Yoda's Jedi force design contributed mightily to the ultimate outcome. The stated mission of the Jedi was to "settle conflict" in the galaxy for the

Republic. With such an expansive requirement, one would expect a set of resources equal to the task.

Yet Yoda kept the Jedi vanishingly small. New recruits were only taken in according to an individual's genetic makeup, based on a count of midichlorians in the blood, purported to be as rare as a virgin birth. So small in number were the Jedi that after they made it past the equivalent of elementary school, the training relied entirely on one-on-one mentorship, a system that fundamentally limited growth. The Jedi also styled themselves as "peacekeepers, not soldiers," which further restricted what they could do at war and therefore influenced their ability and willingness to take on critical missions (a common criticism of today's United Nations military efforts). Also, like certain religious orders, the Jedi could not marry. "Attachment and possession [were] forbidden," because, as Yoda counseled, "attachment leads to fear" (and bad things follow fear). Yoda's leadership of the Jedi promulgated rules governing force design that severely restricted Jedi numbers—he ought to have either allowed the Jedi to marry and grow the Force's fighters organically or created a second tier of well-trained but genetically less rare defenders of the Republic. He did neither.

This design constrained the Jedi so much that they were destined to be useful only in niche scenarios. Like small-unit special operations teams, Jedi were great for hard-to-reach places at must-arrive-now times with failure-is-not-an-option diplomatic consequences. This sounds cool, and lightsabers are neat, but it left the Republic vulnerable to its opponent's exponential numerical advantage. As Joseph Stalin is said to have quipped, quantity has a quality all its own. Yoda learned Uncle Joe's lesson the hard way.

FLUBBED FACILITATION

Yoda failed to facilitate important strategic judgments in concert with his lone constituency, the Galactic Senate. The Jedi served the Republic, and the Republic's leadership was the Senate. Yoda owed a duty to this institution and had a standing requirement to coordinate with the Senate. The first three films provide ample and compelling evidence of Yoda's principal charges disparaging the Senate in all manner of speech, which cut a wide trench between political masters and military servants just when coordination was most vulnerable and important. Obi-Wan Kenobi remarked casually in *Episode II*, "politicians are not to be trusted," and then continued this corrosive talk with Anakin Skywalker, his subordinate padawan learner. Eventually, this loose talk carried consequences—Anakin, convinced that all politicians were rotten and untrustworthy, directly stated his preference for dictatorship over democracy. While Palpatine may have been the one to infect Anakin, Yoda enabled the conditions that allowed the disease to grow and fester. This is where coups are born, and the downstream result of Yoda's leadership failure to maintain a nonpartisan, apolitical Jedi ethic was a slow-motion amputation of the Republic's security arm from its political body. Yoda bears culpability in this tragedy.

FAILED JUDGMENT

As a strategist, Yoda's mistakes in anticipation, design, and facilitation led to inferior judgments. Yoda made his tiny bed and had to lie in it, much the same way that General Robert E. Lee of the Confederate army described his own situation in the American Civil War on August 23, 1864: "Without some [change], I cannot see how we are to escape the natural military consequences of the enemy's numerical superiority."[13] The weight of Yoda's previous mistakes had consequences from which he never could, or did, recover.

Toward the end of *Episode II* Yoda decided to bring the bulk of the Jedi forces to the planet Geonosis for a two-pronged mission: to rescue Anakin, Queen Amidala, and Obi-Wan Kenobi and to capture Count Dooku.[14] Yoda's Jedi sustained heavy losses, and while the rescue was successful, Count Dooku escaped. During the fighting, Yoda faced a choice: save Anakin and Obi-Wan Kenobi or capture Dooku. Yoda chose to save his Jedi, a highly questionable decision considering that he had already safeguarded Queen Amidala and that Dooku was so obviously the linchpin to Palpatine's continued efforts. The rescue on Geonosis was anything but a victory; in fact, it was just the opposite, as Yoda himself admitted when he said, "Begun, the Clone War has."

Yoda's most controversial oversight in judgment must be the enormous Jedi losses sustained when Palpatine directed Order 66 and the clones turned on the Jedi. In these clashes, the Jedi were simply overwhelmed because they were deployed in such small numbers relative to their two-timing, murderous clone "comrades" when the vicious Order 66 was executed. In the end, the Jedi were two heartbeats from extinction.

FUTURE LOOKING, THE STRATEGIST MUST BE

He was a great fighter and may have been an even greater teacher. Yet Yoda was, nonetheless, an inferior strategist. For military schools and thought leaders to adopt his moniker is a demonstrable misappreciation of the strategist's craft, because, ultimately, Yoda was marginalized, the Jedi were unimportant, and the Republic was in flames. Having praised Yoda for what he did well and censured him for what he did poorly, it is important to secure lessons from this wreckage. Himself an educator, Yoda might seek solace in imparting a last lecture of sorts.

Yoda's message is that the strategist's first priority is to look to the future—to see over the horizon, recognize the requirements to come, and build the resources to ensure that surprise does not turn to regret. Though Yoda was subpar at each step on the strategist's competency ladder, the first rung was where he hit hardest. If Yoda had thought more about the future and seen the threat more clearly, or even hedged against what might come to pass, then maybe he would not have designed such a miniscule, inadequate force that was ripped apart when war came. Perhaps if that had happened, a strategist, Yoda might have been.

Notes

1. See Robert Scales, "Return of the Jedi," *Armed Forces Journal*, October 1, 2009, http://armedforcesjournal.com/return-of-the-jedi/; Mark Rountree, "Jedi Knights of the Army," *Leavenworth Times*, May 28, 2016, http://www.leavenworthtimes.com/article/20160528/NEWS/160529426.
2. See Ryan Evans, "Aspiring Yodas: Apply to Fill Andy Marshall's Shoes on USAJOBS," *War on the Rocks*, January 3, 2015, http://warontherocks.com/2015/01/aspiring-yodas-apply-to-fill-andy-marshalls-shoes-on-usajobs/; Jeffrey Lewis, "Yoda Has Left the Building," *Foreign Policy*, October 24, 2014, http://foreignpolicy.com/2014/10/24/yoda-has-left-the-building/; Craig

Whitlock, "Yoda Still Standing: Office of Pentagon Futurist Andrew Marshall, 92, Survives Budget Ax," *Washington Post*, December 4, 2013, https://www.washingtonpost.com/world /national-security/yoda-still-standing-office-of-pentagon-futurist-andrew-marshall-92-survives -budget-ax/2013/12/04/df99b3c6-5d24-11e3-be07-006c776266ed_story.html.

3. B. H. Liddell Hart, "What Is Military Genius?," *Strand Magazine*, October 1941.

4. Colin S. Gray, *The Strategy Bridge: Theory for Practice* (Oxford: Oxford University Press, 2016), 208.

5. Colin S. Gray, "The Strategist as Hero," *Joint Forces Quarterly* 62 (July 2011): 44–45.

6. Steven Jermy, "Strategy for Action: Using Force Wisely in the 21st Century," University of Oxford podcast, 41:30, Ethics, Law and Armed Conflict seminar series, October 26, 2011, http://podcasts.ox.ac.uk/strategy-action-using-force-wisely-21st-century.

7. Clausewitz writes, in describing the steps to proper critical analysis: "First, the discovery and interpretation of equivocal facts . . . historical research proper. . . . Second, the tracing of effects back to their causes. . . . It is essential for theory; for whatever in theory is to be defined, supported, or simply described by reference to experience. . . . Third, the investigation and evaluation of means employed . . . involving praise and censure . . . [meant to find] the lessons to be drawn from history." Carl von Clausewitz, *On War*, ed. and trans. Michael Howard and Peter Paret (Princeton NJ: Princeton University Press, 1976), 156.

8. ML Cavanaugh, "The Strategist's Core Competency," *Commentary and Analysis*, Modern War Institute, May 1, 2015, https://mwi.usma.edu/201551the-strategists-core-competency/.

9. G. K. Chesterton, cited in "Quotations of G. K. Chesterton," s.v. "War and Politics," American Chesterton Society, www.chesterton.org/quotations-of-g-k-chesterton.

10. Task Force Smith was the ill-prepared, ill-equipped first U.S. military unit in the Korean War, and over time, it has become shorthand for an inadequately ready military force.

11. Whatever text or tradition told, Jedi teachings on future gazing, as with that of other religions adjusting to new environments, were (and are) always up to interpretation, and so Yoda may be fairly blamed for not adapting to meet modern needs and threats.

12. David G. Perkins, "Preface," in *The U.S. Army Operating Concept: Win in a Complex World*, TRADOC pamphlet 525-3-1 (Fort Eustis VA: Department of the Army, 2014), iii.

13. Robert E. Lee to James Seddon, August 23, 1864, in *The Wartime Papers of R. E. Lee*, ed. Clifford Dowdey (Boston: Little, Brown, 1961), 843–44.

14. Yoda orders his troops, "Around the survivors a perimeter create," and reasons that "if Dooku escapes, more systems will he bring to his cause."

Epilogue

The Lessons of *Star Wars*

ML CAVANAUGH

Even among the stars, war demands death.

The *Star Wars* list of the lost is long and lamentable: Master Qui-Gon Jinn, Shmi Skywalker, Master Mace Windu, Queen Padme Amidala, Captain Cassian Andor, Jyn Erso, Master Obi-Wan Kenobi, the nameless tauntauns and unknown soldiers of Hoth, Master Yoda, Anakin Skywalker, and Han Solo. And others we knew not: noncombatant civilians, combatant storm-troopers, and collateral wreckage strewn across the galaxy. Death's registry could go on (and on).

Perhaps the most meaningful, if overlooked, lesson of *Star Wars* is the essential loss of life in the conduct of war. This often gets missed in a big conflict filled with clones, droids, and Jedi who don't really seem to mind death.

But Jedi or not, they're still gone.

Awareness of war's casualties instills dread in those who remain, as seen in the only line that's been used in all the films: "I've got a bad feeling about this"—a sick-stomach sentiment felt by anyone who has experienced war death and continues to face the sobering choices that come with conflict.

So war is for the highest stakes. This knowledge wards off hubris; war's costs and consequences should humble us to our core. We're only human.

And even with fancy computers and extra droids, strategy is still essentially a human endeavor. Clausewitz correctly dismissed numbers-driven, dispassionate "war by algebra," just as Harry Summers once ridiculed the notion that war could be predicted by computer calculation.[1] We can see why, vividly, on the *Star Wars* screen—those with hope and "a sharp stick," as Jyn Erso says in *Rogue One*, can outlast technically and numerically superior forces.

This book has tried to make strategic studies relatable and interesting; and while we don't take our films seriously (except *The Big Lebowski*), we do take strategy very seriously. Unless and until political violence goes extinct, our society's solemn duty is to ensure that when such violence happens, it is undertaken with care and thought and only as a last resort.

So with a sense of gravity and modesty, this book has attempted to collect and harmonize some lessons for real-world use. With so many chapters, containing such big ideas, this epilogue won't rehash them all but instead distill them and propose some broad maxims that might apply as sound advice from each of the four sections.

The first section, "Society and War," suggests aiming for balance. Societies must have security, but this security must always be weighed against other vital, societal considerations. Neither militarism nor naked disarmament is the answer. Also, though slightly tilted, Eliot Cohen's "unequal dialogue" formulation describing the appropriate balance in senior-subordinate relations between civilian leaders and military commanders is a useful rule of thumb.[2]

"Preparation for War," the second section, urges aiming for careful prudence. The future is unknowable, but this should never prevent the preparation that propels a society to achieve "minimum regrets."[3]

In "Waging a War," the third section, the aim of strategy should always be sustainable, relative advantage. With limited resources, in harsh environments, and against sharp adversaries, there is no "perfect"—there is only better than the opponent. The goal is to be the "good enough strategist," because, in the end, all war is relative.[4]

In the last section, "Evaluating a War," the aim is empathy. First gather facts; then mentally reenact key moments at war to "approximate, if not replicate," actual strategic decisions made under challenging conditions.[5] Empathy serves two purposes: fairness to those being criticized and self-improvement for future endeavors.

Even armed with these maxims, what makes strategy so complex is that the challenges compound, layering atop one another. With endless permutations, the world at war is difficult to predict. So what can this book, as a whole, tell us about future conflict?

Not as much as we'd like but more than we need. We'll always wish we knew more about a war to come. But if you look closely, there's enough to go on. Consider the statement often attributed to author William Gibson: "The future is already here. It's just not evenly distributed yet."[6] Many of this book's concepts will impact different warfighting groups differently. Today, there are three general categories in the practice of war. There's the top shelf, with the greatest resources and the most destructive power: the United States, Russia, and China. Next are many in the middle, several punch-above-our-weight countries possessing some expeditionary capability, including the United Kingdom, France, Australia, South Korea, New Zealand, and Israel, among others. And then there's the bargain basement, the smallest states and the stateless—mostly guys with trucks and guns.

The future will impact these three groups unevenly. Toward the top, the technophiles will invest in technology—advanced artificial intelligence, brainy bullets, and smarter weapons that further remove practitioners from harm. The bottom, out of necessity, will become more human than human—they'll use humanity itself as weapons and shields, apply simple tools not far removed from days long past, and fight inspired by other means (faith and pharmaceutical).[7] The middle will split the difference.

Some will trend toward tech and "human-machine collaborative combat networks."[8] Others will advance to a higher human plane of fighting. Sound like anything you've seen (or read) lately? Are we on a real-world path to Darth Vader and the Death Star versus Jedi Knights with lightsabers?

It's easy enough to spot this trajectory, but we cannot see the net result of the dynamic interactions between the two. Will sophisticated weapons platforms succeed or backfire? What's the right balance between man and machine? Luke Skywalker shut down his targeting system in favor of his own superior senses, which enabled a successful strike. Should we do the same with our smartphones?

Tough to predict. But despite Yoda's advice to the contrary—try, we must. And we must do so with balance, care, and empathy, to achieve the strategic advantage we need. Because someday, as it was for those in the *Star Wars* universe, it may just be for everything we hold dear.

George Lucas, creator of these films, in an unguarded moment, described "the secret, the bottom line" to *Star Wars*. He said, "There are two kinds of people in the world: compassionate people and selfish people. Selfish people live on the dark side, and compassionate people live on the light side."[9]

So use this book and these lessons for others and for the right reasons. Nothing could be nobler.

If you do, your own story might prove to be the moment—when things are at their worst and the dark side closes in—that strategy strikes back.

Notes

1. Carl von Clausewitz, *On War*, ed. and trans. Michael Howard and Peter Paret (Princeton NJ: Princeton University Press, 1976), 76. See also Harry Summers's widely respected assessment of the Vietnam War, which included this story that "made the rounds [among American military officers] during the closing days of the Vietnam war":

   "When the Nixon administration took over in 1969 all the data on North Vietnam and on the United States was fed into a Pentagon computer—population, gross national product, manufacturing capability, number of tanks, ships, and aircraft, size of the armed forces, and the like.

   "The computer was then asked, 'When will we win?'

   "It took only a moment to give the answer: 'You won in 1964!'

   "The story had a bite; by every quantifiable assessment, there simply was no contest between the United States, the most powerful nation on the face of the earth, and a tenth-rate backward nation like North Vietnam. Yet there was one thing that didn't fit into the computer—national will, what Clausewitz calls the moral factor." Harry G. Summers, *On Strategy: A Critical Analysis of the Vietnam War* (1982; repr., New York: Presidio Press, 1995), 18.

2. Cohen says of dialogue and inequality, respectively, "Both sides expressed their views bluntly . . . and repeatedly," and, "Final authority of the civilian leader was unambiguous and unquestioned."

Eliot A. Cohen, *Supreme Command: Soldiers, Statesmen, and Leadership in Wartime* (New York: Free Press, 2002), 209.

3. Colin S. Gray, "Transformation and Strategic Surprise" (paper for the Strategic Studies Institute, Army War College Press, Carlisle PA, April 2005), viii, https://ssi.armywarcollege.edu/pdffiles/PUB602.pdf.

4. Colin S. Gray, *The Strategy Bridge: Theory for Practice* (Oxford: Oxford University Press, 2010), 223.

5. Jon Tetsuro Sumida, *Decoding Clausewitz: A New Approach to* On War (Lawrence: University Press of Kansas, 2008), 195–96.

6. This quotation is often attributed to William Gibson but without specific reference. See Pagan Kennedy, "William Gibson's Future Is Now," *New York Times Book Review*, January 13, 2012, http://www.nytimes.com/2012/01/15/books/review/distrust-that-particular-flavor-by-william-gibson-book-review.html.

7. Regarding additional means of inspiring troops, David Axe writes, "Patrick Lin, a professor at California Polytechnic State, notes the military's 'ongoing interest in using pharmaceuticals, such as modafinil (a cognitive enhancer), dietary supplements, as well as gene therapy to boost the performance of warfighters.'" David Axe, "This Scientist Wants Tomorrow's Troops to Be Mutant-Powered," *Wired*, December 26, 2012, https://www.wired.com/2012/12/andrew-herr/.

8. Sydney J. Freedberg Jr., "People, Not Tech: DepSecDef Work on 3rd Offset, JICSPOC," *Breaking Defense*, February 9, 2016, http://breakingdefense.com/2016/02/its-not-about-technology-bob-work-on-the-3rd-offset-strategy/.

9. "George Lucas: The Force Be with You," interview by Academy of Achievement, *What It Takes* podcast, 35 minutes, December 7, 2015, https://itunes.apple.com/us/podcast/what-it-takes/id1025864075?mt=2.

CONTRIBUTORS

JOHN AMBLE is the editorial director of the Modern War Institute at West Point. Previously, he was managing editor and chief operating officer of *War on the Rocks*. A veteran of the wars in Iraq and Afghanistan, he is a military intelligence officer in the U.S. Army Reserve. He has been featured in both print and broadcast media and writes on defense issues, terrorism, and intelligence. He holds a BA from the University of Minnesota and an MA from King's College London.

BJ ARMSTRONG serves as an assistant professor of war studies and naval history at the U.S. Naval Academy. He holds a PhD from King's College London and is an active-duty U.S. Navy commander. Previously, he served as a helicopter pilot in search and rescue and in naval special warfare, as the officer in charge of an amphibious-helicopter gunship detachment, and as a strategic analyst and staff officer in the Pentagon. He is an award-winning historian, a senior editor with *War on the Rocks*, and the editor of the 21st Century Foundations series from the Naval Institute Press.

KELSEY D. ATHERTON is a journalist covering war, robots, and other bad futures. His work has appeared in *Popular Science, Politico, The Verge*, and elsewhere. When not writing about the laser drones of tomorrow's wars, he runs *Grand Blog Tarkin*, an online forum for political science fiction and strategy discussions in a galaxy far, far away.

CHUCK BIES is an armor officer in the U.S. Army, currently serving in the rank of major. He holds a BSE in mechanical engineering from Duke University and an MA in diplomacy and military studies from Hawaii Pacific University. Recently, he served as an assistant professor in the Department of History at the United States Military Academy. He won the 2016 General George S. Patton Award at the U.S. Army Command and General Staff School as the best tactician in his class of 1,300 officers.

JONATHAN BRATTEN is an officer in the Army National Guard and a veteran of Afghanistan. A U.S. Army historian with a BA and an MA in history, he is a frequent contributor to the Army Historical Foundation's journal *On Point* and *ARMY Magazine*.

MAX BROOKS is an author, public speaker, nonresident fellow at the Modern War Institute, and senior resident fellow at the Atlantic Council's Art of Future Warfare Project. He is the author of *World War Z* (New York: Three Rivers Press, 2006) and *The Harlem Hellfighters* (New York: Broadway Books, 2014).

CRISPIN J. BURKE is a U.S. Army aviator who is qualified in the UH-60 Black Hawk and the LUH-72 Lakota. His writings on the future of war, *Star Wars*, and sometimes both at once can be found in blogs throughout the Internet.

ML CAVANAUGH is a U.S. Army strategist with global experience in assignments ranging from the Pentagon to Korea and Iraq to Army Space and Missile Defense Command. A nonresident fellow with the Modern War Institute at West Point, he has written for the *New York Times, Washington Post*, and *Wall Street Journal*, among other publications. For more, visit MLCavanaugh.com.

AUGUST COLE is an author and analyst exploring the future of conflict. He is a nonresident senior fellow with the Art of the Future Project at the Atlantic Council's Brent Scowcroft Center on International Security. He is also writer-in-residence at Avascent, an independent strategy and management consulting firm focused on government-oriented industries. His first book, *Ghost Fleet: A Novel of the Next World War* (New York: Houghton Mifflin Harcourt, 2015), was written with Peter W. Singer. He is a former defense-industry reporter for the *Wall Street Journal* in Washington DC.

LIAM COLLINS is a career Special Forces officer who has served in a variety of special operations assignments and conducted multiple combat operations to Afghanistan and Iraq as well as operational deployments to Bosnia, Africa, and South America. He is a graduate of numerous military courses, including Ranger School, and his military awards and decorations include two valorous awards for actions in combat. He is the director of the Modern War Institute at West Point and previously served as the director of the Combating Terrorism Center at West Point. He has a BS in mechanical engineering from the U.S. Military Academy and an MPA and PhD from the Woodrow Wilson School at Princeton University. He saw *Star Wars* for the first time in the theater as a six-year-old in 1977.

MICK COOK is an officer in the Royal Regiment of Australian Artillery and hosts *The Dead Prussian* podcast. He holds a BA in English and history and an MA in strategy and security studies from the University of New South Wales and a master's degree in criminology and criminal justice from Griffith University. He is passionate about encouraging critical thought on war among military professionals and policy makers.

B. A. FRIEDMAN is an officer of field artillery in the U.S. Marine Corps Reserve, currently serving at the Marine Corps Warfighting Lab in Quantico, Virginia. He holds a BA in history from The Ohio State University and an MA in national security and strategic studies from the U.S. Naval War College. He is the editor of *21st Century Ellis: Operational Art and Strategic Prophecy* (Annapolis MD: Naval Institute Press, 2015) and the author of *On Tactics: A Theory of Victory in Battle* (Annapolis MD: Naval Institute Press, 2017).

JAYM GATES has spent nearly a decade as a science fiction editor and author, with over a dozen anthologies and more than fifty published short pieces of fiction and nonfiction to her credit. She is a coeditor of *War Stories: New Military Science Fiction* (Lexington KY: Apex, 2014) with Andrew Liptak, has judged writing contests for the Atlantic Council, and is a juror for the Canopus Award for Interstellar Fiction. She is currently a creative lead on Harrisburg University's Crisis Response Simulation, an in-depth course aimed at developing real-time awareness and strategies for crisis response.

JIM GOLBY is an active-duty U.S. Army strategist who currently serves as a defense operations policy advisor in the Office of the Defense Advisor at the United States Mission to NATO. Jim previously served as a special advisor to the vice president of the United States, a special assistant to the chairman of the Joint Chiefs of Staff, and an assistant professor in the Department of Social Sciences at West Point. Before becoming a U.S. Army strategist, he commanded a security company in combat in Iraq (2006–7) and led a scout platoon in combat in Iraq (2004–5). He has also served in various leadership positions and staff assignments as a cavalry officer during tours in Europe and the Pacific. Jim holds a PhD in political science from Stanford University and has published numerous articles on American foreign policy, strategy, and civil-military relations.

THERESA HITCHENS is a senior research scholar at the Center for International and Security Studies at the University of Maryland, where she focuses on space security, cyber security, and governance issues surrounding disruptive technologies. From 2009 through 2014 Hitchens was the director of the United Nations Institute for Disarmament Research.

ERICA IVERSON is a U.S. Army strategist with a range of strategic career assignments spanning the globe in Asia, Europe, and the Middle East. An experienced speechwriter for several U.S. Army four-star commands, she has also served as a fellow with Congress and the State Department.

VAN JACKSON, PhD, is a senior lecturer in international relations at Victoria University of Wellington and the Defence and Strategy Fellow at the Centre for Strategic Studies, also in Wellington, New Zealand. He also hosts the *Pacific Pundit* podcast series and is a senior editor at *War on the Rocks*. From 2009 to 2014, Van held several policy positions in the Office of the Secretary of Defense, including as a defense strategist and the director of Korea policy. He is a former Council on Foreign Relations International Affairs Fellow. His research interests include East Asian security, defense strategy, and exploring the intersection of fiction and world politics.

STEVE LEONARD is a former senior military strategist and the creative force behind *Doctrine Man!!*, the popular military web-comic site. A career writer and speaker with a passion for developing and mentoring the next generation of thinking leaders, he is a nonresident fellow with the Modern War Institute at West Point, cofounder and board member of the Military Writers Guild, cofounder of the national security blog *Divergent Options*, and a frequent contributor to the Atlantic Council's Art of the Future Project. Published extensively, he writes on foreign policy, national security, strategy and planning, leadership and leader development, military history, and, on occasion, fiction.

ANDREW LIPTAK is a writer and historian. He is the weekend editor for *The Verge* and has written for *Armchair General* magazine, *io9*, *Kirkus Reviews*, *Lightspeed* magazine, *VentureBeat*, and others. His first short story, "Fragmented," appeared in *Galaxy's Edge* magazine in 2014. He published his first anthology (coedited with Jaym Gates), *War Stories: New Military Science Fiction* (Lexington KY: Apex), in 2014. He has a BA in history and an MA in military history from Norwich University and is a 2014 attendee of the Launch Pad Astronomy Workshop.

DANIEL D. MAURER is an active-duty U.S. Army major. After serving as a combat engineer platoon leader in Iraq, he earned his law degree from The Ohio State University and has since served as a judge advocate prosecutor, senior legal counsel to a deployed brigade, appellate counsel in Washington DC, chief of criminal law for a large U.S. Army installation, and chief of operational law at a U.S. Army Service

Component Command headquarters in Europe. Dan was the first judge advocate or lawyer to be selected as a strategist fellow for the U.S. Army chief of staff's Strategic Studies Group. He is a contributing writer at the U.S. Military Academy's Modern War Institute; is the author of *Crisis, Agency, and Law in U.S. Civil-Military Relations* (Basingstoke, UK: Palgrave Macmillan, 2017); and has published essays, a monograph from the Army War College Press, and law review articles on a wide range of subjects, including military justice, social network analysis, innovation, and military theory. *The Empire Strikes Back* was the first film he ever saw in a movie theater.

GENERAL (RET.) STANLEY MCCHRYSTAL is a senior fellow at Yale University's Jackson Institute for Global Affairs, where he teaches a popular course on leadership. Throughout his military career, he commanded U.S. and International Security Assistance Forces in Afghanistan, the nation's premier military counterterrorism force; Joint Special Operations Command; and the Seventy-Fifth Ranger Regiment. From 9/11 until his retirement in 2010, he spent more than six years deployed to combat in a variety of leadership positions. After retiring from the military, he cofounded McChrystal Group, where he is part of a unique team of professionals focused on helping firms develop and implement innovative leadership solutions in order to help them transform and succeed in challenging, dynamic environments. He is the author of two *New York Times* best-selling books: *My Share of the Task—A Memoir* (New York: Penguin, 2013) and *Team of Teams: New Rules of Engagement for a Complex World* (New York: Penguin, 2015).

KATHLEEN J. MCINNIS, PhD, is the international-security analyst for the Congressional Research Service and is a senior nonresident fellow at the Atlantic Council of the United States.

STEVE METZ is director of research at the U.S. Army War College Strategic Studies Institute and writes a weekly column on defense and security for *World Politics Review*.

MICK RYAN is a major general in the Australian Army, where he is currently commander of the Australian Defence College.

JOHN SPENCER is a U.S. Army infantry major currently serving as the deputy director of the Modern War Institute at West Point. During his twenty-five years of active service, he also served as a fellow with the chief of staff of the U.S. Army's Strategic Studies Group. He holds a master of policy management degree from Georgetown University. His writing has appeared in the *New York Times*, the *Wall Street Journal*, the *Los Angeles Times*, *USA Today*, and other publications.

ADMIRAL (RET.) JAMES STAVRIDIS is the twelfth and current dean of The Fletcher School of Law and Diplomacy at Tufts University. He served in the U.S. Navy for more than thirty years and retired in 2013 after completing a four-year tour as supreme allied commander of NATO. He has published six books, including most recently *The Leader's Bookshelf* (Annapolis MD: Naval Institute Press, 2017) with R. Manning Ancell and *Sea Power: The History and Geopolitics of the World's Oceans* (New York: Penguin, 2017). He received his PhD from The Fletcher School.

COLIN STEELE completed his MA in law and diplomacy at The Fletcher School in 2018. He received his bachelor's degree in foreign service from Georgetown University in 2012 and is an AmeriCorps alumnus. He has also worked with *War on the Rocks* and published at *The Strategy Bridge*.

DAN WARD is the author of *The Simplicity Cycle: A Field Guide to Making Things Better without Making Them Worse* (New York: HarperCollins, 2015) and *F.I.R.E.: How Fast, Inexpensive, Restrained, and Elegant Methods Ignite Innovation* (New York: HarperCollins, 2014). He served in the U.S. Air Force and retired at the rank of lieutenant colonel. Dan holds three engineering degrees and received the Bronze Star for his service in Afghanistan.

JEAN MARIE WARD is a science fiction and fantasy author. The one-time freelance reporter entered civil service as a writer and editor for the U.S. Army Development and Readiness Command before becoming the founding public affairs officer for both the Navy Accounting and Finance Center and the Defense Finance and Accounting Service.

CRAIG WHITESIDE is an associate professor at the Naval War College, where he teaches national security affairs to military officers as part of their professional military education. He is a fellow at the International Centre for Counter-terrorism–The Hague. Whiteside's current research focuses on the doctrinal influences on the leadership of the so-called Islamic State movement and its evolving strategies. He has a PhD in political science from Washington State University and is a former U.S. Army officer.

FRAN WILDE has been a technology consultant, is an award-winning science fiction author, and has published three novels. Her stories have appeared in *Asimov's*, *Nature* magazine, and Tor.com. She is a writer for the *Washington Post*, *GeekMom*, and *Clarkesworld Magazine*, on topics including technology, monsters, artificial intelligence, and virtual reality.

RAQ WINCHESTER is the CEO of Ximerae Consulting. She has worked for and with the U.S. intelligence community for eighteen years, currently serving as a strategic innovation expert and futurist. She has served in multiple overseas posts in positions ranging from counterterrorism to support. Her current work involves the military, diplomacy, analysis, collection, and security tradecraft. She writes for the Center for the Study of Intelligence and has the second most popular blog on the intelligence community's internal network.